GOSE

"I have over ten years' experience in sour beer production, including Gose. There is much I have learned from this book that will continue to help me in my professional career. Fal writes with such simple clarity and depth that brewers of all levels and beer enthusiasts alike can enjoy and benefit from this book."

—RON GANSBERG, Brewmaster, Cascade Brewing

"There is more to Gose than just coriander and salt. Fal Allen reveals its rich history while giving the reader an in-depth introduction to both modern and historic Gose-style beers, their ingredients, and their quirks. Follow Gose on its journey from the imperial city of Goslar into the *Gosenschänke* of Leipzig and on to craft breweries in the US and the world."

—BENEDIKT RAUSCH, *Wilder Wald*, http://wilder-wald.com

"Fal takes us on a Dickensian journey through time, detailing what was, what is, and what may become of our beloved and mostly misunderstood Gose. Fal covers the depth and breadth of brewing Gose, with tips, clever tricks, and tasty anecdotes along the way. Whether you're a beer newbie or a master brewer, this book is required reading for all."

—KRISTEN ENGLAND, Head Brewer, Bent Brewstillery

T0169029

GOSE

BREWING A CLASSIC GERMAN BEER FOR THE MODERN ERA

BY FAL ALLEN

BREWERS
PUBLICATIONS™

Brewers Publications™
A Division of the Brewers Association
PO Box 1679, Boulder, Colorado 80306-1679
BrewersAssociation.org
BrewersPublications.com

Proudly printed in the United States of America.

10 9 8 7 6 5 4 3 2 1
ISBN-13: 978-1-938469-49-7
Ebook ISBN-13: 978-1-938469-50-3
Library of Congress Cataloging-in-Publication Data

Names: Allen, Fal, author.
Title: Gose : brewing a classic German beer for the modern era / by Fal Allen.
Description: | Includes bibliographical references and index.
Identifiers: LCCN 2018020718 | ISBN 9781938469497 (pbk.)
Subjects: LCSH: Gose--Germany--History. | Brewing--Amateurs' manuals.
Classification: LCC TP577 .A383 2018 | DDC 663/.3--dc23 LC record available at
https://lccn.loc.gov/2018020718

Publisher: Kristi Switzer
Technical Editor: Benedikt Rausch, Kristen England, Ron Gansberg
Copyediting: Amahl Turczyn
Proofreading: Iain Cox
Indexing: Doug Easton
Art Direction: Jason Smith
Cover and Interior Design: Danny Harms
Production: Justin Petersen
Cover Photo: Luke Trautwein
Interior Photos: Fal Allen unless otherwise noted.

I would like to dedicate this book to my fellow brewers; to all the brewers who came before us—they are our foundation—and to all the brewers who have walked with me for a time along this meandering path. Their generosity and friendship has allowed me to continue the journey.

TABLE OF CONTENTS

FOREWORD

Putting it mildly, Gose is not a beer style that Americans grew up with, or were even aware of until relatively recently. I first heard of it in passing back in 1992, when my then wife, who was and is a curator at the Seattle Art Museum, and I were out to dinner with a visiting German art historical dignitary. Being German, our visitor was interested in the fact that I was a brewer, and he spoke fondly of a beer he recalled from his younger days in his hometown of Leipzig. The beer was flavored with coriander, he told me, and had salt in it. I don't remember whether he mentioned its tartness specifically. In any case, I was intrigued, said that it sounded like fun to brew, and filed it away in the part of my brain that serves as a funny little backwater of brewing, right next to where Pennsylvania Swankey resides.

At that time I was working alongside Fal Allen at the tiny, roughly 800-square-foot Pike Place Brewery, where we turned out about 1600 barrels of beer a year in three-and-a-half-barrel batches. (We were somewhat chagrined that there was an even smaller licensed brewery in Kalamazoo, Michigan run by Larry Bell.) But with the pressures of producing our signature pale ale and not much else, there would be no Gose brewing for us, no Pennsylvania Swankey. We did develop an IPA, and once a year brewed barleywine, along with an occasional batch of stout. Once, for a visit by Michael Jackson, who was good friends with the brewery owners, Charles and Rose Ann Finkel, we brewed a ginger molasses brown ale. It was a simpler time. Those of us who were working at Pike Place continued to be avid homebrewers, where we were able to take advantage of the interesting imported malts sold down the street at our sister homebrewing shop, Liberty Malt Supply, to brew styles of beer that the constraints of professional brewing didn't allow into the schedule. Still, none of us brewed a Gose.

But we did experiment. At one point, having been inspired by Dutch still lifes of dead fowl, oysters, cut lemons, and glasses of beer, I set out to brew a historically accurate seventeenth-century Dutch beer, and served it, with a label that Charles made specially, at a Seattle Art Museum opening for a show devoted to the golden age of Dutch painting. And Fal used to have Polynesian-themed parties at his house near the Greenwood neighborhood of Seattle. He would brew a beer in an open bucket, using everything in the house he could find that was fermentable, its excesses evened out by prodigious fistfuls of hops. It was required that everyone drink the resulting beer from a coconut shell. I also recall that Fal, asserting his Hawaiian bona fides, was the only one to wear a sarong.

Fast forward to the later stages of our careers. . .

In his first stint at Anderson Valley Brewing Company, Fal pretty much brewed the party line— classic beers, such as golden ale, amber ale, and oatmeal stout, boldly rendered in the California style, but representative of the chromatic Holy Trinity of craft brewing's early days. Anderson Valley did do new beers, mostly for sale at the brewery tap room in Boonville, and it came out with an IPA for general sale. But no Gose. Not yet.

When Fal lit out for Singapore to brew at Archipelago Brewing Company within the Asia Pacific Breweries behemoth, he was encouraged to experiment and develop new beers, either new styles altogether or quirky variations on the familiar. He came to Seattle to brew some test batches with me, since at Elysian's Tangletown location I had a three-barrel brewery on which I fooled around, developing beers made with jasmine, rosemary, yuzu, and occasionally pumpkin. At one point I remember Fal being impressed that I had brewed a Berliner *weiss* and run the wort directly to the fermentor without bringing it to a boil. Fal was planning to introduce common or indigenous Asian ingredients to appeal to adventurous craft drinkers in Singapore. Later, his blog entries, posted from all over south Asia, were downright Bourdainian in their search for exotic ingredients and experiences. One of the experimental batches we made was a nominally Belgian-style *witbier*; it had coriander and orange peel, sure, but the orange peel was Chinese, and there was also lemongrass and tamarind. Another was a brown ale made with either regular ginger or galangal and gula melaka, a type of coconut sugar. Later, when I finally visited Fal in Singapore, I drank a lot of Archipelago's Straits Pale Ale. It was one of the first beers I had that used Nelson Sauvin hops.

After five years, when Archipelago's experiments were determined to be maybe too edgy for the Singapore craft masses—to say nothing of the corrupt system of kickbacks from bars that didn't support anything particularly innovative or odd—and he was no longer permitted to spread his creative wings quite so much, Fal returned to Anderson Valley. (Happily, I was able to buy all the unused and unwanted Nelson Sauvin from Doug Donelan at New Zealand Hops Ltd for an IPA I had come up with, which was first called Idiot Sauvin and later changed to Savant.) This time around at Anderson Valley, Fal's experimenting side got heavily into wood-aged beers and some of the other labor-intensive and quirky styles that the craft world had come to love and demand. One of my favorite happy accidents from this time, both conceptually and to actually drink, was a sour wheat beer called Horse Tongue, aged in wood and supposedly, famously, inoculated by a horse licking around the barrel's bung. It kind of reminded me of the time when we were traveling in England doing research for the book we wrote together on barleywine and opened a bottle of *geuze* in which a couple of maggots were floating—we fished them out and threw them away, but we drank the beer, for sure.

It's funny how often the things we come to be known for don't even originate with us, or fall into our laps innocently and sometimes even grudgingly. The first pumpkin beer we brewed at Elysian was because one of my brewers, Markus Stinson, nagged me to brew one (I figured we'd do it once). The idea for Avatar, the jasmine IPA I used to make at Elysian, came from my first-ever Great American Beer Festival® (GABF) judging session, when Mark Dorber, one of my fellow judges and the then proprietor of the White Horse in Parsons Green, commented that one of the IPAs we were judging reminded him of jasmine tea. Similarly, as well-known for their Goses as Anderson Valley is these days, it wasn't Fal who first came up with the idea to brew one. As Fal describes in this book, it was a local homebrewer named Mike Luparello who suggested it, and the rest is California brewing history.

These days no brewer or brewery can rest on their laurels, their past accomplishments and portfolios of beers merely delicious and well-crafted. Those who do may end up with nothing but their memories to grow old with, or perhaps get to the ripe old age of five or six years of professional operation. Fal deserves a lot of credit, if you ask me, for bringing Anderson Valley into the modern age. And with the Gose lines Anderson Valley has created and brought to market, the world has been shown variations on this old style that could only have been possible in the ferment, so to speak, of New World craft brewing. And now, from not even having considered brewing one, Fal has become one of the world's leading experts on Gose.

If you don't know him or haven't picked up on this already, Fal's is an inquiring mind where brewing exploration is concerned, figuring out what's what and sharing it with his fellow brewers. Hence this book, and hence some of the most interesting discussions I've had as a judge at the GABF and World Beer Cup[SM] have been with Fal, judging in categories variously called indigenous or historical beer. These are eggheaded, conceptually driven styles, harking back to beers exhumed from brewing's footnote graveyards, styles like *momme*, *hond*, Grätzer, *grisette*, and Adambier, like Pennsylvania Swankey, like Gose. Or they are new beers, fantasy beers, crafted from whole geographical or historical cloth, beers which might once have been, and are irrefutably now, in your hand and in your face. The trick with many of these, as with many Goses, is to build an idea into a delicious beer, despite not having many of the source materials and benchmarks from which to work. Now, with this book in your hand, Fal's research and travel should provide some of that. The raw materials are the easy part, *Reinheitsgebot* purists be damned; to me the interesting stuff covers the various methods of inoculation for these very interesting and, these days, very popular beers. For who would have thought just a few years ago that even non-beer geeks would stride confidently up to the bar in a craft brewery taproom and ask, "Do you have any Goses?"

Well, do you? You might. But after reading this book you almost certainly will.

Dick Cantwell
Magnolia Brewing Co., San Francisco

ACKNOWLEDGMENTS

I would like to give a special thanks to Benedikt Rausch of
Wilder Wald, Frankfurt, Germany (http://wilder-wald.com).

I would also like to thank the following people and companies:

Lily Apfel—California, USA
Paul Benner and Garret Conley—Platform Brewing Co., Ohio, USA
Sam Bennett and Jim Woods—Woods Beer Co., California, USA
Christopher Bird—Awesome Guy, USA
Ryan Blocker—Galmegi Brewing, South Korea
Sam Calagione—Dogfish Head Craft Brewery, Delaware, USA
Jim Crooks—Firestone Walker Brewing Company/Barrelworks, California, USA
Eric Drew—Casa Agria Specialty Ales, California, USA
Jenna Dutton—Union Craft Brewing, Maryland, USA
Kristen England—Bent Brewstillery, Minnesota, USA
Teri Fahrendorf—Great Western Malting, Washington, USA
Ron Gansberg—Cascade Brewing Barrel House, Oregon, USA
Lars Marius Garshol—www.garshol.priv.no/blog/, Norway
Ulrike Genz and Peter Schnitz—Schneeeule Brauerei, Berlin, Germany
Jens Gröger—Gosenshenke Ohne Bedenken, Leipzig, Germany

Federico Guazzone—Anderson Valley Brewing Co., California, USA

Tiffany Harrington—Berlin, Germany

Mike Heinrich—Great Western Malting, Washington, USA

Lucas Taylor Hendricks—The Cebruery Artisanal Ales and Lagers, Philippines

Andy Hooper—Seismic Brewing Co., California, USA

Norman Jung—Ratskeller Braumanufaktur, Leipzig, Germany

Greg Knox—Anderson Valley Brewing Co., California, USA

Evan W. Lewis—Ægir BrewPub, Flam, Norway

Brad Loukes—Great Western Malting, Washington, USA

Cody Martin—Martin House Brewing Company, Texas, USA

Jeff Mello—Bootleg Biology, Tennessee, USA

Will Meyers—Cambridge Brewing Company, Massachusetts, USA

Randy Mosher—Five Rabbit Cervecerìa, Illinois, USA

Roger Mussche—Belgian Fine Technology International, Belgium

Kailey Partin—Rising Tide Brewing Company, Maine, USA

Ron Pattinson—Author/Historian, England

Matthias Richter—Gasthaus & Gosebrauerei Bayerischer Bahnhof, Leipzig, Germany

Adam Robbings—Reuben's Brews, Washington, USA

Eric Rose—Hollister Brewing Co., California, USA

Sebastian Sauer—Bierkompass / Freigeist Bierkultur, Germany

Edgar Schmidke—Gosenschenke Ohne Bedenken, Germany

Tom Schmidlin—Postdoc Brewing, Washington, USA

Andrew Schwartz—Modern Times Beer, California, USA

Gordon Strong—Beer Judge Certification Program (BJCP), Mid-Atlantic Region USA

Terence Sullivan—Sierra Nevada Brewing Co., California, USA

Kristi Switzer—Brewers Association, Colorado, USA

Jennifer Talley—Brewing Consultant, California, USA

Trey White—Anderson Valley Brewing Co., California, USA

INTRODUCTION

When I started brewing in 1985, small breweries made something light, something dark, and (if you were lucky) sometimes something with wheat. The variations depended on which tradition you were representing—something light British was a pale ale, something light German was a pale lager, and dark beers were stout or *dunkel,* respectively. Wheat beer was a German thing, and sometimes, if you got very lucky, the British dark was a porter. The 1985 Great American Beer Festival® (GABF) winners list was three beers long: lager, amber lager, and *dunkelweizen.* The first year the GABF had style categories was 1987, and there were 12. One of the new ones was Continental Pilsner (leading me at the time to believe there must be other types of Pilsners to be found—why else specify this Pilsner as Continental?). Clearly I needed to know more. I talked to other brewers (the few who were around back then), I began to acquire books (even fewer of those), and I pestered the homebrew shop owner.

I started brewing professionally in 1988 for Redhook Ale Brewery, and in 1989 I went to work for Pike Brewing. Merchant du Vin owned Pike Brewing; it was an importer of classic European craft beers, and this is when I was really exposed to beer styles. Owners Charles and Rose Ann Finkel took me with them on visits to their imports' breweries: Samuel Smith's, Ayinger Privatbrauerei, Lindemans, Caledonian, Traquair House, and others. We met with brewery owners, talked to brewers, and we drank a wide variety of great beers. I was bitten by the brewing bug; once again, I wanted to know more. I started collecting books on beer and brewing. It became a kind of an obsession—I am a bit of a collector, and I may have gotten a little carried away. I ended up with a pretty extensive library of a few hundred books, many of them pretty old. And over my years as a professional brewer, I have done a lot of research in my quest to develop new beers.

So the first time I heard of Gose, I was honestly a little annoyed with myself. How had I missed this style of beer? I went back to my books, starting with the obvious ones: *Michael Jackson's Beer Companion, Michael Jackson's New World Guide to Beer, The Oxford Companion to Beer, The Encyclopedia of Beer, German Wheat Beer,* and *Prost! The Story of German Beer.* Nothing. Maybe I needed to go old school; *The Curiosities of Ale & Beer, Origins and History of Beer and Brewing?* Nada, no entries for Gose. Maybe I was not the only one who had missed Gose. Then, finally, while digging through *One Hundred Years of Brewing,* I found two brief mentions: "Goslar and Halberstadt Gose," and later, "The Gose was named after its home city, Goslar." Then I found two entries in *The Oxford Companion to Beer;* my friend (and excellent brewer) Brian Hunt mentioned Gose in his discussion on sodium chloride: "However some craft breweries have recently recreated the previously extinct Leipzig Gose beer style, which contains notable salt." And then a few pages later Wolfgang Stempfl, while discussing sourness, states, "Sour ales such as Berliner weisse and Leipziger Gose are inoculated with *Lactobacillus* bacteria." Now I knew that Gose-style beers were sour and contained notable amounts of salt, and that they came from either Goslar or Leipzig. Clearly other brewers knew about Gose. I needed to catch up.

Until very recently, little was written about Gose in any language except German. The issue then became finding these old German books and getting good translations. To complicate matters, Gose's history is long, complicated, and sometimes confusing. There are twists and turns, dark patches, and dead ends. Over the more than 600 years that brewers and beer aficionados have written about Gose, much of what has been chronicled created almost as many questions as it did answers. Maybe this would be true of any beer style that spans approximately a millennium, but Gose had moved not just through time but through various locations as well. Over the years, Gose has been sour and not sour; salted and (maybe) not salted; made with 100 percent wheat or 50 percent wheat, or possibly 75 percent; spontaneously fermented or inoculated; spiced with coriander, spruce, and at some points other spices; and named after a huntsman's wife or a river. You have to glean each piece of information with a grain of salt, both figuratively and literally. Each written account needs to be examined through the lens of the appropriate time, using an understanding of the technology and scientific knowledge of the day. And maybe most importantly, you need to realize that all beer styles are fluid and bound to change a little (or a lot) over time. What follows is my endeavor to make sense of what I have learned about Gose, and in turn tell you, gentle reader. We will explore what Gose was like during its heyday, through its darkest hours of near-extinction, and plot out the most likely path it took from Goslar through Halberstadt, Leipzig, across the pond to America, and around the world. I hope you enjoy the journey!

1

THE HISTORY OF GOSE

When asking a Gose-drinker about his favorite drink, as you can see his eyes light up. A well-matured Gose is for the expert, who explored and got to know the nuances in taste at length, above everything, he calls it his "Göttergetränk" ["Gods Drink"]. Tasty and thirst-quenching, seemingly sour but full-flavored and at the same time stimulating digestion, this golden bright drink invites to cheerful pleasure.

—Otto Kröber, *Die Geschichte der Gose und die Chronik der Gosenschänke Leipzig-Eutritzsch* (Translated by Adept Content Solutions)

"Gose" is German and is pronounced "GO-zuh." The name is derived from the river that flows through Goslar, which is named Gose. The Gose name is not derived from the Flemish-named *gueuze*, since Gose predates gueuze by many hundreds of years (Unger 2004). As with most of the classic beer styles, it is difficult to say exactly when a beer style originated or what that original beer looked, smelled, and tasted like. This may be especially true of Gose, as Gose has a lineage that extends well into the hallowed past before most beer styles. Another thing that makes it hard to know what Gose was like traditionally is that today's Gose is not the Gose of many, many years ago. We need to define which iteration of Gose we are talking about.

Which of these Gose traditions are we defining? The early ale brewed in Goslar (between the years AD 950 and the 1300s);[1] the Gose beer of 1470;[2] the Leipzig Goses of the 1600s, 1700s, and 1800s (d'Elvert 1870); the Gose reborn after World War II that died in 1966; the Gose that was again resurrected in the 1980s; or the modern Gose-style beers that we are brewing today? We will discuss all these iterations in as much detail as we can and I will try to categorize them into three general periods: Gose brewed in the Middle Ages (AD 500–1500), those produced in the early modern times (1500–1750), and the Gose of today (1750 to present).

Gose beer was first brewed more than 1,000 years ago in Goslar, a small town that sprung up near the silver mines of the Rammelsberg mountain in central northern Germany. That beer was probably significantly different from the Gose we are drinking today. With the exception of the kettle, almost all the brewing equipment used 1,000 years ago would have been made of wood. My opinion, based on many sources, is that the original Goslar beer was almost certainly spontaneously fermented or fermented from a mixed wild culture that had taken up residency in the wood vessels used for brewing and fermenting the beer. There are many citations that state Gose was fermented without pitching yeast—these citations are from the twelfth until well into the sixteenth century, and some from as late as the nineteenth century (H.S. Rich & Co. [1903] 1974, 32).

Generally speaking, the brewing process prior to the 1400s was very different from that of today. Sparging and boiling were sometimes not even part of the process. Many brewers did not sparge the mash. In some cases brewers did not boil the wort at all, and in other cases boiling the wort was not for very long. The benefits of boiling the wort were not well understood and it was a labor and resource intensive process (keep in mind that any fuel used to fire the boil had to be harvested and prepared by hand). In areas like Goslar, where there was an abundance of metals from mining, copper vessels came into use earlier than in some other areas—in those areas boiling was probably more common.

We can be almost positive Gose was originally brewed with *gruit* or some sort of spice mix and not with hops (Corran 1975). Around roughly AD 500 to 1000 not only were hops not yet used in brewing, but there were laws that decreed brewers use gruit in their beers (Unger 2004). Additionally,

---

[1]   http://www.leipziger-gose.com/gose-geschichte.html

[2]   Goslar Council Regulations *(Goslarer Ratsverordnungen)* of 1470

it was the Holy Roman Emperor, Otto III, that held the *Gruitrecht* ("Gruit Right") which allowed ONLY him or his direct agents to levy tax on the sale and use of gruit. It would have been only the very poor or the exceedingly foolish brewer that would transgress against a king who was also the Holy Roman Emperor (Unger 2004). One can draw the conclusion that these early beers from Goslar would have been fermented by multiple kinds of organisms, probably several strains of *Saccharomyces cerevisiae*, as well as lactic acid bacteria, *Brettanomyces*, other wild yeast, and probably even a bit of *Acetobacter* if the beer was left to age.

Figure 1.1. Portrait of Otto III—a detail from *Gospel of Emperor Otto III, The Enthroned Ruler*, Master of the Reichenau School. Reproduction part of a collection by The Yorck Project, [Public domain], via Wikimedia Commons.

Later iterations of Gose would count on lactic acid bacteria before and during fermentation to create its sourness. By the 1800s, brewers were adding extraneous powder possibly to acidify the beer that today we sour with *Lactobacillus* bacteria in the brewhouse (Frey et al. 1999). Many of the ingredients have changed over time as well (Hornsey 2003). Gruit or herbs, spruce, hops, and coriander have all been used at one point—or not. The malt was wheat, barley, and in some cases some oats—all used in differing proportions during different time periods of the beer's evolution. This includes early versions that were 100 percent wheat.[3] Malt would have been dried over a source of heat, potentially making it smoky, or the malt could have been dried in the air with no heat, leaving it very light in color but without the bready or toasty flavors we associate with malt today. Finally, of course, there were different water sources when Gose was brewed in different towns.

BREWING GOSE IN 1733

By Benedikt Rausch

The origin of Gose lies in a small town in the beautiful Harz Mountains called Goslar. Some time ago I visited the town to recreate one of the oldest beer styles in existence. I was overwhelmed by the beauty of the area. The city and the small river from where the Gose got its name lie deep in gloomy spruce woods. In these surroundings, it is not difficult to imagine how life would have been 300 years ago.

We go back to the summer of 1733 and today is one of 261 brewing days this year (Brinkmann 1925). The brewer, a distant ancestor of the Siemens family, is one of several privileged citizens with the right to brew (Steckhahn 1882). Every year he has one chance to brew a Gose with equipment that he shares with other brewers; today, it is his turn, although this year another citizen has transferred his right to brew to him and in doing so has given him yet another chance (Brinkmann 1925).

The grain he needs to brew was bought directly from farms neighboring Goslar—200 years earlier it would have most certainly been imported. The grain he uses is only the finest quality wheat and nothing else. The wheat is malted by the brewer himself in the attic of his house in the city's center (Brinkmann 1925). After soaking the grain, it is left to sprout in heaps and occasionally raked to keep grains separated and to control the temperature. It is then left to dry in open air but never kilned; hence the name, Luftmalz. A quantity of 3½ Wispel is weighed out, moistened, and brought to the mill (Bibra 1791, 362).

The brewer and his many helpers fill four large copper kettles with water and begin to heat them. Then, they mix a large portion of the malt with heated water from two of the four kettles in a wooden mash tun using long sticks called Krücken *(Zückert 1762). While mixing the mash, the lauter tun is prepared by placing a wooden screen at the bottom and adding*

---

[3]   Jürgen Reuß, "Die Goslarer Gose," Bier aus eigener Küche (website), September 28, 2004, http://www.bierauseigenerkueche.de/Goslarer%20Gose.html.

rye straw on top of it (Brinkmann 1925). Straw is wrapped around a stick and stuck into a hole in the bottom of the lauter tun from which the clear wort will come out later (Zückert 1762; Steckhahn 1882).

After the backbreaking work of mashing in is done, the brewer and his helpers rest for an hour and sing a song (Steckhahn 1882). Then, the brewer loosens the stick and slowly lets clear wort run from the bottom of the tun. He controls the flow with how far he lifts the stick out of the hole. The wort flows into a hollow sandstone vessel that is buried beneath the lauter tun and is then ladled into one of the empty copper kettles until it is half full (Zückert 1762).

Now, two sacks of hops are added to this wort and the mixture is boiled for two hours (Zückert 1762). This very hoppy brew, called Hopfkrug, contains all the flavor the beer needs (Brückmann 1735) and is later blended into the other brews of the day (Zückert 1762).

During the making of the Hopfkrug, wort is ladled into the next pan and boiled for two hours. This wort will become the Bestekrug, or first runnings. During the boil, a basket full of spruce twigs is prepared for the finished wort to be filtered through. Wooden chutes bring the beer into the cellar. There, it runs into wooden fermentors that were cleaned the day before with a hot extract of spruce twigs (Steckhahn 1882).

The process is repeated: water is heated in pans, the rest of the malt is thrown into the mash tun, the mash is mixed and put into the lauter tun, then lautered and boiled for two hours. These less and less potent runnings of wort are the second and third runnings (Brinkmann 1925), and, finally ending with the Hüppig, which is not to be boiled at all (Steckhahn 1882).

The Hopfkrug is distributed evenly into the different runnings, with some kept to blend into the finished beer (Brückmann and Kohl 1735). Now the beer is left to ferment without pitching any yeast. After 12 to 24 hours, the beer has begun to ferment (Zückert 1762).

The still-fermenting beer is blended and moved into wooden barrels made of spruce. Different barrels are filled with different blends, some more potent than others. When transporting the beer to Braunschweig, the driver needs to vent the barrels often to keep them from exploding. It takes an entire day to deliver the barrels to the local pub by horse and cart (Brinkmann 1925).

After making his deliveries, the driver orders a Gose from the pub. If the malt and hops were good, the brewing equipment clean, the wood used to fire the kettles dry, and the Gose not too old, it is a marvelous beer to drink (Brinkmann 1925). When young, the beer has a slight bitterness, but after a while it fades and a slight sweetness becomes evident (Zückert 1762). With a prickly tartness on the tongue, it has a taste similar to wine (Brinkmann 1925). The color is straw yellow and the appearance slightly hazy (Zückert 1762). This thirst-quenching beer goes down the hatch quickly.

After this trip to Gose's past, we can take a step back and analyze the scene with the benefit of today's historical knowledge. Brewing as described above, with lautering, mashing, and fermenting in wooden vessels, is still done to this day in remote areas of

Estonia or Norway where the advancements in brewing technology have yet to penetrate.[4] This progress in brewing technology has achieved some marvelous things, but it has also changed the beers we make today.

With modern technology, nobody would want to produce a 100 percent wheat beer, because it's hard. There is no need to use straw and maybe impart a peculiar flavor. The spruce twigs and barrels are gone, replaced by more modern stainless and oak equivalents. The beer that we make today is different—it is polished, but not necessarily better. Sometimes a nod to history and the introduction of some archaic methods can lead to a stunning beer. I encourage every brewer to step out of their comfort zone and try to reproduce old beer styles by incorporating wooden vessels, straw, spruce, or even spontaneous fermentation. It is worth it!

THE LEGEND OF GOSE

Legend has it that during the rule of the Saxon Emperor, Otto the Great, a hunting party, led by his most favored hunter Ramm, was tracking a deer through the forest in the foothills of the Harz mountains. The terrain became steep and the forest thick, so Ramm decided to dismount from his horse and proceed on foot. He tied his horse off to a nearby tree and went on to pursue the deer for some time. In Ramm's absence his horse became agitated and nervously pawed at the ground. In repeatedly doing so the horse unearthed a large nugget of metallic ore. Upon Ramm's return he found the nugget, which he immediately took to his king. By the color and weight of the ore, King Otto could tell it was of great value. He called for his miners to be sent out to investigate. The miners found silver and other metals of such quality and in such quantity as had never before been seen in all of Christendom. The Emperor was so pleased that he named the mountain Rammelsberg after Ramm, and he declared the stream that ran nearby the mines to be named after Ramm's wife, Gosa (Goslarer Museum 2017). The town that grew up around the stream was called Goslar and the beer that was brewed from the stream's water was called Gose.

Although I do like the legend that Gose was named after Ramm's wife, there is another more plausible explanation: the name Goslar came into use in the tenth century. If you take a close look at the name Goslar, you can see that this name is composed of two syllables. The first is "gos-" or "gose-." *Gose* is of Germanic origin and means "fast flowing, or bubbling water." The second syllable "-lar" means "a vacancy in a forest, at which one can settle and graze." That's how it works out to Goslar, which aptly translates as "a camp or settlement at the fast flowing stream."[5]

---

[4]   Lars Marius Garshol, "Brewing koduõlu on Hiiumaa," Larsblog, March 11, 2018, http://www.garshol.priv.no/blog/386.html.

[5]   "An der Gose," Goslarer Straßennamenkatalog [Goslar street name catalog], Goslar (website), copyright 2016, http://www.goslar.de/strassenverzeichnis/pdf/an_der_gose.pdf

Figure 1.2. The city of Goslar lies in the modern day Goslar district (shaded) of Lower Saxony. Leipzig lies over 90 miles (112 km) to the southeast.

Figure 1.3. The Gose river meandering its way toward Goslar.

Today it is the Abzucht river that runs through Goslar, not the river Gose. There are street names in the town of Goslar that suggest this was not always the case: the Gosestraße (Gose Street) and An der Gose (On the Gose). At one time the Gose river had five arms that ran through Goslar before they met with the Abzucht. In the early days of Goslar's development, it was deemed that the Gose river would supply the fresh or potable water to the mills, breweries, and residences and the Abzucht river would be used to take away waste products from the town and mining operations.[6] This of course made the waters of the Abzucht contaminated and unsuitable for brewing. This is just one more way we know it was the Gose river and not the Abzucht river that was used for brewing Gose beers. Over time the arms of the Gose were diverted and conjoined as needed and eventually these canals were covered over. In later years the canals were replaced by a piping system to supply fresh water to the local community (Brinkmannn 1925). The Gose river canal and piping system for fresh water lasted until the twentieth century before being replaced with a different water supply.

We know that the Gose river's water was supplied to breweries and used in the brewing of Gose beer, thus, we can assume that both the town and its beer derive their names from the river Gose. And so, the town of Goslar—birthplace of Gose beer.

GOSLAR: THE TOWN AND ITS BEER

Archeological remains showcased at the Goslarer Museum show that humans have lived in and around the area of Goslar since the Stone Age over 5,500 ago. Excavations there found the remains of prey, including wooly rhinoceros and mammoth, reindeer, wild horse, bear, wolf, and bison; all with obvious signs of being butchered.

Figure 1.4. Coat of Arms of the district of Goslar. Image by Patzi / Wikimedia Commons / Public Domain.

To give some historical perspective, one thousand years ago there were barely 10 million people on the entire planet (as opposed to the 7.5 *billion* there are today). In central Europe at that time civilization was struggling

6   "Thema: Gose oder Abzucht?", comment thread, Goslarer Geschichten (website), http://www.goslarer-geschichten.de/showthread.php?891-Gose-oder-Abzucht.

since the failure of the Roman Empire's central government, which had mostly dissolved. Feudalism came to control most of what little government there was. There were no schools, records were not kept for most things, the vast majority of people (even most of the aristocracy) could not read or write, and the invention of the printing press was a distant 400 years in the future. Wars and invasions were an almost constant threat, and life was short. All but the youngest (or strongest) of beers were a least slightly sour (Nelson 2005). It is around this time that Gose was probably first brewed, although it is hard to be certain exactly when due to the lack of early records.

According to the Goslarer Museum, Otto the Great first founded the town of Goslar in the tenth century after the discovery of silver deposits in the nearby mountain of Rammelsberg. The mining operations for silver, copper, and lead brought the town great wealth, recognition, and status. By the eleventh century the Salian emperors built the Kaiserpfalz (Imperial Palace) in Goslar. This palace became the sometime residence for the German kings and Holy Roman emperors. These were turbulent times in northern Europe, but even during the greatest difficulties one needs respite. Goslar and its surroundings was where the Salian royalty would take a hiatus. It is said that the (very short-lived) Emperor Otto III (b. 980, d. 1002) sang the praises of the Gose beer from Goslar, thereby supporting the claim that Gose has been around for at least 1,000 years.

Throughout the Middle Ages Goslar was a very important town. The wealth and status that Goslar gained brought it the distinction of being an imperial city of the Holy Roman Empire and as such the city was granted some autonomy, special high status, and the right to mint its own currency.

Eventually, mining production declined as the silver ran out, and as the wealth declined so did Goslar's fortunes. Goslar is tucked away up against the Harz Mountains and away from any of the main trade routes. Without the mines Goslar's population gradually shrank. For a time brewing exports helped buoy up Goslar's economy, but eventually brewing fell on hard times too and Goslar settled into being just another small town in Saxony. Today, Goslar is one of the better preserved historic towns in Germany. Many of its buildings date from the late Middle Ages.

GOSE IN GOSLAR

If sources are to be believed, Gose is one of the oldest distinct beer styles known. It is thought to have first been brewed late in the tenth century. The earliest record of beer being brewed in Goslar is in 1181 (in a medieval manuscript of the city's archives) and again in 1239 (Albers 2017; Doebner 1882, 21). The oldest surviving document from outside of Goslar that makes specific mention of a Goslar beer comes from the monastery of Ilsenburg and is dated March 23, 1332.[7] The monastery had been built on royal lands deeded in 995 by Otto III. Elysynaburg, as the site was called before being converted to the Ilsenburg monastery in 1030, was the sometime residence of Otto III when he was not waging war to keep his rule intact.[8]

In 1381, in order to curb a flood of imported beers, the town council of Hamburg set a tax rate for foreign beers that could be as much as four times that of local beers. It appears that this tax increase in foreign beers was a result of Gose's popularity, and the record mentions Goslar beer is mentioned as the most popular beer imported to Hamburg during the 1300s (Unger 2004). Finally, the beer is mentioned by the "Gose" name in the Goslar city council records of 1470.

With Goslar's great wealth and special status we can be certain that beer was being brewed in the city some time shortly after its founding. Although we cannot be certain of the style's existence prior to its mention in the 1400s, we can be sure that the antecedents of the 1470 "Gose" beer were being brewed in and around the Goslar area long before that. From this perspective, a claim of a Goslar style of beer (i.e., Gose) being brewed 1,000 years ago does seem well within the realm of possibility.

At the height of Gose's popularity in Goslar during the mid-sixteenth century there were 387 houses that had been granted licenses to brew (Brinkmann 1925).[9] The beer had become a phenomenon. "By the end of the 1500s, the entire Harz region was covered by Gose fever and the beer was an export hit of the city."[10] As the style's popularity grew, the Gose name was used not just in Goslar but also in reference to beers being brewed by the same or similar recipe in other cities. The cities of Wernigerode, Quedlinburg, Blankenburg, Halberstadt, Halle, Glauzig, Spören, and (of course) Leipzig all had breweries that made a Gose. Sometimes these beers were just referred to as *weissbier* (white beer). That is, as opposed to the *braunbier* (brown beer) or *Gerstenbier* (beers made only with barley and no wheat) that were also produced in the region. Interestingly, during the height of

---

[7]   "Die Geschichte der Gose," Ritterguts Gose (website), copyright 2018, http://www.leipziger-gose.com /gose-geschichte.html.

[8]   Encyclopaedia Britannica, 11th ed. (1911), s.v. "Otto III."

[9]   Reuß, "Die Goslarer Gose" (see page 8, n. 3).

      Brewing was different in those days and a right to brew did not mean you owned a brick-and-mortar brewery. Brewery space was often shared and a brewer not owning an actual brewery might take a turn using the equipment of the town council or of a shared brewery. Often a town had two or more shared kettles that would be moved from one location to another. But no matter the number of actual breweries, 387 licenses to brew was a lot.

[10]   "Goslarer Straßennamenkatalog - Stadtteil Goslar" ["Goslar street name catalog - Goslar district"]. http://www.goslar.de/strassenverzeichnis/goslar

Goslar's Gose production and export, the brewing of braunbier and Gerstenbier was restricted to the early months of the year so as not to interfere with the brewing of Gose for export (McGregor and McGregor 2017).

By the 1800s there was no more Gose being brewed in Goslar. I have read many reasons for why brewing stopped in Goslar even at a time when Gose was seeing impressive growth in Leipzig. The decline in Goslar's brewing started in the mid-seventeenth century, brought on in part by the Thirty Year's War, which was one of the longest and most destructive wars in human history. During the 1600s and 1700s there was a shift away from beer to the drinking of wine (for the rich) and spirits (for the poor). The introduction of coffee and tea also played a part in the decline of beer's ubiquity in everyday life. Then, in the mid-eighteenth century, the French occupied Goslar during the Seven Years' War. The brewing houses were ruined by the long occupation of the wine-drinking French. The Goslar currency was depressed and the devaluation of circulating money forced the brewers to further reduce the quality of their beer, which resulted in less and less exported Gose.

Figure 1.5. Brauerei von Fritz Natermann helped revive Gose in the town of Goslar from 1935 until it closed in 1939. Photo courtesy Odin Paul, Brauhaus Goslar.

In the 1770s there was a brief revival of Gose, but then in 1780 came the harshest blow. That year there was a great fire that claimed many of the remaining breweries in Goslar. By 1790 there were only 60 breweries operating. The Napoleonic Wars started in the early part of the 1800s; by their end in 1815 Gose production in Goslar and in many of the towns to the southeast had all but died. By 1840 brewing had ceased altogether in Goslar. Even after the demise of Gose brewing in Goslar, the Gose name lived on and remained in use throughout the region, from naming streets to naming the beer being brewed in surrounding towns (Brinkmann 1925).

Gose in Goslar had a brief revival in the years 1935–1939 when it was brewed by the brewery Fritz Natermann. In 1939 the brewery closed, and the old brewery building was turned into a movie theatre and later into a supermarket.[11] Oddly, today in Goslar you will not find any mention of the town's former brewing glory. In a tour of Goslar you will find no plaques commemorating a building holding a former brewery; there is no mention of beer in the entire Goslar museum; and when I asked the museum curator and her assistant about the 387 breweries that once existed there all I got were raised eyebrows, shaking heads, and an answer of, "I've no idea".

GOSE OUT OF GOSLAR: THE 1500s THROUGH THE EARLY 1900s

During the sixteenth century Gose's popularity increased and breweries in the surrounding areas began to copy the style. During the Late Middle Ages beers were often affiliated with the towns they were brewed in; thus, besides the Goslarian Gose, there was the Wernigeröder Gose, Aschersleber Gose, Blankenburger Gose, Halberstädter Gose, and others (Kröber 1912). By the 1600s the center for Gose brewing was shifting from Goslar to the town of Leipzig (around 90 miles southeast of Goslar). Gose's popularity continued to grow in Leipzig and the surrounding areas even as its production waned in its home town of Goslar. By the mid-1800s the area in and around Leipzig boasted over 80 *Gosenschänke,* or Gose taverns, and Gose was the most popular beer in the region.[12] The people of Leipzig were enthralled by the tart, refreshing taste of Gose.

Leipzig

The town of Leipzig was first documented in AD 1015 in the chronicles of Bishop Thietmar of Merseburg (b. 975, d. 1018). Leipzig is located about 90 miles southwest of Berlin where the Pleisse, Parthe, and White Elster rivers

---

[11]   "Die Geschichte der Gose," (see page 14, n. 7).

[12]   Emily Monaco, "The Story of Gose, Germany's Salty Coriander Beer," *Eater,* October 30, 2015, https://www.eater.com/drinks/2015/10/30/9643780/gose-beer-germany.

converge. Leipzig sits at the intersection of two very important medieval trade routes. By 1165 Leipzig had been endowed with city and market privileges. Its importance eventually led to Leipzig becoming one of the leading centers of learning, music, and publishing in Europe. As early as 1499 a city council resolution allowed some of the taverns of Eutritzsch (just on the northern outskirts of Leipzig) to serve the beer of Leipzig.

Figure 1.6. The Leipzig coat of arms. Image by Madden / Wikimedia Commons / Public Domain.

Eutritzsch and the Gosenschänke

Gose was the favorite drink of Prussian military commander Prince Leopold I of Anhalt-Dessau (b. 1676, d. 1747). Prince Leopold, nicknamed "the Old Dessauer," was well known throughout Germany. At that time Gose was very popular in the area around Anhalt and was brewed in many towns of that region. In 1712 Leopold was having Gose brewed on his royal estate in Glauzig. The beer was known as *Gludscher Gose* (the Gose from Glauzig) and Leopold served it to his royal friends (Keil 1872). The beer garnered accolades and continued to spread quickly with the help of the royal recommendation.

During his travels in 1738, Prince Leopold visited the city of Leipzig. To get there, he travelled through what was then the small town of Eutritzsch just to the north of Leipzig (today Eutritzsch is considered part of Leipzig). Leopold stopped for a beer in the local tavern owned by his old friend Gieseke. Gieseke had served as a soldier under Leopold in the Prussian regiment of Halberstadt. Gieseke's soldiering had so impressed the prince that after Gieseke's service the prince asked him to become his personal valet. After many years of service to the prince, Gieseke and his wife (whom he met during his time as Leopold's valet) moved together to Eutritzsch, where they bought the tavern on Heerstrasse (Kröber 1912).

Leopold had been looking forward to visiting his friend, but when the prince arrived to drink in Gieseke's tavern, the beer was most definitely not to his liking. He is said to have spat out the beer together with a number of expletives. The barkeep apologized, but explained that they were not allowed to serve a different beer due to local laws controlling what beers a tavern got and how much. Every tavern within a designated distance of Leipzig's center was

Figure 1.7. The Gose Tavern of Otto Kröber in Eutritzsch, Leipzig. Note the Ritterguts Döllnitz casks of Gose being delivered.

Figure 1.8. Inside the Gosenschänke. Note the longneck bottles of Gose.

only allowed to serve beer selected for them by the Leipzig city council. Prince Leopold was outraged, and he promised to send to Gieseke a few barrels of the Gose brewed at his estate in Glauzig. Soon, as promised, Leopold's Glauzig Gose arrived. When presented to the Leipzig town council, Glauzig Gose's flavors and Prince Leopold's pressure persuaded the council to grant permission for the tavern in Eutritzsch to serve the new Gose beer. Once Gieseke was awarded permission to serve the Prince's Gose, Gieseke renamed his tavern. Now he would call it the Gosenschänke (the Gose Tavern).

Soon Gieseke's business began to take off. People in Leipzig learned about the special beer being served in a tavern in Eutritzsch. People from all walks of life began trekking to the tavern where Gose was served; students, residents, visitors, politicians, and craftsmen—all made the trip to visit the Gosenschänke (Kröber 1912). The trek to Eutritzsch became a highlight of visiting the town of Leipzig. (Even today there are tours of the Gose tavern trail, where you can stop at selected taverns along the way and drink Gose.) With the success of Gieseke's Gosenschänke, other taverns began to ask for and serve Gose.

In 1781, Udolf Audenar Keitzinger published a song, "The Gose-Brother and the Return to Eutritzsch," which describes the Gose-brothers will never become extinct:

> *Many have died*
> *but Eutritzsch's (drinking) army*
> *is not ruined yet*
> *New sprouts come endlessly*
> *every year continuously*
> *who can take in the*
> *soothing Gose beer!*

—Excerpt from "The Gose-brother and the return to Eutritzsch," by Udolf Audenar Keitzinger (1781), quoted in Otto Kröber, *Die Geschichte der Gose und die Chronik der Gosenschänke Leipzig-Eutritzsch* (Translated by Adept Content Solutions) (Leipzig, 1912).

FIGHTING GOSE AS THE COMPETITION

Suspicious that there might be a violation of his Gose serving monopoly in his area, Johann Gottlieb Hermann of the Castle Cellar Tavern wrote to the Leipzig town council on September 23rd, 1776:

"A wheat beer which is known as Gose and is brewed in Glauzig located in Deßau receives high popularity in this local city. With councilman permission I am willing to store this beer in the castle cellar in order to increase interest as well as to improve servings a bit at all sides. However, I was secretly made aware that the tavern host in Eutritzsch, Eckardt, has made a contract with

the leaseholder of Glauzig in such a manner that in an area only two hours from this location nobody is allowed to deliver and sell such beer and the first-mentioned is solely able to serve this beer. This hinders my intention and more importantly affects the councilman's serve privilege given to the castle cellar in such a manner that it turns into a prohibition contract.

Therefore, I kindly ask to defeat the mentioned contract and to forbid Eckardt in Eutrizsch to serve foreign beers, which should solely be permitted to be served in the Dero castle cellar." (Frey et al. 1999)

Throughout the 1700s Gose's popularity continued to grow in and around Leipzig. But by the end of the Napoleonic Wars things looked pretty bleak for Gose. Many of the breweries in the small towns of Anhalt shuttered their doors and Gose production in Goslar diminished to a trickle. In 1812, during the closing days of Napoleon's German campaign, a Leipzig merchant named Johann Gottlieb Goedecke acquired the Döllnitz manor estate. On the manor grounds there was a small wheat and brown beer brewery. Goedecke wanted to try his hand at brewing Gose, but his attempt at a satisfactory brew did not find the right mix of ingredients and know-how. In 1824, Goedecke was able to entice brewer Johann Philipp Ledermann away from an unnamed brewery in Goslar to his estate brewery just outside of Leipzig. Ledermann was brought in to improve the brewing situation. He was said to have directly supervised every brew and soon he was able to get the brewery moving in the right direction. Late in 1824 the brewery began to produce Rittergut Döllnitz Gose (*Rittergut* is a German word for "manor house"). Ledermann worked there until his passing in 1852. After Ledermann's death his wife, Frau Ledermann, took over supervision of the brewery and she ran it until her passing in 1883.[13] By the early 1880s the Ritterguts Brauerei Döllnitz had managed to corner a significant share of Leipzig's Gose beer market. It had displaced the Anhalt Goses almost completely. And although several other breweries tried to imitate and brew Gose

Figure 1.9. Brewmaster Joannes Philipp Ledermann of Döllnitz brewery.

---

13   Ron Pattinson, Leipzig Pub Guide "Leipziger Gose" (website), copyright 2011.
      https://www.europeanbeerguide.net/leippubs.htm#gose

Figure 1.10. A 1908 advertisement for the Ritterguts Brewery in Leipzig. Image courtesy of Shelton Brothers Inc.

themselves, the Ritterguts Döllnitz Gose remained the market leader.[14]

An important reason that the Döllnitz brewery was so successful was the self-sufficient manner in which it operated. Barley and wheat were cultivated on the manor's own 900 acres, then malted and dried in their own malthouse.

---

14   "Die Geschichte der Gose," (see page 14, n. 7).

The coal required for heating in the malt house and brewhouse was extracted from a pit on the manor property. Even the horses that were pulling the carriages filled with beer to Leipzig were raised on the manor property. Another reason for their success was that the Döllnitz brewery intentionally limited its production to keep demand high. Through most of the latter half of the nineteenth century the brewery produced about ~8,522 bbl. (10,000 hL) of Gose per year, much of that in bottles (Frey et al. 1999).[15]

During this time the Gose taverns played an integral part in the beer's life. It was here that the beer was not just served, but completed its fermentation and was packaged for sale. Although Gose was brewed at the brewery, after fermentation started the young beer was quickly transferred to wooden barrels and shipped off to the taverns while still fermenting. The Gose would go through its initial fermentation in those barrels. Toward the end of fermentation the beer would be transferred to its unique longneck bottles, where it would age for a few more days and develop carbonation before being served. The fermenting bottle would remain uncorked. The reason for the special longneck bottles was that the yeast (and/or other fermenting organisms) would form a plug at the top of the long neck as the final fermentation was finishing up and act as a stopper (Frey et al. 1999). This bottle conditioning took about 12 days (somewhat faster in the summer and somewhat slower in the winter months).

AN ODE TO GOSE

A beer brewed in Leipzig
Which they call Gose,
Goes to your head at times
And sometimes in your ... pants
—Anon. Berlin 1856

As the passage suggests, for those not accustomed to a live wheat beer with yeast, the first encounter with Gose can be ... well, a bit difficult on the stomach. It is reputed that even the strongest of men (and women) can encounter some rather unexpected gastric issues and should always be mindful of where the water closet might be.

A more gentle perspective comes from a plaque on the smoke-darkened walls of the Gose tavern Ohne Bedenken that states, "You can peacefully laugh where Gose is drunk; Bad guys drink the stronger beverages."

---

[15]   To give the reader some perspective: during that same time Munich's smaller breweries were producing about twice that annually and the bigger brewers were producing about 50 times that amount.

Throughout the latter half of the nineteenth century, and even into the early years of the twentieth century, Leipzig was known as the Gosestadt (Gose City).[16] At the height of Gose's popularity there were more than 80 Gose taverns in Leipzig alone.[17] There was a whole culture surrounding the drinking of Gose. Terms like *gemütlichkeit* (cozy, conviviality) and *stammtische* (a table for regular customers) took on larger meaning when applied to the *Gosebrüdern,* or Gose brotherhood. Members of the loosely associated Gosebrüdern were said to be able to distinguish those bottles of Gose stored by the cellar wall, where it was cooler, from those bottles stored in the center of the room.

By the beginning of the 1920s Gose's popularity had started to decline again. Pilsner beer, due to easier storage as a lager, was steadily encroaching on the Gose market. The First World War was hard on all German brewers and it seemed to be especially hard on those older styles of beer that were regional specialties. After the war, Gose's popularity was a shadow of its former self.

GOSE IN POST-WAR GERMANY

In the late 1930s the Ritterguts Brauerei Döllnitz was the last production brewery still making Gose. In 1945, after the Second World War, Germany was divided in two, with Ritterguts Brauerei Döllnitz falling in the Soviet Occupation zone where supplies were rationed and priority for grain was to be used for bread. The communist government took over Döllnitz manor and the Ritterguts Brauerei Döllnitz. It was first nationalized and then control was given to Volkseigener Betrieb (VEB) Sachsenbräu. The very large state-owned VEB Sachsenbräu had no interest in running a miniature brewery. This was the final blow for Gose. Soon after, the brewery was shuttered and dismantled. There was no interest whatsoever in preserving an old Leipzig tradition, especially not by the government who considered Gose and its culture as "petty, bourgeois and backwards thinking" (Frey et al. 1999, 52). Gose culture, with its strong regional ties, did not fit in with the concept of the homeland being "the socialist world system [of mother Russia]" (ibid., 52). After the Second World War and through the 1950s, it was only a few very passionate brewers that kept the Gose style alive in just a handful of small pubs. In 1949, Leipzig brewmaster Friedrich Wurzler, using the old Döllnitz recipe, started making Gose at his brewery.

Wurzler had worked at the Ritterguts Brauerei Döllnitz and was the son-in-law of their last brewmaster, who, as fortune would have it, left his brewing

---

[16]   "Die Geschichte der Gose," (see page 18, n. 7).

[17]   Michael Jackson, "Salty trail of Germany's link with wild beer," Beer Hunter (website), May 9, 2000, http://beerhunter.com/documents/19133-000844.html.

notebook to Wurzler. Soon, Wurzler's tiny brewery at Arthur-Hoffmann Strasse 94 in Leipzig was the only brewery making Gose. At that time there were only about 18 pubs in Leipzig that even wanted Gose. In 1958, Karl Matthes closed the most famous of the Gose taverns, the Ohne Bedenken. By the early 1960s there were just a couple of pubs that still took Gose. In 1966 the Wurzler brewery was closed when the brewer, Guido Pfnister (Wurzler's stepson), died of a heart attack while gardening. Another small brewery, Brauerei Ermisch, considered taking over the Gose production; they even went so far as to take possession of Pfnister's brewing notebook. Unfortunately, their enthusiasm was short lived and soon they decided against taking on such an unusual beer.

In the end the brewing notebook also disappeared. The notebook might have been lost or it might have been accidentally destroyed—the people at Brauerei Ermisch were unable to produce the last known notes on how to brew Gose.

On March 31, 1966 the very last barrel of Wurzler Gose was delivered to the last remaining patron, the Hotel Fröhlich. The hotel still carried on the tradition of filling the longneck bottles from the barrel; and so, the hotel served bottled Gose for a short time, but was closed and demolished in 1968 (Frey et. al. 1999).[18] Again, Gose died.

Figure 1.11. Leipziger Gose label from Friedrich Wurzler Brewery.

Without a Concern

One of the most famous Gose taverns in Leipzig was Carl Cajeri's Ohne Bedenken (which translates to "without concern"). Carl opened the *Gosenstube* (Gose room) in 1899, but moved to a new location in the early 1900s. The current Ohne Bedenken was opened in 1905 and run by Carjeri until 1920. It survived the pre-war, First World War, and post-war difficulties—all very difficult times in German history. Around 1921, August Kurz became the owner and served guests there for ten years until 1932. The tavern was bought by Karl Matthes in 1936 and he ran it until its final day in 1958, some 53 years after its opening. Karl Matthes passed away in a retirement home in Leipzig in 1981; sadly, he did not live to see Gose's rebirth.

---

[18]   Pattinson, Leipzig Pub Guide, (see p. 24, n. 13).

IS THIS STUFF DRINKABLE?

In 1905 Carl Cajeri built a new Gose house on Menckestraße, with a cozy tavern room lined with dark wood on the ground floor. He named it Ohne Bedenken (Without a Concern) after an inspiring word with the popular waiter, Karl Schmidt. When Schmidt was asked fearfully, or in a provocation, whether one could even drink the Gose beer due to its reputed devastating effects, Schmidt replied calmly, "Without a concern," (Frey et al. 1999).

This phrase has also been attributed by others to Dr. Hartmut Hennebach, who became the tavern's owner in 1994. Michael Jackson says, "When Gose was first introduced there [at the Ohne Bedenken tavern], a customer, shocked by the taste, asked proprietor Hartmut Hennebach: 'Is this stuff drinkable?' To which Dr. Hennebach replied, 'Ohne Bedenken.' Although this may have happened as reported by Michael Jackson, it may have happened many a time when customers only accustomed to Pilsners or Bavarian wheat beers got their first taste of Gose (Jackson 1996). It is more probable that the exchange between Karl Schmidt and a customer was the original instance—and thus the quip that the tavern was named after—since the tavern and its name date back to long before Dr. Hennebach worked there or became the proprietor. It is also the explanation given on the Ohne Bedenken website.

That might have been the end of the Gose story if not for one gentleman by the name of Lothar Goldhahn. I don't think it would be an exaggeration to say that without Herr Goldhahn's zeal for this beer style, Gose would have disappeared forever. Luckily for the beer drinking world, in 1985 Goldhahn read an article in a local newspaper about the Gose culture in Leipzig's past. He had the idea to purchase and reopen the old Gosenschänke named Ohne Bedenken.

Goldhahn's objective was to restore the tavern to its former glory as a Gose haven—to restore it as it had been in the in the early 1900s—but the job would not be an easy one. A large part of the beer garden had been damaged in bombings during the Second World War. After the Communist party's takeover of Germany in 1949, the Ohne Bedenken had fallen on hard times. This culminated with its closure in 1958, after which the tavern was stripped, and the rooms left empty for the spiders to move in. Eventually, around 1960, the German Democratic Republic (GDR) government converted the tavern into a cultural center. The great tiled stove was thrown out and the main room was separated into two smaller rooms by a dividing wall. A television set was put up in the front room (a rare commodity at that time). People had to pay a small entrance fee to come in off the streets and watch the television.

In the beer garden a small stage had been set up to host concerts, but it was infrequently used. The cultural center never became very popular. Later, a small library was set up, and then some time after that a small X-ray examination room. In the 1970s the building was abandoned and left completely empty. Nothing was left of the once convivial atmosphere that inhabited the tavern.

In the late 1970s, Lothar Goldhahn was working in a bookbindery, but he had been educated as a "gastronomical host and hotel economist." He wanted to open a tavern of his own. He had been looking for, and hoped to find, a pub with a special character. In the autumn of 1984 Goldhahn applied for a business license to run a privately owned restaurant. This was quite a provocative move during the era of a state-planned, state-owned, state-run economy. Private ventures were not the norm. But Goldhahn had a leg up because he knew the rules well. He knew that in the GDR economic success must always go hand in hand with politics, and he had become a member of the liberal party of the GDR as his special way in. When the party's newspaper, the *Sächsische Tagesblatt,* reported on Goldhahn's plan, it mentioned that he had the support of the trade and supply division of the municipal administration . . . and that he would be spending about 3,000 hours of his own time refurbishing the long abandoned building. Goldhahn had decided to reopen the Gosenschänke.

Over the next two years, Goldhahn collected everything that he could find about Gose: advertisement signs, postcards, books, bottles, glasses, coasters, menus, ashtrays; everything. He hoped this would help him get a better understanding of the Gose beer and form the better part of his new endeavor's decorations. One day in 1985, Goldhahn went to a swap meet looking for Gose memorabilia and there he met Dr. Hartmut Hennebach (who had been a biologist before the end of the war and the rise of the GDR). Hennebach had a collection of things related to the history of Leipzig and in among them Goldhahn found some interesting items related to Gose. The two men got to talking about Leipzig and its great history and soon they were friends. Goldhahn, assisted by Hennebach, began doing extensive research and they were able, through records and interviews, to gather up enough information to develop what they felt was a traditional Gose recipe.

Goldhahn felt strongly that the Gose should be brewed in Leipzig, but no local brewery wanted anything to do with this odd, top-fermented sour beer. He had to look further afield. In 1985, he was able to convince the Schultheiss Berliner-Weisse-Brauerei in East Berlin to brew a Gose for his establishment. In a tasting held some days after the first test brew was finished, a gathering of a few of the Gosebrüdern and other "old school" experienced Gose drinkers declared the new beer a real Gose. Production brewing started in early 1986.

After the tavern's opening in mid-May of 1986 enthusiasm quickly spread. One commentator complained in the Goslar town newspaper, "Why didn't we come up with the idea to revive our old exported beer Gose, and attract large number of tourists (Frey et al. 1999)?"

The Schultheiss Berliner-Weisse-Brauerei stopped producing the Gose in 1988 because (they said) of the need to prepare for the 750th anniversary of the city of Berlin. Goldhahn had to revert to selling just Berliner *weisse* at his tavern (sometimes adulterated with salt and coriander to mimic a Gose), but Goldhahn still was adamant that there was a need for real Gose, not just another beer with the Gose name. Goldhahn and Hennebach became partners of sorts early the next year, and in 1990 Hennebach was made the manager of the Ohne Bedenken tavern, but fairly early on they fell into disagreement about how the business should be run (Frey et al. 1999). Eventually, it was agreed that Hennebach would rent the Ohne Bedenken from Goldhahn and that Goldhahn would concentrate on the beer. In 1991, Goldhahn was able to purchase the small Löwenbrauerei in Dahlen (about 25 miles from Leipzig) and he started brewing his Gose again there. In November of 1989 the Berlin Wall came down and East Germany was again open and free.

In the early 1990s, after decades of oppression of Saxon culture by the Communist Party, a rebirth of the Free State of Saxon was creating a boom in anything and everything regional. For a time, Goldhahn's Ohne Bedenken flourished. It became so popular that during the mid-1990s it was impossible to get a seat without a reservation. It was so busy, in fact, that the tavern was able to expand the beer garden to its original size—"Leipzig's most beautiful beer garden" raved the Leipzig newspapers. But by 1995 economic pressures caused Goldhahn to close the little brewery in Dahlen and the tavern had to find someone new to contract brew its Gose. The Andreas Schneider brewery in Weissenburg took up that challenge. Today, not much has changed at the Ohne Bedenken since the mid 1990s. Hennebach felt a certain obligation to represent the 1990s when Gose became a Leipzig staple again.

Enthusiasm for Gose Grows

Thomas Schneider (of the Andreas Schneider brewery) became so intrigued by the Gose beer style that in 1999 he decided to convert the derelict former Bavarian train station in Leipzig, the Bayerischer Bahnhof, into a Gose brewery.[19] The train station had once been part of Germany's most important north-south routes, the Saxony to Bavaria railroad line. The current Bayerischer Bahnhof pub and brewery houses a 15 hL copper brewhouse, a large bar, a *bierstube*, several private

---

[19] Pattinson, Leipzig Pub Guide "Leipziger Gose," (see p. 24, n. 13).

rooms, a performance hall, and a beer garden. Once the defunct train station was turned into the Bayerischer Bahnhof Brewery, people began to take notice. The Bayerischer Bahnhof Brewery now has a yearly production of about 2000 hL (~1700 bbl.), of which about 90 percent is consumed on the premises.

Figure 1.12. Bayerischer Bahnhof Brewery's brewmaster, Matthias Richter, and the author, Fal Allen, at Bayerischer Bahnhof Brewery, 2017.

In 1999, homebrewer-turned-professional, Tilo Jänichen, and Adolf Goedecke (great-great-grandson of the original Ritterguts Brauerei Döllnitz owner, Johann Gottlieb Goedecke) formed a business venture to brew the Ritterguts Gose again. They had no brewery, since the original had been dismantled after the Second World War. Jänichen and Goedecke decided that the beer would be produced according to the Ritterguts Gose profile from 1824, and they were lucky enough to find a few old bottles of beer from which they could culture yeast and *Lactobacillus* to use in the fermentation (McGregor and McGregor 2017). They started brewing at the Microbrewery Leipzig, but soon it became apparent that they needed more capacity to keep up with demand. They tried several other breweries, before finally settling on the Brauerei Reichenbrand in Chemnitz, just east of Leipzig, to make their Gose.

In 2009, the Brauhaus Goslar opened under the direction of brewmaster Odin Paul. Brauhaus Goslar is now the producer of the new Goslarian beer. The brewery can be found at Goslar's marketplace, just few minutes' walk from the famous Kaiserpfalz. Brauhaus Goslar makes both a light *(helles)* and a dark (dunkel) version of their Gose. The Gose they make is not sour. Brewmaster Paul Odin claims that the Gose from Goslar never was sour, but there is ample documentation to the contrary (discussed later in this book). Odin does add coriander and salt to spice up Brauhaus Goslar's version of Gose.

THE WORLD DISCOVERS GOSE

In the mid-1990s a few people outside of Saxony started taking notice of this unusual style, Gose beer. Randy Mosher talked about Gose in a presentation he gave in 1995 at a "Home Brew U" conference put on by Charles and Rose Ann Finkel (the owners of Merchant du Vin and the Pike Place Brewery). I was at that presentation, but the idea of a salty, sour German wheat beer was so outlandish that no one gave it much consideration. Remember, back in 1995 we were just beginning to grasp the IPA style (with varying degrees of success). Beer writer and guru Michael Jackson wrote about Gose in two separate articles. The first was in October of 1996 in the Campaign for Real Ale (CAMRA) magazine, *What's Brewing*, and it was titled "Salty Trail of Germany's Link with Wild Beer."[20] The next was in 2000 for his Beer Hunter website and was titled "Going for Gose."[21] Both these articles chronicled the recent rebirth of Gose. Randy and Michael teamed up in 1997 in Chicago to do a presentation on Gose, *sahti,* and Grodziskie—Michael talked (and digressed) while Randy brewed beer.[22]

Figure 1.13. Brauhaus Goslar's Helles Gose.

But even with luminaries the likes of Michael Jackson and Randy Mosher applauding the style, not many brewers outside of Saxony showed much interest in Gose. If you look through the beer and brewing books published in the 1990s and early 2000s there is scant mention of Gose. In 2004 Randy Mosher included the style in his *Radical Brewing* book. A year later in 2005, Lars Marius Garshol wrote in his excellent blog, "There seems to be only three Gose beers in existence today: two from Leipzig and one from a US microbrewer."[23] Ron Pattinson wrote a more in-depth blog post on Gose in 2007. He outlined the Leipzig history of Gose and his blog post got the attention of a few more brewers.[24] In 2008 Lars again wrote about Gose, this time he was able to report, "It [Gose] is extremely rare today. RateBeer lists nine Gose beers, 5 in Germany and 4 in the US, all of which are hard to find."[25]

[20] Michael Jackson, "Salty trail of Germany's link with wild beer," *What's Brewing*, October 1, 1996.

[21] Michael Jackson, "Going for Gose," Beer Hunter, August 31, 2000, http://www.beerhunter.com/documents/19133-001353.html.

[22] personal discussion with Randy Mosher, 2017

[23] "Gose," *Larsblog*, accessed June 14, 2018, http://www.garshol.priv.no/blog/19.html.

[24] Ron Pattinson, Leipzig Pub Guide "Leipziger Gose" (website), copyright 2011.

[25] Randy Mosher, pers. comm., 2017.

Even into the early part of the 2010s, Gose was still almost unknown in the beer industry both in Germany and in the USA. In early 2012 Westbrook Brewing released their interpretation of a Leipzig Gose. It was the first release of a Gose that got any real traction in the USA, and for many people (especially on America's East Coast) this was their first introduction to the style. In October of that same year Dr. Hennebach passed away and Gose lost one of its most ardent advocates. Without Dr. Hennebach and the help he gave to Lothar Goldhahn, and later his fervent almost singular support of the style, Gose might have been relegated to the beer scrap heap like so many other unusual beer styles that have been lost over the centuries.

Within a few years of Dr. Hennebach's passing the beer landscape would begin to see a slight shift. The international craft beer obsession with IPAs would start to wane (albeit very slowly) and brewers would begin to seek out things other than the next new hop. Brewers and consumers started to become fascinated with sour beers and this slight shift would turn into a full blown movement. Gose would ride this wave from the brink of extinction to common place. Gose's popularity has been driven by many factors: drinkability, being a great palate for other flavors, by consumers' desires for "something new," and by ease of production (well, ease relative to other styles of sour beer at least).

JOY AND DELIRIUM

Gose good gifts of God; Joy and delirium.
We strive to be lazy, Gose becomes our sanctuary.
Our fingers grasp what has been ripened in the cellar.
All become Gose brothers who drink the gentle drink here.
—An ode to Gose by the Gose Host of Ohne Bedenken, Dr. Hartmut Hennebach.

In 2011 our lab manager Andy Hooper wanted to try making a sour mash beer. He didn't really have a particular style of beer in mind, he just thought it could make an interesting beer. I had tried sour mashing before with only negative results, but I thought, if Andy wanted to try, then why not see if he could triumph where I had failed. Andy gave it a try. The resulting beer lacked drinkability in a gym-locker-meets-rotting-grain sort of way. I did not find the results that surprising, since my results at sour mashing had been similar. I asked Andy what he thought had gone wrong and what we might try differently. He said he was not sure, but that he was going to find out as he wanted to try it again. Andy is a really smart guy, and I thought I had better do some research too if I hoped to be able to discuss it intelligently with him in the future. A few weeks later we were having a beer after work, discussing what we might do to improve our sour mash beer project. We came up with several good ideas that eventually worked their way into how we brew Gose today. As we were talking, a local homebrewer, Mike

Luparello, sat down at the table and after a few minutes said, "That sounds like a great method for making a Gose." I said, "A what?" Neither Andy or I had ever heard of a Gose.

After 25 years of craft brewing, I thought that I had at least heard of most styles of beer, but here was one I certainly had missed. Mike told us a little bit about the style, and we all agreed that it did, in fact, sound like a good method for making a sour beer that only minutes before we knew absolutely nothing about. Now going forward we had a style goal in mind. We went out and bought the few Goses we could find. We did more research about the style and about brewhouse souring in the hopes that we would be better able to tailor our new process to the new beer style we were making. Ultimately, we came up with a process that we think makes a pretty good Gose (it is outlined in the "Souring the Beer" section of chapter 4). We brewed Anderson Valley's first Gose in July 2013.

Figure 1.14. The Gosenschenke Ohne Bedenken, Menckestraße 5, in the Gohlis neighborhood of Leipzig, Germany.

During my trip to Leipzig in 2017, I sought out the Holy Grail of Gose, the Gosenschenke Ohne Bedenken. It has resided in the same location for over a hundred years. The outside looks a bit modern, but the interior remains pretty much the same; the beer garden out back is still very popular during the summer months and consistently wins awards for being one of the best in Germany. In my bad German I ordered a Gose and something to eat. As I sat there pondering my next brewery visit, two older gentlemen at the next table finished their beer and said their goodbyes to the bartender. As they were about to leave one of them turned to me and asked in English, "What do you think of the beer?" (Yes, it was that obvious that I was not a native German speaker.) I replied that I liked it very much, that I had come all the way from California to drink a Gose here at the Ohne Bedenken and that I was not disappointed. His face broke into a big smile and he beamed, "I am the brewer here." I did not know that Ohne Bedenken had a brewer or a brewery. The Ohne Bedenken's new brewer was Edgar Schmidke, and he told me that up until about six months earlier the Gose they served had been made by Ritterguts Brauerei Döllnitz brewery. Edgar said that he had been coming to the Ohne Bedenken for many years. He was a former hobby brewer and now a retiree following a career in engineering. He told me that over the years he had gotten to know the owner, chef, and staff. In early 2017, chef Jens Gröger asked him about helping him brew a Gose for them and Edgar had happily agreed, so they bought a small brewery and began making Gose specifically for the Gosenschenke Ohne Bedenken. And, once again, the Ohne Bedenken had its own beer. The beer is made using a sufficient amount of sour malt, sea salt, and coriander. It is mildly sour, soft yet effervescent, and very bready, with overtones of a German wheat beer. Drinking it was the first time that I fully understood what Napoleon and his troops had meant when he called Berliner weisse beer the "Champagne of the North."

Figure 1.15. From left to right, Fal Allen (author), Edgar Schmidke (Ohne Bedenken brewer), and Andreas Heinz (Ohne Bedenken patron and Gose drinker).

The following day Edgar took me around to several other breweries, notably the Bayerischer Bahnhof and the Ratskeller (which opened in March of 2017). Both of these breweries make very nice renditions of Gose as well as several other traditional beer selections. It was nice to see that Leipzig is once again the home of Gose and I felt (in some small way) part of the Gosebrüdern, or Gose brethren.

As of September 2017, Rate Beer has over one thousand Goses listed. Gose is no longer just an unusual "Saxon niche product," as called by the GDR. Gose-style beers are now being brewed all over the world: Europe, North America, Asia, Australia, and Africa. Today Gose has moved from the realm of near extinction to the realm of near ubiquity. So much so that you never know where you might find one. You might even stumble across a Gose (or two) on your travels through Perm, Russia, over 700 miles east of Moscow—and it would be an oak-smoked tomato Gose no less (fig. 1.16).

Figure 1.16. The backboard from a pub in Perm, Russia. #1 and #9 are both Gose beers. Photo courtesy of Lars Marius Garshol.

2

FLAVOR PROFILES OF GOSE

The new Gose tastes better than the old one, which was, in its pure state, barely enjoyable.

—This comment from an experienced Gose drinker in 1986 appeared in the *Berliner Zeitung* newspaper, regarding Lothar Goldhahn's resurrected Gose of that year, contract brewed by the Schultheiss brewery in Berlin.

The [new] Gose is now more vinous, has a slight acidic character, and lactic acid air and flavor; the foam is very acid with little hops, the beer is yeast-cloudy, fresh, and very refreshing because of its still considerable acidity.

—This description of the same 1986 Gose also appeared in the *Berliner Zeitung.*

The Gose beer style is over 1,000 years old, and during that time the beer has changed in innumerable ways. I have tried to capture an "average" of what Gose was probably like during three separate eras: the Middle Ages (AD 950–1400), the modern period (1600–1900), and the contemporary period (mid to late 1900s into present day). During each of these periods, Gose-style beers were notably different than they were at other times, although each of these three renditions of Gose would have shared many similar characteristics. Throughout all three periods, the beer remained a moderately low-gravity, slightly saline, sour wheat beer.

The flavors and aromas listed here are for Gose beers made without unusual additional flavorings, such as non-traditional spices or fruit. Obviously, additions of fruit or spices will greatly alter the beer's flavor profile. The fact that Gose-style beers easily lend themselves to being flavored with spices or fruit makes it difficult to cover all possible flavor variations.

ACIDITY AND pH

Since acidity is such a big part of Gose, I felt it should be addressed before looking at the other specifications of the beer's flavor profile. Acidity is the main thing that has defined the Gose style since its beginning and also what makes it so unusual as a German beer.

To better understand a Gose-style beer, you need to know a little about acidity, how it is usually measured, and how it works. There are two ways to measure acidity, namely pH and titratable acidity (TA). We will discuss pH first. Acidity is the effective strength of an acid in solution. We use the pH scale to measure that level of acidity or basicity. For the more scientifically minded, acidity is the concentration of hydronium (H_3O^+) in an aqueous solution and pH is one of the scales we use to measure that concentration.

The pH scale was developed at the Carlsberg Laboratory in Denmark by Søren Sørensen in 1909. The p stands for "power of" or "potential of" and the H stands for hydrogen. The pH scale is the negative logarithm of hydrogen ion concentration, and it runs from zero (very acidic) to 14 (very alkaline, or basic), with 7.0 being neutral. At room temperature (25°C), pure water is pH 7. Accordingly, a pH below 7 is acidic, and a pH above 7 is alkaline.

The pH scale is logarithmic, like the Richter scale that measures earthquake intensity, and uses base 10. Each increase or decrease of 1.0 on the pH scale indicates a ten-fold change of hydrogen ion concentration. Thus, a solution of pH 4 is 10 times more acidic than a solution of pH 5, and 100 times more acidic than a solution of pH 6. Remember, the lower the number, the more acidic it is.

Temperature will affect pH, so pH readings should be taken at or calibrated to a temperature of 77°F (25°C). As the temperature rises, pH decreases. For example, at 32°F (0°C) the pH of pure water is 7.47; at 77°F (25°C) its pH is 7.00; and at 212°F (100°C) its pH is 6.14. Be sure to adjust your pH reading accordingly if the temperature of your solution is greater or less than 77°F (25°C).

pH plays an important role in the brewhouse, both in the mash tun, where it will have an effect on enzymatic activity, and in the kettle, where it will affect protein coagulation, hop utilization, and Maillard reactions. Keeping track of pH can also give you vital information on the progress of fermentation. As fermentation progresses, pH decreases. In sour beers, the acidity level can tell you how far bacterial activity has progressed. Because of the many ways pH can affect your beer's flavor, good brewing practice dictates that pH should be measured and tracked throughout the process. To brew Gose-style beers reliably and consistently, you will need a way to measure pH. I would suggest investing in a decent digital pH meter. A pH meter is much easier to read than pH strips and leaves no room for interpretation. They are also much more accurate than pH strips, although pH meters do need to be kept properly calibrated—a relatively easy process—by checking their accuracy against two standard buffer solutions of known pH.

The pH range for most finished, unsoured beers runs between 4.0 and 4.5. Sour beers will run in the range of about 2.9 to 3.9 pH.

TYPICAL pH VALUES IN NORMAL BREWING

Water pH	6.7 to 7.6 optimum
Mash pH	5.0 to 5.7 optimum (should not go below 4.8)
Sparge water over grain	<6.0
Wort pH	4.9 to 5.5 optimum
Beer pH	3.9 to 4.6 optimum
Rinse water pH	pH same as source water

APPROXIMATE pH OF COMMERCIALLY AVAILABLE GOSE BEERS

Anderson Valley Holly Gose	3.3
Lindeman's Cuvee Rene Gueuze	3.4
Lost Abbey Duck Duck Gose	3.3
New Belgian Clutch	4.0
Rueben's Gose	3.2
Russian River Consecration	3.3
Westbrook Gose	3.4
Widmer Marionberry Hibiscus Gose	3.8

Perception and Titratable Acidity

The other main way to measure acidity in liquids is titratable acidity (TA). While pH is an easier and more common method of measurement, TA will give you a more accurate measurement of how the beverage will be perceived. Both are measures of acidity, but TA is a more accurate measure of what you will taste. The general rule is, the lower the pH, the higher the TA, but in actuality these two measurement scales cannot be correlated very well. This is because pH measures only part of what TA measures. Titratable acidity is usually expressed in grams per liter (g/L).

These concepts of pH and TA can be confusing, but I will try to keep it as simple as possible. The more acid you add or create in a solution, the lower the pH, and the higher the titratable acidity. For weak acids, which includes organic acids found in wort or beer, this relation can be explained in the formula:

$$\text{pH} = \text{p}K_a + \log \left(\frac{\text{conc. base}}{\text{conc. acid}} \right)$$

where $\text{p}K_a$ is the negative log of the disassociation constant of the organic acid being measured.

True, a great many people, myself included, struggle to understand this. So, if you don't get it, don't worry about it too much, just keep reading.

In a solution there is both free and bound hydrogen. The pH scale is a measurement of how many free, positively charged hydrogen ions are in the solution. When we measure titratable acidity (TA), we add sodium hydroxide (an alkali, or base) to the solution. What occurs in the solution is that the sodium hydroxide (NaOH) first neutralizes the free, positively charged hydrogen ions, those measured by the pH scale. Once all the free hydrogen ions are neutralized, the sodium hydroxide begins to start to unhook bound hydrogens that are attached to the remaining organic acids in the solution, and by doing so renders them free to be measured. As this happens, we gradually add more sodium hydroxide to the solution. The sodium hydroxide continues to unhook and neutralize hydrogen ions. Only when you have added a sufficient amount of sodium hydroxide to unhook all the accessible hydrogens is our measurement of the titratable acidity complete. At that time your solution pH will be neutral (see below). Titratable acidity does not just measure a specific acid in a solution, for example, lactic or acetic acid; TA measures all the acids in that solution.

Since the proportion of free and bound hydrogen varies greatly according to several variables, most notably the type of acid, so then does the relationship between pH and TA. Both measurements can be important, because they are measuring different, but certainly related, things.

There are many different kinds of acids, and each is made up a little differently. It is important to understand that each acid has a different strength of tartness on the tongue. Some acids are very sharp, others much less so.

With this background on the perception of acidity, it should be easier to understand that how tart a beer tastes is not solely a function of its pH. Different acids will contribute different amounts of TA. And each type of acid will contribute its own unique character to beer. For example, lactic acid, produced by *Lactobacillus* or *Pediococcus* bacteria, is described as much softer on the pallet than acetic acid (produced by *Acetobacter* bacteria). Acetic acid is often described as harsh, burning or biting. To give you a better idea, lactic acid is the main acid in yogurt; acetic acid is the main acid in vinegar. Imagine two beers with the same pH of 3.3. One gets 20 percent of its total acidity from acetic acid, the other gets 100 percent of its total acidity from lactic acid. The acetic acid beer will have a much sharper level of perceived acidity than the 100 percent lactic acid beer.

The harshness of acetic acid is one reason many brewers say it is a flaw in almost all beers and should be kept to very low levels, even in the few styles, like *oud bruin* (sour Flanders brown ale) in which it is an accepted part of the flavor profile. Flavor perception is the reason we care about TA. The pH scale only quantifies the amount of free hydrogen ions in solution; however, your sense of taste interprets not just the free hydrogen ions, but also some of the bound hydrogen that is subsequently released by the acids in the beer. Most people agree that TA is a more accurate representation of how acidic something will taste. Again, keep in mind that different acids are perceived to have different levels of sourness intensity, so two beers with the same TA may taste very different—for example, a Gose with 100 percent lactic acid versus a Flanders Brown with 20 percent acetic acid. Both have the same TA, but taste very, very different. Keep in mind that there are many other factors that can affect one's perception of acidity level, including residual malt sweetness, herbs, flavorings, temperature, and carbonation.

One may wonder, if TA is the measurement we taste, why bother with pH at all? There are many processes that are pH dependent: saccharification during mashing, hop utilization and protein coagulation during the boil, and healthy yeast metabolism. All these activities require specific pH ranges. If we are to assure that these processes progress in the manner desired, we need to provide the optimal pH range for them. Also, a pH reading is much easier to take and does not taint the sample with sodium hydroxide. But both measurement processes are valuable—the TA measurement, for example, can be a good tool for use in blending.

Figure 2.1. An artist's rendering of a delivery from Dollnitz brewery at the back door of Ohne Bedenken Gose tavern. Artist Fritz Brändel.

PERFORMING A TITRATABLE ACIDITY TEST

To perform a test for titratable acidity (TA) you will need a good pH meter, a solution of sodium hydroxide (NaOH) at a known strength, a pipette (in the 0.1 mL range), some glassware, and safety gear (plastic, latex, or nitrile gloves, and safety glasses).

You will need a precise volume of the beer at a specific gravity—but small differences in specific gravity don't greatly impact the results of the equation too much, so don't stress about it if you are not exact. The beer sample should be degassed by agitation. You will need to add small amounts of sodium hydroxide (0.1 or 0.2 mL at a time) to your beer sample. Stir vigorously after every drop and take a pH reading. Do this until you get a pH reading of 8.2—this is the American Society of Brewing Chemists (ASBC) standard. Sodium hydroxide can be purchased in 0.1 M form or blended yourself. Once you reach a pH of 8.3 you will need to do the math.

$$\text{TA (as lactic acid)} = \frac{\text{mL 0.1M NaOH} \times 0.9}{\text{mL beer} \times \text{specific grav of beer}}$$

As a side note, there are many people who use titratable acidity and total acidity as interchangeable terms, but they are not interchangeable. Total acidity is the total number of positively charged hydrogen ions that the organic acids of all types would release if they were fully dissociated. The titratable acidity is always going to be less than the total acidity, because not all of the hydrogen ions expected from the acids are found (or dissociated) during the determination of titratable acidity.

Tools: pH Meters and Strips

pH meter: The best tool for measuring pH is a pH meter. A pH meter measures the voltage between two electrodes, then converts the result and displays it as the corresponding pH value. To ensure accuracy, a pH meter must be kept clean, stored in a dedicated storage solution, and be calibrated regularly in a solution with a known pH value, preferably before each use. Usually, the more expensive a meter is, the longer it will last and the more accurate its readings will be. More expensive pH meters are often equipped with automatic temperature compensation, which can make taking readings even easier.

pH strips: These are a relatively inexpensive and fairly accurate way to measure pH. The strips are calibrated and will measure both acid and base sides of the pH scale. They change color after being exposed to a solution. The color can then be matched to the color chart that comes with the kit to identify the pH of the solution.

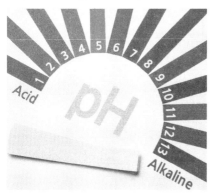

Figure 2.2. Color chart for pH strips. Getty Images/phototake.

GOSE IN THE CONTEMPORARY PERIOD (MID-1900S TO PRESENT DAY)

This section introduces the specifications of the contemporary period in which Gose-style beers are modeled after the Leipzig Gose beers that are now brewed worldwide.

Specifications of Contemporary Gose

Carbonation

Carbonation should be on the higher side of 2.55–3.0 volumes CO_2.

Starting and Finishing Gravities

Original Gravity (OG): These are not big beers, so your starting gravity should be no higher than about 14°P (1.057), and could be as low as 8°P (1.032). Typical starting gravities should be about 10°P (1.040).

Final Gravity (FG): Gose should finish dry, between 1.25°P (1.005) and 3°P (1.012), and certainly not above 3.25°P (1.013). Typically, final gravities should be about 2.25°P (1.009).

Alcohol

The alcohol by volume (ABV) on these beers is fairly low, between 3 and 5 percent.

Color

The color of Gose should be relatively pale, in the range of 1.5 to 6.0 SRM (3 to 12 EBC). This might be a little higher if brewers decide to use a small amount of specialty malt.

Certainly, Gose-style beers will be hazier than German Pilsners, at 0–4 nephelometric turbidity units (NTU). They can range from as low as 20 to as high as 800 NTU, but they should not be milky or opaque. Some haze is acceptable, but Gose should not be as hazy as *hefeweizen*-style beer.

pH

The pH should fall between 3.2 and 3.6. Sourness should be low to medium-high, but should complement the overall beer.

Bitterness

Bitterness should be low—between 5 and 15 IBUs—although some brewers in the US have produced hoppy Gose-style beers. The hoppy versions fall far outside the guidelines of the Leipzig Gose tradition.

Flavor Profile

Flavor

Gose is a tart wheat beer with low bitterness and a restrained touch of seasoning, most often that of coriander. This beer is brewed with both barley and wheat in equal amounts and the flavor reflects this mix. The beer has a mild salinity. The overall impression from the salt should be a light mineral quality and not one of saltiness. Gose-

Wie zwei alte Gosen kosen.

Figure 2.3. An old advertisement that shows two kissing Gose bottles. Notice the stange (glasses) for legs.

style beers usually have a high carbonation level. The tartness is the result of lactic acid and this is often described as a lemon or citrus tartness. Bitterness should be low and generally go unnoticed. Gose-style beers have bright, sharp flavors that make it refreshing to drink. They are highly attenuated and should finish dry and crisp, never full-bodied or flabby. The restrained acidity and sourness should balance the bready, doughy, wheat malt character.

Aroma

Gose-style beer aromas are often light to moderately fruity. The malt aroma is reminiscent of sourdough bread dough. There may be a cider quality to the overall aroma. The use of coriander can give the beer a floral and sometimes lemony note. These coriander notes, when mingled with the fruitiness and sourness, create a pleasing aroma. Hop aroma should be low and when noticeable should complement the other aromatic components. The fermentation (both bacterial and yeast) should be clean, with very low levels of funkiness to none at all. The aromatic qualities should be mild to moderate and should blend together to create an overall impression of being fresh and spritely.

Appearance

Gose-style beers are a very light straw to medium amber color. Typical Gose beers are light golden with a white head. They are unfiltered wheat beers, and as such may range from fairly hazy to bordering on almost bright. High carbonation levels should lend a pleasing effervescence. They may have good head retention from the wheat, but due to lactic acid fermentation, some may also have very little foam at all.

Mouthfeel

The body of these beers is light to medium-full. The overall impression should not be heavy.

GOSE IN THE MODERN PERIOD (1600–1900)

These specifications cover the period of 1600–1900 for Gose as it was brewed in southern Anhalt, Quedlinburg, Halle, Glauzig, and then Leipzig. This was a period of great flux in the brewing world. At the period's start, beers were being made in a fairly similar fashion to those of the era before them, but by the end, brewing had come into the modern age replete with much of the scientific knowledge and brewing equipment that we have and use today.

A SECRET IN THE WORLD OF BEER

We owe this precise description of Gose at three stages of maturity, and its vastly different effects on the drinker, to Friedrich Hofmann, who uncovered "A secret in the world of beer" (Keil 1872):

> *Premature Gose is described as Birnbrühe, too-old Gose sometimes even as vinegar, but Gose with the just right degree of maturity is warmly welcomed with glowing eyes and praised as lemonade with a spirit, the happy spirit of wine. The most gentle effects for the soul and mind are introduced by this middle-aged Gose: The devout regular drinker is seized by emotions of immense serenity and good nature, only joyful talks can be heard at the tables, bright faces all around are pleasing to the eye, blood is pumping lightly through the veins, the soothing and comfortable feeling of a spirit that is not disturbed by any physical discomfort but indulges oneself in relief. It becomes clear to everyone that 'Gose is peace!'*

> *If the stranger now starts to wonder about destroyed chairs and similar things that he might spot in the corner of the tavern, these are only the result of Birnbrühe or vinegar, which are capable of turning the milky source of the most devoted and peaceful mind into fermented dragon poison.*

Specifications of Modern Period Gose

Carbonation
Carbonation should be on the medium to medium-high side of 2.2 to 2.6 volumes CO_2.

Starting and Finishing Gravities
Original Gravity (OG): The starting gravity would be moderate—a maximum of about 12 to 14°P (1.048 to 1.057) and as low as 7°P (1.028). The typical starting gravity should be about 11°P (1.044).

Final Gravity (FG): These beers should finish dry, between 1.5 and 2.5°P (1.006 and 1.010), and certainly not above 3°P (1.012). Typical final gravity should be about 2.0°P (1.008).

Alcohol
The ABV on these beers is fairly low, between 2.8 and 4.8 percent.

Color
The color of these Goses should be relatively pale to white, in the range of 1.5 to 8.0 SRM (5 to 16 EBC). The malt that they were using would have been similar to the

> *A middle course is pursued by the brewers of Gose (light Gose) in Goslar in the Duchy of Anhalt as in Sondersleben, Glauzig and Wendorf. They also take air dried-malt of wheat for brewing, but they add a small amount of the decoction of hops, which is hardly, or not at all, tasted in the drinking of it. This keeps better, and our nature gradually, so easily and so fully accustoms itself to the small quantity of hops that it eventually produces no difference in the effect of the homoeopathic doses of medicine. The lighter beer of Kirchberg, however and in other similar light beers, have an intoxicating, injurious ingredient in them. Even Brown beer, which in itself I cannot recommend, if it only contains hops and no other bitter herb or intoxicating growth, but only hops in a limited quantity, may yet, in default of a better, be permitted, if the patient was before used to it, whereby it becomes pretty much indifferent.* (Dr. Samuel Christian Frederic Hahnemann M.D. [1755–1843] in a letter to his colleague, Dr. Johannes Schweikert, November 24, 1826, quoted in Bradford [1999].

base malts we use today in many ways. In the early part of this period it appears that Gose-style beers were usually 100 percent wheat malt; later in this period that percentage shifts and we see more barley being used. We can be fairly certain that they were using some *Luftmalz* (air-dried malt). Some references put the amount of Luftmalz at about 30 percent of the malt used, others suggest up to 100 percent. Whichever the case, the Luftmalz has less color and produces a light colored, often cloudy beer, not unlike Belgian *witbier*.

pH

The pH should fall between 3.2 and 3.8. Sourness ranges from medium to medium high, but should complement the overall beer. It should be noted that, in the early modern period, most Gose beers were spontaneously fermented by a mixed culture of microbes that resided in the wooden brewing equipment. These mixed cultures would have contained some *Acetobacter* bacteria and, if exposed to air over time, would have developed a distinct acetic acid flavor in aged or older Gose. This may have changed in the mid-1800s when brewing moved to using specific mixed culture additions.

Bitterness

Bitterness should be low, between 3 and 12 IBUs.

Flavor Profile

Flavor

This era's Gose is a tart wheat beer with low bitterness and a restrained touch of seasoning, most often that of coriander. They have a mild salinity—the overall impression from the salt should be a light mineral quality, noticeable, but not one of saltiness. Salt was generally used to enhance flavor and body. These beers were highly attenuated and dry. They usually had a medium-high carbonation level, somewhat lower before mechanical stoppers were introduced. Gose's tartness is predominately the result of lactic acid fermentation or, in some cases, the addition of lactic acid—this was often described as a lemon or citrus tartness. Bitterness would have been low and generally gone unnoticed. Hops were used, but at very low rates. Gose displayed bright, sharp flavors that made it

At table he [Dr. Hahnemann] drank some good wine when he had guests; but his daily drink was sweetened Gose, a kind of mild beer. (Bradford 1999)

refreshing to drink. These beers should finish relatively dry and crisp, not full or round. The restrained acidity and sourness should balance the bready, doughy malt character.

Aroma

Aromas during this timeframe were light and moderately fruity. They were often described as having a white-wine aroma. The malt aroma was reminiscent of bread dough, most notably sourdough. They were sometimes described as having a cider-like aromatic quality. The use of Luftmalz would have contributed a slight grassy note. Coriander or other herbs and spices gave the beer an herbal and sometimes lemony quality. These coriander notes, when mingled with the

Figure 2.4. A postcard from the Gosenschenke with greetings from Leipzig. The artwork shows the unique shape of Gose bottles.

fruitiness and sourness, create a pleasing aroma. Hop aroma was not present. The fermentation, both bacterial and yeast, would be clean with low to very low levels of funkiness in younger versions. Generally speaking, in older, aged versions of Gose you might find that *Brettanomyces* contributed some fruity or light horsey aromas, and bacteria may have contributed aromas of funk or acetic acid.

Appearance

Visually, this era's Gose was very light straw colored to light amber. A good percentage of the malts were air-dried and produced a very light color, making what was often described as white beer with a white head. They were unfiltered wheat beers, and as such were fairly hazy to semi-hazy. Higher carbonation produced a pleasing effervescence. The beers were reported to have a good foam head.

Mouthfeel

The body of these beers was light to medium-full, somewhat heavier than later versions due to the use of Luftmalz, but not heavy.

GOSE IN THE MIDDLE AGES

These are the general specifications for the Gose beers brewed in Goslar and neighboring towns from AD 950–1400.

There were many differences between beers brewed in the early Middle Ages and beers brewed today. In the early Middle Ages there were no hops used in brewing. Brewers often used gruit or an herb and spice mix as a bittering agent and for flavor. The brewing equipment was mostly made of unlined wood, with all its potential for adding tannins and microbiological contamination. There were no thermometers, no hydrometers, no conical tanks. The malting process, although recognizable by today's standards, was quite different. The resulting malts would therefore also have been fairly different. Malt was kilned with less heat for longer periods of time than today's malt.[1] The kilning process is what gives malt, even pale malt, much of its flavor; with less kilning there would be fewer Maillard reactions and fewer bready or biscuit flavors. Gravities would have been higher and the beers heavier, because alcohol was the beer's only real preservative (Corran 1975).

The brewers did not pitch yeast, although they may have used the "leavings" from one batch to start the fermentation of the next. The beer might have been spontaneously fermented, but much more likely fermentation was started by a mixed culture that had taken up residency in the wooden vessels.

This quote from a nineteenth century newspaper article about Gose suggests that not only was the yeast not pitched, but that there were other bacteria and probably wild yeast like *Brettanomyces* active in the ferment as well: "There is no yeast pitched into the beer. Due to that fact, a thick layer of mold builds on top of it. The thicker this leather-like layer gets, the better the stability of the beer. The reason is that the mold layer blocks oxygen from getting into the beer. Only when the beer is given away is yeast pitched."[2]

The brewing process would have been quite different as well. Very few brewers owned their own brew kettle, so much of the equipment was shared and sometimes community-owned. Brewers used the parti-gyle brewing system well into the eighteenth century. They would mash

> The process differed some—"During the first mash, a song was sung during a break, usually, 'Thus Far God Has Brought Us Here,' and then the mash was finished. (Reuß 2007)

---

[1]   Personal discussion with Randy Mosher.

[2]   From "Lokales aus der Provinz und aus den Nachbarstaaten: Goslarsche Gose," *Goslarsche Zeitung*, February 17, 1882, quoted by Benedikt Rausch [nacron, pseud.], "Gosslarsche Gose," *Wilder Wald* (blog), February 15, 2017, http://wilder-wald.com/2017/02/15/gosslarsche-gose/.

the same grain several times to achieve beers of differing gravities. Lautering was done through straw or spruce branches or twigs. There was no sparging of the mash. They would prepare four or five versions of the beer from one milling of grain. The *Frehmtenbestekrug* (best-made jug) was made with the first runnings, and this was the best Gose—and it was often heavily spiced with other herbs. This beer was only given to the best pub customers. The second mash created the second wort, then a third wort was produced, and finally a fourth wort, or *Hüppig*. Additional malt and salt were sometimes added to the last wort. Each type of beer came in specially marked vessels at the time of sale. The beer made with the last runnings would have obviously tasted much different from the one with the first.

The kettles were wood fired, thus making the process somewhat smoky, and although there are some references to the wort having a limited or possibly no boil at all, others say the wort was usually boiled, even as long as two hours. If the wort was boiled for any length of time, the direct-fired kettle would have led to some notable caramelization of the wort. There was no temperature control of any kind for wort cooling, so the wort sat out waiting to get cool enough for fermentation to start. This also meant there was no cooling to control fermentation temperatures. In all likelihood, the beer was fermented in relatively shallow vessels, allowing for sufficient heat dissipation. There was also no cooling of the beer after fermentation was complete. It is hard to know what organisms were involved in the fermentation—certainly yeast, and certainly some bacteria. Top-fermenting yeast was probably the main fermentation organism. Whatever fermented the beer, we can be certain that it was not a pure strain culture like most brewers use today. It was probably several strains, and there was probably a fair dose of lactic acid bacteria involved as well. In all likelihood, if aged long enough, there was probably some *Acetobacter* as well as *Brettanomyces* involved at some point too.

Once the beer was finished, there was the service of the beer. The drinking experience would have been significantly different from that of today. Carbonation would have been lower, because in the Middle Ages there were no vessels or bottles that sealed well enough to hold very much pressure. There was also no glassware—drinking vessels would have been made of wood, horn, leather, gourds, or, for the wealthier consumers, maybe ceramics or metal. The beer would have been served fairly warm, as there was no refrigeration. It would have been served in a house, tavern, or inn among the (literally) unwashed masses, where the acidic aroma of the beer might have been a welcome change over the piquant aroma of your neighbor at the table.

Figure 2.5. Typical activity outside of a tavern during the Middle Ages. *Flemish Kermess* by David Teniers the Younger, 1640. Staatliche Museen, Berlin, Germany.

> *Boiled water from the kettle is poured on top of the malt and is mixed thoroughly through. After it will be boiled for some hours. This extract is the best wort and is called* Beste Krug.
>
> *Water is again added to the grist in the vat. After this, the runnings are cooked and then they are stored in separate vessels in the cellar since every infusion is weaker than the one before. The beer is filled into casks with a certain proportion of each running. (The beer has to be fermenting before it is filled.) The filling is done by selected and sworn-in people. This is the source of the different kinds of Gose. Each has a different amount of the* Beste Krug *in them. The prices for these types are also different. The Gose types that are drunk at the table are sold for four* Pfennig *a Maaß [large mug], the ones that are better cost 6 Pfennig, and the strongest kind is the* Mariengroschen. *The* Mariengroschen *is a strong drink which should not be drunk till fully matured, otherwise you would get too drunk.*
>
> —*Journal von und für Deutschland* edited by Sigmund von Bibra, 1791, p.363; (Translation by Benedikt Rausch and Fal Allen.)

Specifications of Middle Ages Gose

Carbonation

Carbonation of these early beers would be lower, coming in around 1.1 to 2.0 volumes CO_2. There were not very many vessels that could hold much more than about 2.2 volumes of pressure, which is about 12 psi (83 kPa) at 45°F (7°C). Even if the first beer out of a pressurized cask was at 2.2 volumes, once the beer started to be dispensed it would lose its condition fairly quickly. More likely the beer would have been about 1.6 volumes (8 psi , or 55 kPa) at around 55°F (13°C).

Starting and Finishing Gravities

Original Gravity (OG): Starting gravity would probably have been higher than 14 or 15°P (1.057 or 1.061) for the *beste Krug* (best jug) beer, and then lower for the subsequent beers. Likely 12–13°P (1.046–1.053) for the second brew and down in descending order until that last beer probably had an OG of about 8°P (1.032). The higher gravity for the first two brews would be partly because, until the thirteenth century, the common beers of northern Europe were spiced ales that needed alcohol as a preservative—often beers were "a heavy and thick drink" (Lawrence 1990). Toward the end of this period, when hops came into use, beer could be brewed with less malt to achieve the same balance and longevity (Hieronymus 2012, 55).

Final Gravity (FG): These beers finished somewhat drier, between 2.0 and 3.2°P (1.008 and 1.013) and not much above 3.3°P (1.013), given wild yeast and bacterial fermentation. The last brew would have finished in the range of 0.5–0.8°P (1.002–1.003).

Alcohol

The alcohol by volume (ABV) on these beers would have been a little higher, between 3.8 and 5.5 percent, maybe a little higher for the Frehmtenbestekrug, and of course lower for the last brew. They were made to be consumed fairly quickly after fermentation and not meant to be stored, thus we can deduce that the alcohol was probably lower than that of contemporary "brown beers."

Color

This is a tricky question. On one hand it has been suggested that the beers were being brewed with air-dried wheat malt, a process in which the malt is dried in the sun or air without ever being kilned. This malt would have been relatively light in color and would produce a light and cloudy beer. On the other hand, the color of the earliest Gose or those beers brewed to the south of Goslar might have been somewhat darker than today, in the range of 3 to 10 SRM (6 to 20 EBC), because during the early Middle Ages malting was often done on a small scale at home or on a farm, and most of that type of kilning used a wood-burning heat source. These beers probably were brewed with mostly wheat malt, but may have had lesser amounts of barley or even oats. Certainly, these Gose beers would have been hazy with such a malt bill. Additionally, there was no cooling of the beer to precipitate chill haze or assist in yeast flocculation. The lack of hops and short boil times would have limited protein coagulation and probably created a very hazy beer.

pH

The pH probably ranged between 3.2 and 3.6. Sourness would have been low to medium-high depending on the age of the beer, but it would have complemented the overall beer. Acidity would have come from multiple microbiological sources, including *Lactobacillus* and probably *Acetobacter,* as the beer aged. There are written accounts from the later part of this period that describe a thick, leathery layer forming on top of the beer as it fermented. This leathery layer might have been the result of *Gluconobacter, Pichia,* or other heavy pellicle-forming microorganisms in the fermenting mixed culture. The pellicle would have initially protected the beer from oxygen, suppressing *Acetobacter* growth and reducing acetic acid formation. Thus, young Gose was probably much less acidic than older, aged versions.

Bitterness

The bitterness in beers from this era would have come from the herbs, spices, or tree barks used in the gruit or other herb mixtures. These beers were probably not boiled for an hour or more as we do today. They might not have even been boiled at all, since there were no hops to extract bitterness from, and sterilization from boiling was not a concept understood at that time. Hops weren't introduced until around the 1200s, and even then use varied from location to location.

Flavor Profile

Flavor

These Gose beers would have been tart wheat beers with very low bitterness, seasoned most likely with gruit herbs and spices. They were

Figure 2.6. "With the girl good-looking and slender, While drinking Gose the cooling drink, When the stuff is sparkling in the glass, The uncle is quite amused."

probably made with 100 percent air-dried wheat malt. The air-dried malt would have given them a raw, grassy clover or alfalfa flavor (see the section on Luftmalz in chapter 3). There would have been a mild, mineral salinity from the water source or from small amounts of added salt.[3] Highly attenuated and dry due to the lactic bacteria fermentation, the tartness would be mostly the result of lactic acid, but during these years there might have been some acetic acid produced as well due to contact with the open air. This acidic tartness would have mingled with the more funky aromas and flavors of the wild yeast that assisted with fermentation. Balance of these beers came from acid then, as it does in modern Gose. Acetic acid, as we've noted, is more biting and vinegar-like. Lactic acid has bright, citrus-like flavors that lend an element of refreshment to beer. This refreshing quality may be one reason that Gose gained such popularity over other beers—they were balanced by the lactic acid and not sweet and heavy as the brown beers of this period are said to be. There was probably a white-wine or cider-like quality to the overall aroma and flavor (meaning with the aroma of grapes, pear, or apple). There are many accounts describing Gose as white-wine like. Because they were open-fermented and stored in wood, if they were left for too long they would have become more acetic and eventually very vinegar-like. There are many accounts from later periods of Gose not aging well and taking on aggressive vinegar flavors. Spruce boughs may have been used in the lautering process and, potentially, spruce barrels may have contributed some flavors.

Aroma

Aromas of the Gose of this time would have been moderately fruity, or maybe a bit more than moderate—remember they had no temperature control during fermentation. The malt aroma would have been reminiscent of sourdough with a hint of vinegar and a slightly grassy or alfalfa note. There was probably a white-wine or cider quality to the overall aroma and flavor. The use of herbs or gruit would give the beer an herbal aroma, which hopefully would have blended with the fruitiness of the fermentation esters. It is doubtful, but of course possible, that coriander was used in these early versions of Gose. Coriander was known in Saxony during this era, but was not common (Weicker 1899). Coriander may also have been part of the gruit mix. Spruce tips and branches were probably part of the overall flavor profile. The fermentation, both bacterial and yeast, would

---

[3]   Caroline Southern, "The Somewhat Disgusting Origin of the Gose, America's New Favorite Beer," Hop Culture, February 9, 2017, https://www.hopculture.com/the-history-of-gose-beer/.

have produced low to medium levels of funkiness. *Brettanomyces* might have contributed some fruity or light horsey aromas in aged versions of the beer. Older versions might also have had aromas of acetic acid from exposure to *Acetobacter* and air. The aromatic qualities should be mild to moderate, and should blend together to create an overall impression of fresh, bready, and spritely.

Figure 2.7. "Without a doubt" the perfect Gose pour at Gosenshenke Ohne Bedenken in Leipzig, Germany. Courtesy of Edgar Schmidke.

Appearance

These beers were unfiltered, unchilled wheat beers, and as such would have been hazy.

Mouthfeel

The body would have been medium-light to medium. There might have been small amounts of oats or other grains used in these beers, giving them a bit more body and mouthfeel.

PUBLISHED DESCRIPTIONS OF GOSE

Döllnitzer (Leipziger) Gose.
Original wort: 7-8°P. Infusion procedure.
The Gose is a cloudy, slightly acidic beer and was already mentioned as an export beer in 1755, but originally came from Goslar and was later produced in Döllnitz. Nowadays it is produced in the Leipzig area by a number of breweries, but the yeast is taken from the distillery Libertwolkwitz.

—"Die Fabrikation obergäriger Biere in Praxis und Theorie" by Braumeister Grenell, 1907, page 74. (Translation by Ron Pattinson)

The brew (3.8 percent ABW, 4.8 percent ABV) has an original gravity of (1.050–1.051), though historically the style varied from 9–14°P (1.036–1.056). The Ohne Bedenken Gose is smooth, spritzy, very fruity and tart. The salt is clearly evident, but not dominant.

—Michael Jackson from *Michael Jackson's Beer Companion*, 1997.

I found Dr. Hennebach's beer very drinkable indeed [at the Ohne Bedenken tavern]. Or was it the salt that sharpened my thirst for more? The orangy-yellow brew is very fruity and lemon-tasting, though neither as sharp as Berliner weisse nor as long as gueuze.

—Michael Jackson, *Beerhunter.com*, May 9, 2000, http://beerhunter.com
/documents/19133-000844.html.

In Leipzig, the modern version of the Gose style has settled into a very distinct flavor profile—a green apple aroma, a ripe plum fruitiness, an herbal coriander finish, and a refreshing hit of salt that makes it very moreish and easy to drink.

—Emily Monaco, *Eater,* October 30, 2015,
https://www.eater.com/drinks/2015/10/30/9643780/gose-beer-germany.

It's not so strong as compared to the Berliner weisse or any of these specialty Belgian beers. It's a relatively medium sourness, and it has a little bit of a fruity flavor. It goes very well together with the coriander, which produces citrus flavors in the beer. It's a nice combination.

—Henryk Szymczak, brewer at Gasthaus & Gosebrauerei Bayerischer Bahnhof as quoted by Emily Monaco, *Eater,* October 30, 2015,
https://www.eater.com/drinks/2015/10/30/9643780/gose-beer-germany.

Elegant golden yellow with a fine turbidity. First impression? Fizzy but sometimes sour as well. Its true nature? Rather bitter and dry. Its greatest strength? That certain something! Its hidden talents? 10.8 % original gravity, 4.5 % alcohol content, lactic fermentation – and a distinctive coriander character.

—Gasthaus & Gosebrauerei Bayerischer Bahnhof, Leipzig, Germany, 2013,
http://www.gose.de/en/.

Rittergut brewed the only genuine Gose. Apple and pear aroma; sour taste with apple, horse blanket and lemon; sour fruit finish with lemon and apple aromas. An outstanding beer with a flavor profile usually unseen outside Belgium.

— Ron Pattinson, "Breweries in the former DDR: Leipziger Familienbrauerei Ernst Bauer KG," European Beer Guide (website), copyright 2014, https://www.europeanbeerguide
.net/ddrbrew.htm#bauer.

RATING AND DESCRIPTION BY LARS MARIUS GARSHOL, 2005

Aroma	Appearance	Flavour	Palate	Overall
6/10	3/5	7/10	3/5	14/20

Medium creamy white head with some big bubbles, which subside quickly. Milky orange body. Aroma is sourish with notes of flour and maybe a hint of coriander. Taste is big, with a citrus-like sourness which balances in the mouth. Aftertaste is thin, lingering sourness. A very unusual beer, and a lot more drinkable than the description of the beer type would have you think. I quite like it, without really thinking it the greatest invention of the beer world.

Source: Lars Marius Garshol, "Gose," *Larsblog*, December 4, 2005, http://www.garshol.priv.no/blog/19.html.

3

INGREDIENTS

The preparation I learned from my time in Goslar—this beer is prepared from the waters of the River Gose. This is where the [Gose beer] name comes from.

—Johann Friedrich Zückert, *Die Naturgeschichte und Bergwerksverfassung des Ober-Harzes.* (Translation by Benedikt Rausch.)

Many things play a part in the formation of a final beer's flavor: specific processes, time, cleanliness, equipment design, the brewer's skill, and ingredients. None can be more important than good ingredients, particularly the water and the yeast you will use. Without good ingredients it is very difficult to make delicious beer—as brewers, making good beer is always our goal.

WATER

Often people take water for granted; it just comes out of your tap (or hose). As far as ingredients go, water makes up the largest percentage of beer and as brewers we need to give it a bit more consideration. Water can be one of the simplest brewing ingredients and the one of the most complicated. On the simple side, if you can drink it and it tastes good, then you can probably make good beer with it. Simple. On the other hand, your water and all its components (or lack thereof) can have fairly dramatic effects on the final flavors in your beer. There are entire books written about it—just ask my friend John Palmer about water, or better yet, buy his book! For people with mathematical minds, water chemistry seems easy and understandable; the rest of us have to struggle through it. However, understanding water chemistry is worth the struggle and it can help us make better beer, and that should always be our goal. And what of the water chemistry for the classic beers and their brewing sites: Burton-on-Trent, London, Dortmund, Pilsen, and Leipzig? Do we need to emulate their waters to brew their beers? Not necessarily—I think you can make a great porter without emulating London's water, but I also think it is always good to know what characteristics an ingredient brings to a beer. So, what do we need to know?

Figure 3.1. The Gose river that runs through the town of Goslar.

I think that the best place to start is with your own taste buds. If you like the way your water tastes then there is a pretty good chance you will like the way it makes your beer taste. If you do not like the way your water tastes then you have some tough decisions to make.

Your brewing water should be chlorine and chloramine free. Even small amounts of free chlorine in your water can end up forming chlorophenols in your beer and even at low levels these can be noticeably unpleasant. Luckily, removal of chlorination is easily accomplished by heating your brewing water before use, using a not-yet-saturated activated carbon filter,[1] or by using ultra-violet light, a technology that some brewers already use to sterilize their house water (Palmer and Kaminski 2013). Usually, the softer your water—meaning the lower the mineral content—the better. Not because minerals are bad, but because it is much easier to add the minerals you want to your water than it is to take out the ones you do not want.

The easiest way to find out what is in your water is to obtain a water report. Every brewer should get an analysis of their water. Whether you are brewing with your own well water or using a reliable municipal water source, you should know what is in your water when it comes out of your tap. For those on private wells, like Anderson Valley Brewing Company, you can send samples to a private lab for analysis. If you are on a municipal water system like most towns, then your local municipality should be able to supply you with a water report.

ANDERSON VALLEY BREWING WATER ANALYSIS

Sodium:	31 ppm
Potassium:	1.0 ppm
Magnesium	17 ppm
Calcium:	40 ppm
Chloride:	24 ppm
Nitrate:	1.2 ppm
Sulfate:	3 ppm
$CaCO_3$:	176 ppm
pH:	7.8

We know from many sources that the water of the Gose river was used to brew the beers in Goslar. In the case of Gose beer, the mineral content of the water, especially the salinity, is a good part of what this beer is all about. So, what of the Gose river and its water?

The Gose is a small river in Lower Saxony, Germany. It is a tributary of the Abzucht river, and is approximately 5 miles (8 km) long with a drainage basin of about 3.9 sq. mi. (10 km²). The Gose's source lies north of Auerhahn in the Harz Mountains, on the eastern slopes of the Bocksberg. The river runs toward the northeast through a steep and narrow valley, and meets the Abzucht on the western edge of the town of Goslar, which is named after the

---

[1] Carbon filters have a limited life span and a fully saturated charcoal filter may not completely remove all chlorine.

river. The area around the Harz Mountains is high in mineral content, one of the most abundant of which was salt (Burnsed 2011). Some of these minerals dissolved into the waterways and this may have originally been the source of Gose's salinity. There are several large salt mines off to the east, which made salt a much less valued commodity in the Harz region than it was in other areas. So, adding a bit of salt might have been a cost-effective way for brewers in Goslar to add a bit of mouthfeel to their beers.

GOSLAR WATER ANALYSIS

Sodium:	28.9 ppm
Potassium:	1.4 ppm
Magnesium	6.3 ppm
Calcium:	20.7 ppm
Chloride:	45 ppm
Nitrate:	6.9 ppm
Sulfate:	22.4 ppm
$CaCO_3$:	76.7 ppm
pH:	7.65

$907 mmol/m^3$
$4.3°dH$, or 4.48 grain $CaCO_3$/gal.
Data courtesy of and much thanks to Benedikt Rausch.
°dH, deutsche Härte (German hardness); ppm, parts per million (1 ppm = 1 mg/L).

As you can see in the Gose river water analysis above, today the waters of the Gose are not very high in mineral content. Where then did the salinity come from? Although there is no definitive answer, it will be discussed more later in the book.

A brewing water analysis for Leipzig is a bit more complicated than that for Goslar. Leipzig draws its water from several different supply sources. The water supply in any particular location in Leipzig may vary from the supply in another part of the city. This variation may also depend on what time of the year it is, or the municipal waterworks' needs at that time. The sources include the supply stations Canitz, Thallwitz, Naunhof 1, Naunhof 2, Belgershain, Probstheida, and Plaussig (Boone and Castenholz 2001). Some of these water supply stations are on the outskirts of the city; others are farther afield. Some of the water profiles vary greatly from the others. The following are averages for those seven locations. The Döllnitz water analysis is for the Döllnitz city water supply.

LEIPZIG WATER ANALYSIS

Sodium:	26.7 ppm
Potassium:	4.4 ppm
Magnesium	<0.1 ppm
Calcium:	78.2 ppm
Chloride:	43.0 ppm
Nitrate:	12.0 ppm
Sulfate:	167.7 ppm
pH:	7.8

14.1°dH (German hardness)
°dH, deutsche Härte (German hardness); ppm, parts per million (1 ppm = 1 mg/L).

DÖLLNITZ WATER ANALYSIS

Sodium:	9.7 ppm
Potassium:	1.0 ppm
Magnesium:	3.3 ppm
Calcium:	22.3 ppm
Chloride:	17.9 ppm
Nitrate:	1.3 ppm
Sulfate:	22.9 ppm
pH:	8.67

3.9 dH (German hardness)
°dH, deutsche Härte (German hardness); ppm, parts per million (1 ppm = 1 mg/L).

With all this discussion of mineral content, salinity, and water analyses, you may be asking yourself, so where does this leave me? Stick with the premise that if your water tastes good, it will make good beer. If you want to do more, there are a few things to consider trying. Homebrewers can start with distilled water and make mineral additions to build the water profile required. That is probably not an economically viable solution for professional brewers. If you want or need to make adjustments, compare your water to the beer style you would like to brew—in our case the water of Leipzig or Goslar. For example, if you would like to emulate a Leipziger Gose, Leipzig water has a rather high sulfate content.[2] This is said to be good for brewing pale beers, to give a beer a sharper bite, showcase the hops, and make malts less sweet. Adjust your sulfate content to around 160–175 ppm by

---

[2] The city of Leipzig water authority publishes annual reports showing average water analyses (see https://www.l.de/wasserwerke).

adding gypsum to your water. Or you might want to increase your calcium content by adding calcium carbonate to your water. Keep in mind that calcium can impart mineral flavors at levels over 200 ppm. However, unless your water has some fairly serious issues, I think it is better to start with the water available to you, make the adjustments you feel are necessary, and always use an even hand.

MALT

Most brewers adhere fairly closely to tradition when creating the malt bill for their Gose-style beer. This malt bill usually consists of wheat and barley in near equal proportions, with wheat sometimes taking a slight lead. There are some recipes prior to 1800 that used 100 percent wheat malt, but not all of them. In the past, oats were sometimes used in small quantities. Specialty malts can be used too, but should be used sparingly. The main focus of this beer is wheat, and if the brewer creates an overly complicated malt bill, it will only distract from the wheat's contribution.

Barley

The barley malt for a Gose should be pale two-row malt, Pilsner malt, or another well-modified pale barley. The pale malt can be either German- or American-grown. The German malts may produce a bit more flavor, but American pale malt will work just as well. If you are trying to recreate a traditional Gose, you will of course need to acquire a German variety for both your

Figure 3.2. Malted barley—brown malt and pale malt.

pale barley malt and wheat malt. It is noteworthy that German malts are usually not as highly modified as American malts and as such will not readily supply as much low molecular weight nitrogen, which makes up a large percentage of the free amino nitrogen (FAN) in wort. To help alleviate this, brewers using German malts (or high percentages of wheat) may choose to have a protein rest at around 122°F (50°C) before moving up to a saccharification rest.

Some brewers like to use two or three different base barley malts to add complexity to the malt flavor profile.

Oats

It has been reported by several sources that during the High and late Middle Ages some brewers used oats in smaller quantities when brewing Gose (Brockhaus 2001, 723). The literature is scant on the subject, but it has been suggested that the proportion was low—possibly up to 20 percent, but not much greater. It has also been suggested that beers made with oats were of a lower quality; these beers were made for the less fortunate in the community. In modern Gose, oats are not used in any appreciable quantity, and most literature maintains that Gose is made using only wheat and barley in near equal proportions. If you do want to use oats, I would suggest using flaked or rolled oats at 10 percent or less. Oats will give the beer more mouthfeel and some greater depth.

Wheat

When brewing a beer with such a large percentage of wheat, it is important to understand a little about this grain. Wheat and barley differ in several ways and it is important to note that the overall protein content of wheat is typically higher than the overall protein content of barley. The most important difference is in the amount of gluten contained as a percentage of the protein content. The protein content of raw barley is in the area of 10–12%, with the fraction of gluten being about 50–55%. Wheat malt, on the other hand, has a protein content of about 13–17%, with about 80% of that being gluten. The higher protein and gluten levels in wheat malt will result in a more turbid beer with greater mouthfeel and better head retention. The more wheat malt you use, the more you will see those components in your finished beer.

The use of more than about 60 percent wheat malt can lead to a deficiency in amino acids. This lack of amino acids can in turn lead to a sluggish or weak fermentation, producing undesirable fermentation flavors and by-products in your final beer. These undesirable components can include excessive diacetyl, worty flavors, and fusel alcohols.

Wheat malt has about twice the high-molecular-weight proteins as does barley. Wheat malt also produces a wort that is more viscous than that of barley—this viscosity can lead to problems during lautering. A 100 percent wheat malt wort is over 50 percent more viscous than that of a wort produced from 100 percent barley. Also remember that wheat is a huskless grain; plan your malt bill accordingly and, if needed, use rice hulls to augment filterability of your grain bed during lautering. I have been told that in Europe rice hulls are not easily available, so if brewing in Europe you might use sorghum hulls or spelt husks.

Your choice of wheat malt variety can make subtle differences in the overall flavor of your Gose. (See "A Short Dissertation on Wheat" sidebar for additional details).

A SHORT DISSERTATION ON WHEAT

Less than one tenth of one percent of the wheat grown in America goes on to be used in brewing. Understandably, almost no one bothers to grow wheat to brewers' specifications, although I have heard tell of farms, such as Skagit Valley Malting in western Washington, who are growing unusual wheat and barley micro-crops for craft brewers. But for the most part, nearly all wheat is grown to bakers' specifications and we brewers must make do with what is available to us.

Red versus White, Hard versus Soft, Winter versus Spring

The differences in the varieties of wheat malt are fairly minor for brewing applications—varietal differences are of much greater importance to the baker—but they matter enough in brewing to warrant some discussion. For those who want to make a more nuanced or delicately complex-tasting wheat-based beer such as Gose, this sidebar may bring you some helpful insights. For brewers wanting a Gose with bold and robust sourness, spice, or fruit flavors, any difference in wheat malt variety will likely be too subtle to make much difference, as the other flavors would overpower them.

Wheat malt can be either red or white. The color refers to the outer seed coat. Red wheat has a more distinctive and robust wheat flavor and character than the milder white varieties. Hard white wheat was developed from hard red wheat by genetic selection that eliminated the genes for bran color while still preserving the other desirable characteristics of red wheat. Depending on the variety, red wheat has from one to three genes that give the bran its red color. White wheat lacks these genes. Their elimination results in fewer phenolic compounds and tannins from the bran, and this in turn reduces husk bitterness.

Winter wheat is planted about six weeks earlier than spring wheat (a.k.a. summer wheat). This means that winter wheat sprouts and is harvested earlier, resulting in a plumper kernel with a lower protein level; approximately 12 percent for winter varieties compared with 15 percent for spring varieties. This lower protein level is preferable, as it translates to slightly higher extracts and a slightly paler beer. Spring wheat also has a slightly higher gluten level.

Hard and soft wheat are terms used mainly in the United States to differentiate between high-protein and low-protein wheat types. The term comes from the baking industry. Hard wheat has higher protein and higher gluten levels than does soft wheat. The gluten it forms is strong and elastic and is better able to trap the carbon dioxide bubbles formed by the yeast, causing dough to rise. Its protein content is usually around 14–15 percent. Hard wheat is prized for baked goods like bread. Soft wheat has a lower protein content, around 10–12 percent, and forms a softer gluten matrix, making it more adequate for cakes, piecrusts, cookies, and other pastries. It will absorb less water than hard wheat flour and cannot take over-kneading. There is no noticeable flavor differences between the two.

Unmalted or raw wheat has not undergone the sprouting and drying process of malting. Some brewers feel that unmalted wheat lends more flavor and body to their beers. I have found it adds more haze to the final product. Unmalted wheat is also cheaper to purchase. When I once asked brewer Pierre Celis, of Hoegaarden *witbier* fame, why traditional witbier used a percentage of unmalted wheat, he replied, "Because it was cheaper." It was such a sensible, down-to-earth answer, it made me realize that traditional may not always mean better. Beware: the use of unmalted wheat can slow the lautering of an already difficult-to-lauter wheat beer.

Pregelatinized, Torrified, Flaked, and Rolled Wheat

These products are all basically the same. They can be used in place of raw wheat with slightly better results. All of them are unmalted, but heat-treated. This heat treatment allows for faster hydration and easier access to the starch for enzymatic degradation. Rolled and flaked wheat are just flattened versions of the whole-kernel grains, and they require no milling. All these products should be used with a malt that has sufficient enzymes to carry out the conversion of their starches. They add body and fullness to a beer, but can also lead to difficulty in lautering (although not as bad a plain raw wheat). I would suggest using them sparingly, less than 15 percent of the total grain bill.

Figure 3.3. Wheat malt is sometimes called "the naked grain."

Historical Use of *Luftmalz* in Gose

As discussed earlier, it can be difficult to know what beers were like historically, as it is difficult to pin down even the most basic information, like what kind of malt was used. Prior to the 1200s, there is a real dearth of documentation, not just about the beers, but about the ingredients of almost any kind. This coupled with the fact that, in the past, brewers were a very secretive group, makes it very difficult to be sure of the facts. But, although it is impossible to be certain, we can make a few assumptions. For example, if people were writing about a process or ingredient and not saying it was an amazing new development, then we can be pretty sure it had been done or used in the recent, or even distant, past. Such is the case with *Luftmalz,* or air-dried malt. People from the area now known as Belgium called it "wind malt," because it was malted at low temperatures and dried in the open air rather than kilned (Hieronymus 2010).

The lack of a strong heat source to dry the malt prevented any color formation or Maillard reaction-derived character. (Maillard reactions are chemical reactions between amino acids and reducing sugars that give browned food its distinctive flavor, and is especially important for developing dark malt flavor in brewing.) It has been suggested by maltster Michael Heinrich of Great Western Malting that malt produced without heat would have very little of the taste we currently associate with malt, because most of the flavors in malt, even today's light pale malts, are created in the kilning process. The flavors of un-kilned malt would probably include grass, a lightly herbal character, and perhaps a bit of sulfur. My experiments of malting and drying without a heat source did in fact have grassy, clover, and alfalfa-like flavors, but no sulfur notes (see "Luftmalz Malting" sidebar below). Air-dried malt would be high in enzymes, and the resulting beers would have been very pale, sometimes described as white or waxy light yellow.

These malts were made specifically to create light-colored beers. Both wheat and barley could be air-dried, making it difficult in some cases to tell which grain Luftmalz referred to. If that ambiguity did not complicate things enough, even well into the nineteenth century some parts of central Europe understood *weissbier* to mean white beer, not necessarily wheat beer. The term white beer could refer to wheat beer, barley beer, or a mixed barley and wheat beer brewed with air-dried malt (Hieronymus 2010). Drying malt in this manner was probably a technique that went back hundreds or even thousands of years prior to its first mention. Certainly, it would have been a less resource-intensive way to go about drying malt; in the Middle Ages, when the maltster often had to supply the heat source, be it wood, coal, or coke, air drying malt would have made a lot of sense. Another important point about Luftmalz is that, because it did not use heat, it could only be produced in the warmer months of the year. In cooler months not only would it not dry properly and be more prone to mold, but in winter the malt could freeze and then the "quality of beer brewed with it suffered" (McGregor and McGregor 2017, Pt.1). Because of its higher moisture content, such malt could not be stored for very long.

Without records, it is impossible for us to know what malts were used in the early Middle Ages, let alone what wheat and barley varieties existed.

Later records tell us of the use of 100 percent wheat malt in some Gose recipes. I would suspect that, because of the difficulty with lautering, 100 percent wheat recipes were the exception, not the norm, but there is no way to be certain. At some point, probably during the eleventh and twelfth centuries, brewers began to shift away from brewing with 100 percent wheat for Gose in favor of using some proportion of barley. There were probably economic reasons behind the change: barley kept better than wheat, it had greater diastatic power, and barley was easier to lauter. The references below speak to this, but bear in mind these are all from later sources.

When barley first started to be used in Gose, its proportion was rather low, but it increased over time. Recipes suggest that by 1700 ratios were about 3 to 1 (wheat to barley). For the last 100 years or so the ratio has been around 1 to 1.

Historical References to Luftmalz Production

If you want to brew a weissbier *from barley, use malt that has been merely air dried and is called* Luftmalz. *The usual* weissbiers, *Gose,* Brenhahn, *are brewed with air-dried malt and oats.*

—Hedenus 1817

If the malt has already dried on the aforementioned kiln floor that there is no need for any kilning, then the malt is called Luftmalz. *This* Luftmalz *is primarily used for weissbier to give it a very light and faint color. However, comparing* Luftmalz *to the quality of everyday kilned malt, it isn't always advantageous to use it alone, namely because 1) Its faint color, 2) On account of the enormous amount required that it is necessary to grow during the most favorable times of the year, 3) The* Luftmalz *is harder to mash in, and 4) The wort is also harder to extract; because the brewer's grains (*Treber*) are very sticky and stick together leading to a slow and imperfect wort runoff.*

—Heiss 1870

One uses air-dried malt and two parts air-dried malt with well-modified kilned malt, but lower quality will also do, as it works just as well [for making Gose].

—Grenell 1907

Air and kiln drying: The moist, green malt comes to a dry, moderately warm, airy loft or attic floor, where it is spread out in thin layers and turned, and partly dried; The germination process is thereby interrupted. The so-called half-dried or air malt with close to 12 percent moisture is further kiln-dried by heating. This Luftmalz is only stable for a short time, does not provide a long-lasting beer and does not contain the necessary flavor for the beer. Kiln drying takes place between 50 and 100°C (122 and 212°F) or higher, and thereby destroys part of the diastatic power, but without disadvantage for the beer, because the green malt contains much more diastatic power than is necessary for saccharification. Green malt is used for distillation. The malt is kiln-dried using hardwood or hard coal (anthracite).

—Heiss 1870

The character of the beer is primarily dependent on the type and degree of malting and kiln drying. For a light and thin beer, for example, Bohemian and light northern German beers, [grain] must be malted at a lower temperature with strong ventilation, so that the carbohydrates remain fermentable and have little browning.

—Ost 1890

100 lb. [45.4 kg] of air-dried barley results in about 92 lb. [71.7 kg] of Luftmalz; eight percent of the barley weight is lost in the malting process. Consequentially:
1.5 lb. [0.68 kg] lost during steeping
3 lb. [1.36 kg] lost during germination
3.5 lb [1.59 kg] lost to rootlets
100 pounds barley Luftmalz contains on average 65 lb. [29.5 kg] whole grain, 35 lb. [15.9 kg] husks, and under dry conditions yields up to 75 lb. [34 kg] of water-free extract.

—Heiss 1870

The malt is never kilned but germinated and dried under the free air. It needs a lot of care to create the malt always in the same quality. The owner has to watch it day and night so he does not miss the right moment to get it out of the growth bed and break it apart.

—Bibra 1791 (Translated by Benedikt Rausch)

Adjuncts

Adjuncts are probably not appropriate in a beer as light as Gose. They would only serve to dry the beer out to a point where the sourness would be unbalanced by the lack of sufficient malt body and sweetness. If a brewer felt compelled to use an adjunct, I would recommend keeping its use below 10 percent of the total grist bill.

TABLE 3.1 DIFFERENCES BETWEEN BARLEY AND WHEAT

	Barley	*Wheat*
Husk:	Yes	No
% Cellulose:	5.7	2.9
% Starch:	71	76
% Lipids:	2.5	2.0
% Protein:	11.8	14.5
% Gluten:	5–8	12–14
	High content of fiber and a stronger taste	Less fiber and lighter taste
% Extract:	85	80

LUFTMALZ *MALTING*

After reading many historical German brewing texts and meeting with several German brewers who made sour wheat beers, I began to wonder about Luftmalz and what its characteristics might be. Since I could find no malting company making Luftmalz, and encouraged by my discussions with maltster Michael Heinrich at Great Western Malting, I thought I might be able to make some myself. I procured some homegrown wheat from my friend, John Keevan-Lynch. It was a variety called Dylan. Dylan is a hard red spring wheat that is well able to handle wet soils (like we find here in the Anderson Valley in winter and spring). I followed instructions I found online to malt the wheat. It was quite easy.

1. Homegrown grain will probably need washing to separate the wheat from the chaff. Cover the grain with water. The chaff will float—remove it. Give the grain a gentle stirring. Remove any other floating debris. Purchased commercial grain will probably not need this step.
2. In a container, cover the grain with an inch or two of water. Cover and let soak for 8–10 hours.
3. Drain and let the grain sit for 8–10 hours.
4. Repeat step 2.
5. Drain and spread the grain out to a thickness of 1–2 in. (2.5–5 cm). At this point the chit should be showing from one end of the grain (see fig. 3.4). Cover the grain and let it sit for 2–4 days (3 days is normal) at room temperature.
6. Turn the malt every 8 to 12 hours. The grain on the bottom will sprout faster and thus the grain needs to be turned. Keep the grain moist but not wet during the first two days

Figure 3.4. Day one sprouting.

Figure 3.5. Day two, rootlets galore!

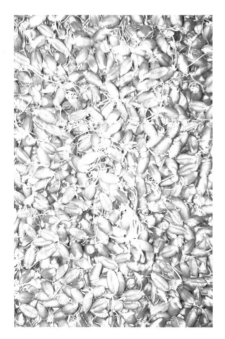

Figure 3.6. Day three you can see the beginning of the sprouts.

Figure 3.7. Day four. Just about ready. I stopped hydrating it at this point and allowed it to air dry.

(fig. 3.5). You can lightly spray it down or lightly rinse and drain it. This can easily be done if the grain is in a perforated pan or colander.

7. Allow the sprouting to continue until the coleoptile (a vegetative sheathed sprout—not to be confused with the rootlet) is 75–100 percent of the length of the kernel (fig. 3.6). Sprouting will occur faster for wheat (2–3 days) than barley (4–6 days). How quickly it sprouts will depend on the wheat variety, temperature, moisture level, and other conditions (fig. 3.7).

8. Drying can be accomplished in the sun, by blowing air on the malt with a fan, or using a food dehydrator. Air movement is important. If drying with only a fan, turn the malt occasionally. The drying should take 16–30 hours depending on the method used.

9. Luftmalz was milled and used both damp and fully dried. The malt should be fully dried if it is to be stored for any length of time.

The malt had an overall impression of being green, with aromas of mown grass, clover, alfalfa, hay, and husks.

WHITE BEERS

It is interesting to think about what connections might have existed across Europe during the Middle Ages, when long distances were traveled infrequently, and records about brewing were scant and jealously guarded. Of the few records we do have, malt was the common denominator in the brewing of white beers. Records were kept on things like gruit, herbs, and hops, but the amounts used changed over time as well as distance. For example, the use of gruit herbs in beer may have remained in use in one area, while hops supplanted them in another. It is tempting to make a connection between similar beers brewed with similar ingredients, but in different places. Many brewing historians have suggested a historical link between Berliner weisse, Broyhan, and Gose. A few others have suggested a link between Gose and witbier. It is tempting to theorize that there might have been a general style of "white beer" that many brewers across Europe adapted to fit their region.

> White beer is brewed in other places, and these beers are called Gose. These
> should be called wrong Gose, because they are not brewed with the Goslar
> water and are not able to come near the Gose from Goslar in taste and quality.

—Zückert , *Die Naturgeschichte und Bergwerksverfassung des Ober-Harzes,* (1762).

There are a number of less well-known beers that probably fall into this white beer category: Lichtenhainer, Broyhan, Grodziskie, witbier, Berliner weisse, and Gose. All these are pale (white) wheat beers with low gravity, and varying levels of lactic sourness. Certainly, each of them today has a unique character, but these differences are regional and fairly nuanced: one slightly smoky and hoppy (Grodziskie), one with another spice (Broyhan), and more than one with coriander (Gose and witbier).

In Stan Hieronymus's book, *Brewing with Wheat,* there is an intriguing sidebar in which Belgian brewer and beer historian Yvan De Baets outlines a historical witbier recipe that contains both coriander and salt (plus 250 grams of stag's antler shavings—but as I said, regional differences). At the bottom of the sidebar De Baets notes, "The lactic fermentation, plus the use of salt and coriander, will inevitably make you think of the Leipzig Gose, which has the same characteristics. It's worth a study on the links between those cities that would show a possible influence in their brewing methods." Could these beers have been related at some point?

Indeed, and it would be interesting to know about the possible links between Goslar and Jena, where Lichtenhainer beer was brewed, and between Hamburg, where Broyhan was brewed, and Berlin, among others. It makes me wonder if brewers really were as secretive as many of the books suggest. Maybe connections were developed by the practice of what in Germany today is called *die Walz,* during which a young hopeful ventures out into the world to find a master to apprentice with, before returning home to start his or her own trade in earnest. Or is it more like modern day brewers, who, when they chance to meet, sit down over a few beers and discuss their mutual interest.

A FAMILY OF WHITE BEERS

Back in 1784, Dr. Knaust, the eighteenth century beer writer, suggested a similar but less widespread notion of a family of white beers. He wrote about as many as 50 of them and profiled each one. "The beer of the mountain town Goslar am Harz is called Gose, just like the river that flows through the city. Dr. Knaust says it's sweet at first, but later turns sour like Hamburg. Several places, of which the book makes Quedlinburg, Halberstadt, Blankenburg, Aschersleben, Werningerode and Osterwyk praised, mimicked the Gose." (Elvert 1870)

HOPS

> *In order to tame the sweetness of the wheat and to prevent the beer from getting sour, some Scheffel of Hops should be added.*
>
> —Sigmund Bibra, *Journal von und für Deutschland* (Translated by Benedikt Rausch and Fal Allen).

In the case of Gose, hops came in mid-game as a replacement player. Gruit and other herbs and spices were the flavorings of the very first Gose beers. But since there are almost no brewing records and certainly no recipes from those early days in Goslar, we will have to make a few assumptions about those beers. Hops probably came into use during the 1200s and possibly a little bit later (Lawrence 1990). We do know that hops were being grown, probably for medicinal purposes, around Goslar by then. In fact the *Ratsapotheke,* or councilor's apothecary of Goslar, was first documented in 1300. It was one of the oldest chemist shops in Germany and hops would certainly have been on one of their shelves (Goslar Museum 2017).

At first, hops may have been a part of a gruit mix. They were worked into the recipe with other spices that had come before them. Then, over time, most of the other spices fell away, leaving only hops and coriander, or maybe sometimes a little spruce.

Gose is not a hop-forward beer style; it's just not. In this current India Pale Ale (IPA) craze, that may be hard to remember. Making a hoppy Gose is a bit like making a blonde stout, or black IPA, or . . . Oh, wait a minute. All right, I know some of you out there won't be able to help yourselves—you will feel compelled to make a hoppy Gose. To all of you in that camp I say do what makes you happy, just don't call it a traditional Gose. Part of writing a style guideline book is defining the style's parameters, and traditional Gose is not a hop-forward beer. Its notably low bitterness is one of the things that helps define the style. To add to that, in my experience, I have found that bitter and sour do not really work all that well together. That is probably one of the reasons Gose is not hop forward. Hops were used—there are many descriptions of their use historically—they were just used in small quantities.

Another reason that Gose is not a hoppy beer is that *Lactobacillus* is not a hop-tolerant bacteria. As little as 5 IBUs can affect the growth of some strains of *Lactobacillus,* and without *Lactobacillus* Gose would not be a sour beer. So it is not all that surprising that a beer traditionally soured by *Lactobacillus* during fermentation didn't contain much hops. This is less of an issue if you are doing a non-traditional souring of your Gose, like using acidified malt or brewhouse souring.

Hop Selection

Traditionally, hops probably would have been added only once, in small amounts. In the early years of using hops, during the late Middle Ages, that addition was probably in the mash tun. This is because the gruit spices were often mixed in with the malt in the mash tun (Corran 1975). In later years, the hop addition probably shifted to the boil, or even after the boil. Hop additions would have been enough to ward off some unwanted bacteria, but low enough to allow *Lactobacillus* to do its work. Hops traditionally would be of a noble German variety, but since the hops play a smaller role they could conceivably be of any variety as long as they are not overly assertive.

When choosing a hop variety, it is important to know what you want out of it. There are three basic characteristics to look at: bitterness, flavor, and aroma. In Gose, bitterness should range from 2–15 IBUs. Bitterness should be mild, not harsh. Look for a mild flavored hop with low cohumulone to impart a softer bitterness. Keep in mind that if you use lower alpha acid (AA) hops, you will need to use a greater quantity of them to achieve the same amount of bitterness than you would with a higher alpha acid hop. For example, you would need roughly twice the amount of Cascade hops (5–7.7% AA) than you would Magnum hops (~10–16% AA) to achieve the same bitterness.[3] This means that if you use Cascade hops you will be boiling twice the vegetal matter than you would with Magnum hops, and doing so will extract more cooked vegetal flavors. These flavors might remain hidden in a bigger beer, but in a low-gravity pale beer like Gose, these unwelcome vegetal flavors could distract from the overall flavor profile. Also note that low gravity beers achieve better hop utilization (alpha acid or hop bitterness extraction) than do higher gravity beers.

Hop flavors and aromas are more subjective choices. Flavors should be mild for the same reasons bitterness should. What you choose for your aroma hops can make a big difference in the overall perception of your beer. For more traditional Gose beers, the classic German aroma varieties Hallertauer Mittelfrüh, Saphir, Hersbrucker, or Perle might be good choices. But whether you choose fruity, spicy, pine of citrus hops, be sure they pair well with the other spices you may be using; traditionally, that would be coriander or maybe spruce. Remember, in most cases you want to make a balanced beer and to do so you will need to use a judicious hand.

YEAST

> *The Gose is a cloudy, slightly acidic beer and was already mentioned as an export beer in 1755, but originally came from Goslar and was later produced in Döllnitz. Nowadays it is produced in the Leipzig area by a number of breweries, but the yeast is taken from the distillery Libertwolkwitz.*
>
> —Braumeister Grenell, *Die Fabrikation obergäriger Biere in Praxis und Theorie* page 74. (Translation by Ron Pattinson.)

---

[3]   Also, Magnum has a lower cohumulone level than does Cascade (~25 vs. ~37% AA respectively) and low cohumulone is a good thing.

A brewer's choice of yeast can have a big impact on any beer style. Bavarian hefeweizen brewed with English ale yeast would taste very out of place. It would lack the signature banana and clove nose traditionally found in a German *weizen*. Or imagine a Pilsner brewed with a Belgian monastery yeast; it would be full of a rich, ripe fruitiness that no lager should have, and it would be lacking the clean crispness and malty backbone associated with Pilsners the world over. If you have any doubt about how much of an impact the chosen yeast strain has on the final beer, try splitting a single run of wort and fermenting it with two or three different yeast strains. The results will surprise you.

For Gose, the choice of yeast is not as dramatic as the examples above, but the choice is still an important one. The six factors that a brewer usually looks at (pretty much in this order) are flavor and aroma, attenuation, alcohol tolerance, temperature range, flocculation, and ability to remain viable during storage.

Flavor is very subjective and so you will need to base yeast selection on the flavors you like, or what you want to bring out in the beer. Gose beers are traditionally top-fermented ales, so although lager yeast could be used, it is not really the best choice. I would recommend a well-known German ale strain, perhaps *Kölsch* or *altbier*. White Labs WLP029 is a good Kölsch strain; under the right conditions it will lend a classic white-wine note, and is a good attenuator. Wyeast 1007 German Ale ferments dry and crisp, with a mild fruitiness at higher temperatures, though it will ferment cleanly closer to 55°F (13°C). You could also use an English ale yeast, but I would avoid ones that are overly fruity. A fruity yeast might bring out more of the spice you use, but a yeast with a relatively neutral flavor profile will let more of the sour brightness show through in the beer. I would also avoid using distinctive strains, like monastery ale or Bavarian weizen ale yeasts, as the ester profile might overpower the other Gose flavors. A Belgian witbier yeast, like White Labs WLP400 Belgian Wit and Wyeast 3944 Belgian Witbier, might bring out interesting notes. Most importantly, find a yeast strain that you think will work well with the Gose you want to brew. Good versions of these strains and others can be found through your favorite yeast supplier or local homebrew supply stores.

Attenuation can be important in this style depending on what you are shooting for. A highly attenuative yeast will leave the beer dry and crisp. Yeast with low attenuation will leave the beer with more sweetness. When looking at yeast specifications, keep these general ranges in mind: high attenuation is 78 percent and above, medium is from 73 to 77 percent, and low attenuation is anything less than 72 percent.

For Gose, alcohol tolerance in not really an issue, as Gose-style beers are low to medium-low alcohol content beers. The same can be said about flocculation, as Gose is not particularly clear.

The one characteristic that is of a concern for Gose is tolerance to acidity. Some yeast will not properly function at pH levels lower than about 3.8. At that point, they may produce off-flavors or they may stop metabolizing sugars and leave the beer underattenuated. Some yeasts (like the house yeast at Anderson Valley Brewing) can adequately ferment low pH wort and produce good flavors, but after fermentation is over that yeast cannot be repitched into another wort with acceptable results. The yeast is essentially burned-out and must be discarded. Still, there are other yeast strains that can produce beer at low pH levels and can easily be repitched. Since this characteristic in not usually listed on yeast performance descriptions, it will need to be tested before taking a Gose to full production.

Terminal Acid Shock

As discussed above, some yeast cannot thrive under low pH conditions. They remain alive, but are not able to proceed with normal fermentation function. This is known as terminal acid shock. However, it may be possible to train or acclimate your yeast so as to tolerate low pH conditions. This can be done by re-propagating your yeast in a series of successively lower pH pitches until the yeast has acclimated to the low pH conditions. This has been successfully done for yeast needed to bottle condition low pH beers, but this method may not yield yeast that can produce satisfactory flavors in a full-scale ferment.

DEFINING SPONTANEOUS, WILD, AND OPEN FERMENTATIONS

Spontaneous when referring to a process or event is defined as "developing [. . .] without apparent external influence, force, cause, or treatment."[4]

Wild when referring to an animal or plant is defined as "living in a state of nature and not ordinarily tame" or "growing or produced without human aid."[5]

The *Milk the Funk* blog defines a spontaneous fermentation as "the inoculation of wort for fermentation with local ambient microbes."[6]

Wine makers define spontaneous as "fermentation that naturally occurs when the

---

[4]   *Merriam-Webster,* s.v. "spontaneous," accessed May 6, 2018, https://www.merriam-webster.com /dictionary/spontaneous.

[5]   *Merriam-Webster,* s.v. "wild," accessed May 6, 2018, https://www.merriam-webster.com/dictionary/

[6]   Milk the Funk Wiki, s.v. "Spontaneous Fermentation," last modified June 3, 2018, 16:23, http://www.milkthefunk.com/wiki/Spontaneous_Fermentation.

wild yeast and microorganisms that the grapes bring in with them from the vineyard are encouraged to propagate."[7]

My opinion is that all of these definitions give about the same answer: a spontaneous or wild fermentation is one that occurs naturally from local microbes not introduced by the brewer. The two key points seem to be that the introduction of the microbes occurs without assistance of the brewer and that these microbes are naturally occurring in the environment. I would venture to agree with *Milk the Funk's* loose interpretation and think that these microorganisms could be blown in on the wind, residents of the wooden barrels and tanks, or existing in the environment that surrounds the coolship or fermenting vessels, as long as they are naturally occurring and indigenous to the surroundings. I would also put open fermentations in the category because, as the name suggests, the wort is left open to the environment to achieve fermentation. All of the above would be considered mixed fermentations, but not all mixed fermentations can be considered spontaneous. A brewer could pitch selected bacteria and *Saccharomyces* yeast and that would be a mixed fermentation, but it would not be naturally occurring and it probably would not be with indigenous microbes. Even if it was pitched with indigenous microbes, they would have been selected by the brewer and not by random occurrence or nature.

Wild Ferments and/or Spontaneous Fermentation

The Goslarsche Gose inoculates itself without the addition of yeast or gest.
—Brückmann and Kohl, *Epistola itineraria XXXVIII.*

It [Gose wort] is then filled in barrels and left to ferment which happens after 12 to 24 hours. This beer needs no foreign additive but inoculates itself.
—Zückert, *Die Naturgeschichte und Bergwerksverfassung des Ober-Harzes.*

There should be some discussion here about not pitching yeast. Originally, Gose beers were almost certainly spontaneously fermented. There are records of Gose fermenting without the addition of yeast as late as the 1700s, yet those fermentations were starting within 24 to 48 hours.[8] So there must have been a more immediate source of microbes to get the beer fermenting so quickly. Additionally, Gose beer was drunk fairly quickly—usually within three weeks—and most 100 percent spontaneously fermented beers take much longer than three weeks to

---

[7]   Simon Von Dieter, "Spontaneous Fermentation – What's It All About?" Bonvinitas (website), October 26, 2011, https://www.bonvinitas.com/de/component/content/article/40-the-art-of-wine/general-topics/155-spontaneous-fermentation-whats-it-all-about.

[8]   This is quite fast, considering that modern day brewers who are spontaneously fermenting their beer often don't see signs of fermentation until 4–7 days after cooling.

Figure 3.8. Wort starting fermentation in the coolship. Photo courtesy of Sebastian Sauer, Bierkompass/Freigeist Bierkultur, Germany.

finish and be safe to consume. It has been suggested that fermentation vessels made of wood, sometimes spruce, were the possible source of bacteria and yeast necessary for fermentation (Brinkmann 1925). These vessels may have acted as a home for resident microbes, and brewers may have intentionally avoided cleaning these vessels too thoroughly, as they would have noticed that a more casual cleaning resulted in the next fermentation starting faster (from the imbedded microbes left behind in the wood). This would be akin to the fashion that Scandinavian brewers used the fast-acting *Kveik* to start their fermentations prior to a good understanding of how fermentation was carried out.

Those brewers today wanting to reproduce a spontaneously fermented Gose have a few options. One would be to build a coolship and allow local wind-borne microbes to ferment your beer. An alternative would be to lightly spray the walls, ceiling, and rafters of the building/shed/garage that holds your coolship.[9] Spray these areas down with a diluted, unfiltered, spontaneously fermented beer of your choice (I prefer Lindemans Cuvée René, after I have enjoyed about half the bottle). To avoid mold, do not spray too much at one time. Let it all dry up and repeat the process. This puts the many, many microbes involved in the spontaneous fermentation of that beer up and soaked into the building in a percentage that you might find them wafting about in the air.[10] Another method would be to naturally inoculate a small wort sample, culture it to assure that there is no mold or other evil present,

---

[9]   If you are planning on trying this in your family garage, I highly recommend you FIRST clear it with your spouse/partner/parents.

[10]   Personal communication with Roger Mussche, *lambic* expert.

and the flavors are not completely unacceptable. Then you can grow up that sample to a sufficiently pitchable quantity, and pitch it into the main body of wort.

Another way to achieve a spontaneous fermentation is to pitch your wort into a wooden vessel, such as a barrel or *foeder,* that previously contained a wild ferment. The microbes responsible for the wild fermentation will be ensconced in the cracks and crevices of the inherently porous wood, and once you introduce the sweet wort they will take over and do what they do best. This method is, of course, only an alternative if you have access to such vessels.

SPICES

In the early part of the Middle Ages, before the Crusades, Asian spices in Europe were costly and mainly used by the wealthy. A pound of saffron cost the same as a horse; a pound of ginger, as much as a sheep; two pounds of mace as much as a cow. A German price table of 1393 lists a pound of nutmeg as worth seven fat oxen. Pepper, as well as other spices and herbs, was commonly used as a monetary source. Eastern Europeans paid 10 pounds of pepper in order to gain access to trade with London merchants. Throughout Europe, peppercorns were accepted as a substitute for money—some landlords would get paid as a "peppercorn rent" (Rosengarten 1969). Peppercorns, counted out one by one, were accepted as currency to pay taxes, tolls, and rents (partly because of a coin shortage). Many European towns kept their accounts in pepper. "If you were an exceptionally lucky bride, your father might give you peppercorns as a dowry" (Moseley 2006)

When Gose beers were first brewed in the Middle Ages there were many herbs and spices used in brewing, including a spice mix called gruit. Gose-style beers from the modern period are spiced with coriander, but other spices have been used in the past. A *Brauwelt International* article written by Nancy and Christopher McGregor explains, "It seems that many herbs—some of them exotic and available only through the town's [Goslar's] links to the Hanseatic League—were employed in the brewing of the beers from Goslar. Some of these herbs included cinnamon, anise, ginger and caraway. However, none of them were employed for very long in the beer . . . except for coriander. The popularity of this herb [coriander] was apparently due to propensity to soothe the stomach" (McGregor and McGregor 2017).

Today the German breweries I have spoken with use only coriander, with one exception: Geisterzug Gose by Freigeist Bierkultur uses spruce. The flavor of coriander is usually mild, but most often overshadows the even milder hop profile of today's Gose. When designing any beer, I think that the spices should be an accent, not a dominant flavor, and so it is with Gose. You want to add enough coriander to lightly spice the beer but not overpower the other flavors. Use a subtle hand and keep the spice as a complement to the beer's other flavors. Of course, you need to be mindful of consumer expectation too. If you create a beer using juniper and call it Juniper Gose, then the consumer will be expecting some juniper flavor in the beer. But better a subtle undertone of juniper than a juniper branch slap in the face.

If you are planning on breaking with tradition, as many American brewers do, Gose is a style of beer that lends itself nicely to other spices. Many brewers have used fruit (addressed later in the book) and unusual spices in their Goses. Experiment, have fun with it, and find your own path.

Spices can be added at any time during the brewing process, depending on the flavors and aromas you want them to provide. You can add spices in the mash tun, the kettle, in the whirlpool, hop back, in the fermentor, or even in the finished beer. Conventional wisdom says that the later you add the spices during the process, the more flavor and aroma will be left in the beer. There are a few exceptions to this rule, where flavor is better extracted on the hot side (in the brewhouse) rather than on the cold side (in the cellar), but by and large the rule holds true. It is important to remember that each spice is different and the best way to extract flavors and aromas from one spice may not be the best way to extract them from another. A hot steep of leaves may be the best way to extract tea flavor and aroma, but something as delicate as basil might best be extracted in cold, finished beer.

GRUIT RIGHTS

Charlemagne, known as Charles the Great (b. 742, d. 814), became King of the Franks in AD 768; he later become King of the Lombards through conquest, and finally, after being crowned Holy Roman Emperor in 800, became ruler of the Carolingian Empire until his death. He played an important role in developing, growing and using local and foreign herbs. He was the first ruler to encourage farmers to plant an abundance of culinary herbs such as anise, fennel, fenugreek, sage, thyme, parsley, and coriander. It was Charlemagne's government during the ninth century that gave the emperor imperial power over all the unexploited lands, and thus by extension, power over all the plants and animals of those lands. The open lands were vast, and this was where most of the herbs and spices used in gruit were found. Charlemagne's power over these unexploited lands and all things from them gave him the right to grant similar power to those he thought worthy—and so he did. This was known as *Gruitrechte,* or gruit rights: the right to manage, tax, and control the herbs found in gruit (Unger 2004).

Hot Side Additions

The obvious advantage to adding spices on the hot side is that they are sterilized by their contact with the hot wort. The down side may be a loss of some of the more subtle, delicate flavors and aromas during the steeping or boiling process. Adding your spices during the active boil is probably not the best choice. A boil sufficiently vigorous for brewing purposes will often drive off more delicate flavors and aromas. Boiling may also extract more of the unpleasant harsh or woody flavors from the spices. So most breweries add spices in one of the following ways: toward the very end of the boil, so that there is a short time of boiling and a longer steep in the whirlpool; at the end of the boil, so there is no actual boil time but a gentler steep in the whirlpool; or in the whirlpool or hop back so that the contact time is shorter, though long enough to extract what the spices have to offer.

The other disadvantage of adding your spices on the hot side is twofold. As mentioned, higher temperatures may extract astringent and harsh flavors. The other issue is that the spices may get carried over into your heat exchanger and get stuck or cause build up. An inline screen upstream of the heat exchange can help alleviate this potential problem. If you use spices in your beers regularly, I would recommend that in addition to installing an inline screen upstream, you also do a reverse clean in place (CIP) after every brew, and that you take apart and clean your heat exchange manually at least two to four times a year.

Cold Side Additions

The obvious down side to adding your spices after cooling the hot wort (the cold side) is that they are not sterilized by coming into contact with the hot wort, and that leaves open the possibility of infection. Adding spices to the cold side can also bring out some different flavors than a hot side addition, though they may or may not be to your liking. Cold side flavor extraction doesn't depend on heat, obviously, but post-fermentation additions may get some help from alcohol extraction.

There are three times during cold side operations that you can add your spices. The first would be before or during fermentation. The main disadvantages of adding the spices at this time is that the evolution of carbon dioxide during fermentation will scrub out a lot of the aromas you are hoping to retain in your beer. Since there is little or no alcohol produced yet, your chances of infection will be higher. The second opportunity to add your spices is very late in fermentation or after fermentation is complete, but before the beer is chilled. The advantage to adding spices here is that the evolution of carbon dioxide is complete (or very near complete) and the more delicate aromas will not likely be scrubbed out. Also, there is now some alcohol in the beer to help ward off infecting bacteria. The pH has also dropped significantly and this too helps reduce the number of bacteria and wild yeast that can prosper in the beer, although this point may be moot for brewhouse-soured or spontaneously fermented Gose beers. The temperature of the beer is still warm enough that the extraction of flavors and aromas will be faster and more effective than they would after the beer has been chilled. And if you add the spices at the very end of fermentation, there is still just enough yeast left in suspension to sequester any oxygen that you might inadvertently introduce to the beer when you add your spices. The third window is after you have chilled the beer. This gives you one more advantage against infection, as most bacteria don't thrive in the cold, but cold temperatures will inhibit extraction, and there is less yeast in suspension to absorb any inadvertently added oxygen.

There is also the option of making up a tincture of the spices you would like to use by soaking them in a solution of at least 40 percent ethanol. This method can be very useful for some spices, but be aware that ethanol may extract flavors that other methods do not, and this method may pose legal issues for professional brewers.

I believe that although Gose-style beers are low in both alcohol and hops, both of which act as preservatives, the one great advantage these beers have is their high acidity, which also has preservative qualities. Gose beers are in a way pre-infected—certainly at this point a *Lactobacillus* infection is not much of a worry. Still, you should remain vigilant, because some strains of bacteria and wild yeast (like *Brettanomyces*) can tolerate pH down to around 2.0.[11]

Coriander

A little about the main spice used in Gose: coriander, or *Coriandrum sativum,* is an annual herb indigenous to southern Europe and the Mediterranean. The leaves are used in cooking, especially in Asian, Latin, and Indian cuisine; most people in the Americas know it as cilantro. The ripe, dried fruit is known as coriander seed. This is what is used in Gose brewing. Coriander seed and cilantro leaves give very different flavors and aromas, and they are not interchangeable. There are also two different varieties of coriander: *C. sativum* var. *microcarpum* is grown in Russia and central Europe, and is spicier and less fruity; and *C. sativum* var. *vulgare* is grown in India, and is

---

[11]   Milk the Funk Wiki, *s.v.* "Brettanomyces," last modified June 3, 2018, 23:59, http://www.milkthefunk.com/wiki/Brettanomyces.

fruitier, with heavier notes of citrus. The aroma of coriander seed is fragrant and distinctive, vaguely sweet and similar to a combination of lemon and sage. During the Middle Ages, coriander was added to love potions and was mentioned in *One Thousand and One Nights* as an aphrodisiac (Rosengarten 1969, 211). Today coriander is used in essential oils, perfumes, candies, pickles, alcoholic beverages, chocolates, tobacco, meats, curries, and pharmaceuticals. Its medicinal properties are said to be anodyne, stimulant, and carminative. Herbal uses are said to include mild pain relief, stimulation of appetite and digestive juices, and reduction of flatulence.[12]

Gruit

There should be further discussion of gruit, as it was the herb and spice mix almost universally used in brewing when Gose was first brewed. Gruit was the herb and spice mixture used in almost all beers during the Middle Ages. In the fourteenth century, hops began to replace gruit, but the replacement of hops by gruit was strongly resisted for many reasons and took many decades. Gruit was a combination of several herbs and spices mixed together and they could vary greatly depending on location, season, and local availability. The most notable of the herbs used were bog myrtle (a.k.a. sweetgale) yarrow, mugwort, and marsh Labrador tea, or wild rosemary *(Ledum palustre)*. Both bog myrtle and wild rosemary provided a similarly sharp taste component to gruit. Other notable gruit herbs and spices might include ginger, cumin, caraway, anise, sage, marjoram, juniper, laurel, mint, wormwood, ivy, and may have even included the bark of certain trees (Unger 2004). The addition of gruit was for flavor, aroma, sometimes color, and effect (Hornsey 2003). Some gruit mixes contained somewhat intoxicating herbs. *Sacred Herbal and Healing Beers* author Stephen Buhner writes that the properties of gruit were "highly intoxicating—narcotic, aphrodisiacal and psychotropic when consumed in sufficient quantities. Gruit ale stimulates the mind, creates euphoria, and enhances sexual drive. The hopped ale that took its place is quite different. Its effects are sedative and anaphrodesiacal" (Buhner 1989). Although I have read several references that suggest some gruit ales were somewhat mildly psychotropic, I have found nothing to give the indication that all were psychotropic or that the level of the effects were as potent as might be inferred from the above quotation. The gruit ales I have myself consumed had no greater effect on me than ales of equal alcohol percentage brewed with hops.

---

[12] A carminative reduces flatulence, which is why coriander may be an enduring spice in Gose, if the reports of some of the Leipzig Gose drinkers can be believed.

We also know that one of the reasons gruit ales were generally more intoxi-cating than hopped ales was because their alcohol content was higher. Whereas alcohol was the main thing that protected "ales" against bacterial infection, "beer" was brewed using hops, which are an antimicrobial. Hops were so much better at preserving beer than gruit spices were at preserving ale that brewers fairly quickly found they could use less malt for making beer than they would in making gruit ales. Using less malt lowered the brewers' costs as well as the alcohol content, and the hopped beer lasted just as long without spoiling. This is discussed in *A Perfect Platform of a Hoppe Garden* by Reginal Scot: "Whereas you cannot make above 8 or 9 gallons of indifferent ale out of one bushel of malt, you can draw 18 or 20 gallons of very good beer." This means you would need about half the malt to brew an agreeable beer as you would to brew the same amount of ale, if you wanted them to last the same amount of time. A similar sentiment is borne out in *Ale, Beer and Brewsters in England* by Judith Bennet (1996).

There were several reasons hops eventually supplanted gruit: substantially lower malt costs, longer shelf life, lower alcohol content, cleaner bitterness to balance the malt, more consistent flavors (remember, one never knew what was in a gruit mix), and consumer preference.

One of the problems you will face when brewing gruit beer is that without hops the risk of infection is much higher. Because of their strong preservative qualities, hops help to keep all those unwanted bacteria, molds, and some of the wild yeast from growing in beer.

When hops began to replace gruit it did not happen all at once; it happened slowly and in different places at different times. As mentioned earlier, it is very likely that hops became an addition to gruit, and other herbs were phased out over time. It is also likely that in the case of Gose, hops came into use as other herbs were discarded, and that eventually coriander was the sole remaining herb besides hops. Coriander gives Gose a pleasing lemon note that works well with both the lactic acid and the mild hop character.

Spruce

It appears that throughout the Middle Ages spruce branches and tips were also used in the brewing of Gose. The branches were used in the lautering process and for separating the hot break. The wort was "filtered through the spruce branches" and this gave the wort "the peculiar taste of spruce needles."[13] Later,

---

[13] Jürgen Reuß, "Die Goslarer Gose," Bier aus eigener Küche (website), September 28, 2004, http://www.bierauseigenerkueche.de/Goslarer%20Gose.html.

when brewing methods changed and spruce branches were no longer used, some brewers continued to use spruce as a spice in Gose. I have not had the opportunity to brew or taste a spruced version of Gose, but I have made other styles of beer using spruce. For the most pleasing spruce flavor, I would suggest waiting until the early spring when the spruce trees begin to shoot out new foliage. These pale green tips have a bright conifer aroma and a pleasant, sweet spruce taste. Older branches will be more woody and bitter.

FRUIT

Traditionally, fruit was not added to Gose, but as with Berliner weisse, flavored syrups were sometimes added to the beer when it was served. American craft brewers have taken that concept and run with it by adding fruits, both natural and as syrups, purees, or flavorings, to their beers before packaging. The potential flavor combinations are nearly limitless. When you add fruit to your beer, in addition to the flavors it contributes, the fruit will also be adding some fermentables. It is important to understand what these additional fermentables can mean for your beer. Most fruits contain a mixture of sugars: fructose, glucose, and sucrose. Limes contain the least amount of sugar, clocking in at about one percent by weight. Dates contain the most sugar at about 50–60 percent. These sugars come from the breakdown of fruit starches during ripening. Ripe fruits still contain some starch (notably amylose and amylopectins) and pectins. When boiling, fruits pectins may be extracted and these pectins can cause haze issues downstream. The pectin content will vary from fruit to fruit.

Pears, apples, plums, guavas, gooseberries, oranges, and other citrus fruits contain large amounts of pectin. Some of the relatively low-pectin fruits include raspberries, strawberries, cherries, apricots, grapes, and peaches. Keep in mind that although some haze is acceptable in the wheat-based Gose style, they should not be a cloudy mess. If you feel your beers have haze or other issues related to fruit pectin, you can use a pectic enzyme (pectinase) to break the pectin down. Pectinases are readily available at most homebrew and winemaking shops.

Color, pH, and Astringency

Most fruits have a pH lower than normal, non-soured beers. The pH of fruit can vary from 4.5 to as low as 2.1 for some citrus fruits. You should bear this in mind when adding fruit to beer. In the case of Gose, a fruit addition might even raise the pH.

Fruit may also bring color to the beer. Most of these colors will be pleasing, but not all. The color in fruits come from either anthocyanins, carotenoids, or chlorophyll. The red, purple, and blue colors come from anthocyanins, which give cherries, raspberries, and blueberries their color. Anthocyanins are pH sensitive; at low pH they are more reddish and at higher pH they exhibit more blue color. In Gose, due to low pH, anthocyanins will be expressed as reddish even when using purple or blue fruit. Carotenoids are what create the yellow, orange, and, in some cases, red colors in plants (the red in tomatoes, for example, comes from carotenoids). Carotenoids are fat-soluble and as such will not transfer much color into your beer. Chlorophyll is responsible for the green colors in fruits, but most fruits do not have a lot of chlorophyll. I have found that chlorophyll can also cause astringent bitterness, so be careful when using green-colored fruits. Seeds, pits, and skins can also cause a lot of unpleasant astringency. I recommend tasting these by themselves and deciding if you think it worth the extra effort of removing them from the fruit. In most cases, if possible, I think it is worth the trouble to peel and pit or de-seed the fruit.

In our experience at Anderson Valley Brewing, fresh fruit almost always tastes best, but fresh fruit has many drawbacks as well. It is labor intensive to process, often requiring peeling, squeezing, zesting, chopping, pureeing, scooping, and mixing. It is often hard to acquire a sufficient amount—imagine asking the local grocer for 65 flats of fresh raspberries. It does not store well, and most fruits are seasonal, thus cannot to be found year round—try getting fresh watermelon in the dead of winter or pumpkin in July. Not only that, fresh fruit is covered with micro- (and sometimes macro-) organisms. If you plan on using fresh fruit, be careful of the rind, peel, skin, and seeds, as they can contain compounds that impart harsh and unwanted flavors, sometimes even toxins. Some seeds can contain toxins too. You might want to check out Stan Hieronymus' *Brewing Local* for safety details on which parts of the plant to avoid using.

Your other options include, in descending order of preference, frozen whole fruit, frozen purees, frozen pasteurized purees, pasteurized juice, pasteurized aseptic non-frozen purees, juices, juice concentrates, extracts, natural flavoring, and artificial flavorings. Each of these has pros and cons. As you descend down that list from frozen whole fruit to artificial flavoring, usually the quality of the flavor decreases and the ease of use increases. One nice thing about using purees, juices, or extracts is they have removed most of the extraneous matter (seeds, pits, stems, etc.). Whichever of these forms you choose, be careful to find a vendor with flavors that you like; puree, juice, syrup, and extract can vary widely in flavor and aroma from one supplier to another.

Hot Side Fruit Additions

The obvious advantage to adding your fruits on the hot side is that they are sterilized by contact with the hot wort. The downside is that there may be a loss of some of the subtle and more delicate flavors and aromas during the boil, whirlpool, or steep. Boiling fruit may also create a more cooked, jam-like flavor. Many fruits also contain seeds, which, if not removed before heating, can be the cause of harsh and bitter flavors in the beer. Boiling fruit may also release pectin that will cause haze issues post fermentation. As with spices, the best way to add fruit on the hot side is at the very end of the boil, just long enough to sterilize the fruit in the whirlpool. Like spices, another disadvantage of adding your fruit on the hot side is that the pulp or seeds may get carried over into your heat exchanger. Again, the use of an inline screen upstream can help alleviate this potential problem. The same cleaning protocols also apply: I recommend a reverse CIP on your heat exchange after every brew with fruit or spices to help flush out any material, and that you also take apart and manually clean your heat exchange at least two to four times a year.

Cold Side Fruit Additions

Adding fresh fruit to your beer on the cold side can give your beer the flavors closest to real, fresh fruit. As with spices, the downside to adding fruit at this time is that it has not been sterilized. And fresh fruit has a lot more bacteria and bugs (micro and macro) than spices. Adding fresh fruit to beer on the cold side will dramatically increase your chances of infection. To alleviate some of this potential, brewers often use frozen fruit, as most bacteria cannot survive any length of time in the deep freeze—but some bacteria can. Safer yet are flash-pasteurized fruit purees that have then been frozen, and even safer are fruit concentrates. Unfortunately, the more stable a fruit product, the farther you are from the real fresh fruit's flavors.

Adding your fruit to the cold side can also bring out some different flavors, and to some extent this will be affected by when you add the fruit. The closer to the beginning of fermentation that fruit is added, the more fruit flavor and aroma is lost during fermentation as a result of the fruit's compounds breaking down. The production of and gassing off of carbon dioxide in particular can be responsible for the loss of many aromatic compounds, just like with hops, and spice aromas. The obvious way to avoid losing aroma and flavor this way is to add the fruit after fermentation is over. But then you might be left with a lot of fruit sugar in your beer. This additional fruit sugar will not only make the beer sweeter, it will leave unfermented sugar in the beer.

If a brewer wants to get fruit flavor and aroma, but does not want the sweetness from the fruit sugar left in the beer, adding the fruit in the last 20–30 percent of fermentation could be a good compromise. At Anderson Valley, we like to add the fruit when fermentation is about 90 percent complete. We do this for several reasons. First, we get good fruit flavor and aroma. True, we do lose a little to carbon dioxide evolution, but not much. Second, the yeast is still active and consumes most, if not all, fruit sugar. Third, because the yeast is still active and in suspension, it absorbs and metabolizes any oxygen that was added during the fruit addition. Fourth, at that point in the fermentation the yeast have already lowered the pH and created alcohol; both suppress the growth of unwanted bacteria. And finally, the beer is still warm enough so that the extraction of flavors and aromas takes place faster and more completely.

The other time you can add fruit to your Gose is after you chill the beer, though it is not advised. Adding the fruit to chilled beer is a double-edged sword; the beer is cold and that offers more protection against spoiling microorganisms (which is good), but the cold temperature means that the flavors and aromas of the fruit will not be extracted as completely or as quickly as they would in warmer beer. All chemical reactions happen faster when they are warmer. Also, since the beer is cold, the yeast will not be able to immediately consume the fruit's sugars. This will leave fermentable sugar in the beer, which may lead to infection issues after packaging. And even if you are not worried about the flavors those unwanted bacteria may produce, the eventual fermentation of sugar in a finished beer can create unexpected additional carbonation. This will lead to gushing bottles and foaming kegs.

In your favor when adding fruit and spices to the cold side, is that Gose, although not hoppy or very alcoholic (both fairly decent preservatives), has a very low pH. A low pH is a natural preservative, because most microorganisms do not grow well at a pH of less than 3.4, and most bacteria that will grow at a low pH mostly only contribute more acid, which in a Gose is not the worst thing in the world. Do not let this lull you into a sense of false security! To make great beer you should always remain vigilant against unwanted microorganisms.

Of course, you could use fruit on both the hot and cold sides and at multiple stages, or even every stage, of the brewing process. Fruit used at different stages will bring out different flavors and each fruit will act in its own unique way depending on when you add it to your beer. Table 3.2 will be of some aid in your fruit selection.

TABLE 3.2 pH AND SUGAR CONTENT IN SOME COMMON FRUIT

	pH	Approx. sugar % by weight
Apples, Golden Delicious	3.60	10
Apples, McIntosh	3.34	10.5
Apricots	3.30–4.80	9
Beets	5.30–6.60	Varies
Blackberries	3.85–4.50	4.88
Blueberries, Maine	3.12–3.33	11
Breadfruit, cooked	5.33	11
Cactus	4.70	4
Cantaloupe	6.13–6.58	N/A
Cherries	4.01–4.54	14
Cherries, frozen	3.32–3.37	15
Ginger	5.60–5.90	N/A
Gooseberries	2.80–3.10	N/A
Grapes, Concord	2.80–3.00	15
Grapes, Malaga	3.71–3.78	14.8
Grapefruit pulp	3.00–3.75	9.2
Guava nectar	5.50	9
Kumquat, Florida	3.64–4.25	9.36
Lemon juice	2.00–2.60	2.53
Lime juice	2.00–2.35	1
Mangoes, ripe	3.40–4.80	11
Mangoes, green	5.80–6.00	4
Mangostine	4.50–5.00	8
Orange juice	3.30–4.19	9.15
Peaches	3.30–4.05	9
Pears, Bartlett	3.50–4.60	9.69
Pineapple	3.20–4.00	9.85
Plums, blue	2.80–3.40	11
Plums, frozen	3.22–3.42	11
Plums, red	3.60–4.30	11
Pomegranate	2.93–3.20	13.67
Rambutan	4.90	N/A
Raspberries	3.22–3.95	7
Raspberries, frozen	3.18–3.26	7
Strawberries	3.00–3.90	7
Watermelon	5.18–5.60	9

SALT

Legend has it that the salinity of Gose once came from the mineral-laden water of the Gose river. It has been postulated that some medieval brewers thought salt enhanced fermentation and the flavors of the beer made with it. And unlike other regions of the world at that time, salt was plentiful in the Harz mountain region around Goslar, and thus salt was not the expensive commodity it was in other brewing centers. A thousand years after the first Gose beers were brewed, it is hard for us to be certain where it first got is mineral saline note.

We do know that later on, as the beers from Goslar gained in popularity, brewers in the nearby towns wanted to emulate their unique character. In order to replicate the Goslar's famous Gose flavor, brewers needed to replicate that mineral salinity. From brewing records, we know that the solution for many of those brewers was to add a little salt.

By the late Middle Ages many of the towns surrounding Goslar, especially to the southeast, were producing a Gose. Records show that the towns of Wernigerode, Quedlinburg, Halberstadt, Aschersleben, Blankenburg, and Sandersleben all made their own versions of Goslar's famous beer. Not much was written about these beers, but we can assume that the further a town was from Goslar, the less likely it was to have similar water. Thus, adjustments would be necessary, and salt became part of the Gose recipe.

Types of Salt

There are many varieties of salt, and you probably should decide what kind of salt you want to use before you decide how much of it you want to use. So let's do a little Salt 101 class. Humans have been using salt for at least as long as they have been brewing beer. The earliest evidence of the harvest of salt comes from China about 6,000 years ago, and salted fish and game birds have been found in Egyptian tombs that date back to circa 2000 BC.[14] Salt's chemical makeup, in its purest form, is sodium chloride ($NaCl$) in a 2:3 ratio by mass of sodium and chlorine. The molar masses are approximately 23 g for sodium and 35.5 g for chlorine. Thus, 100 g of sodium chloride (salt) contains 39.34 g sodium and 60.66 g chloride. This could have implications depending on when in the brewing process you add your salt, but these implications are discussed elsewhere in the book.

Minerals or compounds bound up with the salt are what give different salts their different flavors and colors. The minerals could be calcium, potassium, magnesium,

---

[14]   "A Brief and Fascinating History of Salt," Beyond The Shaker (website), copyright 2018, http://beyondtheshaker.com/pages/salt-guide/salt-guide-history.html.

sulfur, or others. Some salts are intentionally mixed with other components to give them distinctive colors and flavors. Salt is either mined from ancient ocean deposits or evaporated from ocean water. Most of the nearly 200 million metric tons of salt produced each year is mined from terrestrial deposits. Mining salt usually involves sending water underground into the large salt deposits, then pumping the briny solution to the surface, cleaning it, and then vacuum evaporating off the water. This process leaves salt in the form of grains sufficiently small and uniform to fit through the perforations of your household salt shaker. Sea salt is made by evaporating ocean water, which leaves behind coarse salt crystals. Kosher salt can be either mined terrestrial salt or evaporated sea salt. There is a specific evaporating process used to make kosher salt and it creates coarse, irregularly shaped crystals. The irregular shape is desired because it helps the crystals cling more easily to meat, helping to draw out blood, thereby koshering the meat. Kosher salt is produced under rabbinical supervision. Both kosher salt and natural sea salt are non-iodized. In addition to being used in food and beverages, salt is also used in industrial processes and for the deicing of roads.

Salts of the World

Now that we know a little bit about salt and its makeup, we need to determine what variety of salt we want for our beer. One might think that this would be a bit easier to nail down than how much salt we want to use, but there are a lot of options to choose from.

Iodized Salt

Most table salt is iodized. This mean that the salt has had potassium iodide added to it. This addition is to help protect us humans against thyroid disease, which can be caused by iodine deficiency. Some table salts have other additives like dextrose or calcium silicate to help stabilize the salt and keep it from clumping. Iodized salt is good for table use, but most people agree that it is not suitable for curing meats, some types of cooking, or for brewing. This is because the iodine in the salt can contribute unwanted flavors. The salt you use in your brewing should be non-iodized and free of anti-caking agents.

Pink Himalayan Salt

Pink Himalayan salt is a form of halite or rock salt. It comes from in, around, and near the Punjab province of Pakistan. It has a lovely pink color. It is purported to have many great health benefits, none of which, to date, have been scientifically confirmed. It is also said to be 99 percent pure and to contain over 84 different minerals and trace elements, which one must assume make up the other one percent. It is also purported to store vibrational energy (to understand vibrational energy, you'll need to first get your chakra realigned). I think that Dr. Andy Weil, the founder and director of the University of Arizona Center for Integrative Medicine, put it best when he said, "Pink Himalayan salt is nutritionally very similar to regular salt. It's just prettier and more expensive." A lot more expensive.

Persian Blue

Persian blue salt is harvested from an ancient salt lake in Iran. It is a mineral-rich deposit. Its blue color does not come from the mineral content as with many other colored salts, but from the natural compression of the salt's structure over millennia. While visually pleasing, as one of the rarest salts in the world, it is very expensive.

Fleur de Sel

Fleur de sel means "flower of salt" in French. For many chefs, this salt is the Holy Grail. It is hand-harvested along the French coastline in the same pools as Celtic grey sea salt. Fleur de sel comes from the uppermost layer of the saltpans, and is therefore the lightest and most flakey of the hand-harvested French salts. In terms of health, it is an expensive, mineral-rich sea salt with delicate flakes. Did I mention that it was expensive?

Celtic Sea Salt

Sometimes called *sel gris,* this salt is colored by the grey clays of France. It is a naturally evaporated sea salt. It is hand-raked in Brittany, France, and sometimes in other areas where the natural clay and sand create moist, mineral-rich crystals. It comes from the same harvest area as fleur de sel, but from the bottom of the saltpans. Sel gris is said to have alkalizing properties and to prevent muscle cramps. This salt is on the more expensive side, due to the labor-intensive process of hand raking.

Kala Namak / Bire Noon

This is black salt from Nepal (bire noon), India, and Pakistan (kala namak). It is dark purple when whole but becomes pink once ground. It begins as white salt, which is sealed in a ceramic jar with charcoal, sometimes soda ash, and small amounts of harad seed and other spices, and is then fired in a furnace for 24 hours. It develops its color from iron sulfide during this process, which makes it sulfidic in aroma and taste. Thought to be a beneficial digestive aid, black salt is highly prized and is relatively expensive. Kala namak might be good creating some interesting dishes in the kitchen, but I would be reluctant to use it in a Gose. No one wants a beer that smells like boiled eggs.

Hawaiian Black Salt

Another black salt that supposedly originates in Hawaii (although I found no credible source for this claim), Hawaiian black salt is an unrefined sea salt that gets its color from being mixed with activated charcoal. The charcoal is supposedly great for your digestion and for removing impurities in the body. The latter might be true if you've just ingested some toxins, although the amount of this charcoal-laced salt you would need to eat to absorb the toxins would have its own deleterious effects. According to Witchipedia (you can't make this stuff up), this salt is "used in magick [sic] to absorb and trap negative energies."[15] So if you use this salt in your beer you could say your Gose traps and absorbs negative energy, but then again maybe that's not really a good selling point. As you might imagine, magic salt is fairly expensive.

Hawaiian Rock Salt

Also known as alaea salt, Hawaiian rock salt is an unrefined sea salt that is mixed with and gets its color from alaea, or Hawaiian volcanic red clay. In traditional Hawaiian culture it is used to season local cuisine and to purify, or *hi'uwai,* tools, objects, and areas. Most of the Hawaiian rock salt that is sold in the United States is produced in California, not in Hawaii (Bitterman 2010). Real Hawaiian alaea salt made in Hawaii is hard to find and legally cannot be sold there (Bitterman 2010). I grew up in Hawaii, so obviously I think that this salt is the best salt known to man (plus, I no can talk stink 'bout alaea, cuz den bambai da nex time I stay in Hilo, da mokes deah, dey going catch me an buss me up).[16]

Tahitian vanilla salt

Made with hand-harvested sea salt and Tahitian vanilla beans, this has an attractive brown color and a mild vanilla fragrance. Sweet and salty. It is also expensive.

Spruce Tip Salt

I have included spruce tip salt for three reasons: 1) there are a lot of flavors you can infuse into your salt and I thought this was a good example of one such flavor; 2)

---

15   Witchipedia, *s.v.* "Black Salt," last accessed June 9, 2018, http://www.witchipedia.com /mineral:black-salt.

16   Personal communication with some blah'lahs at four miles.

spruce was used in Gose traditionally and I thought that this might be a good way to incorporate some spruce flavor; and 3) it just sounds really yummy. I have had spruce tip beers in the past and I have always enjoyed them, but you can only make them during a very brief period of the year when the spruce trees are putting out new shoots. Using spruce tip salt preserves this flavor for year-round use. I got the following basic recipe from the *Saveur* website: "Dehydrate spruce buds. Grind the dry buds into a powder using a spice grinder; stir them into Maldon flake sea salt. Store at room temperature up to 1 month.[17]"

Smoked salt

Smoky and sour does have its place: think of some of the sour interpretations of the classic smoked beer from Poland, Grodziskie (Grätzer). Smoked salts are sea salts that are smoked at low temperatures over coals. This process gives the salt a light, smoky flavor and a grey or tan color. Smoked salt has no known health benefits over common table salt, in fact, it may actually be bad for you, as it is alleged that smoked products have compounds such as polycyclic aromatic hydrocarbons, which are known to cause cancer in lab animals. So, not as expensive, but may cause cancer.

Natural, Non-Iodized Sea Salt

Natural, non-iodized sea salt is the salt evaporated from the oceans of the world. It contains a very low level of pretentiousness, and yet is made from 100 percent fresh, natural ingredients. Widely available, it can be purchased very inexpensively in bulk or in bags. Perfect for brewing or cooking.

Conclusion

There are some people who claim to be able to taste the difference between common non-iodized table salt and more esoteric salts. That may be true in their dry form, but once dissolved in either food or beer it is pretty unlikely that any difference could be easily distinguished. The mineral content in most salts is so low that any effect these minerals might have on flavor will be lost when even as much as 0.5 oz. (14 g) is mixed into one gallon (3.78 L). This leads me to believe that the value of using an esoteric and expensive salt to make Gose would be almost entirely marketing. For brewing Gose I would suggest an affordable non-iodized sea salt. For further reading on this subject I suggest the excellent article by *Cook's Illustrated*.[18]
https://www.cooksillustrated.com/taste_tests/51-salt

---

[17]   "Spruce Salt," *Saveur*, December, 2014, https://www.saveur.com/article/recipes/spruce-salt.

[18]   "Salt," *Cook's Illustrated*, September, 2002, https://www.cooksillustrated.com/taste_tests/51-salt.

How Much Salt

I believe that, in most of brewing, more can often end up being less. It's a tricky thing, you want your beer to stand out in the crowd, but you also want people to have more than one of them. If the beer is not unusual enough, it won't get noticed; but if it is too unusual people will think, "Well, it was an interesting beer but I don't really want to even finish this pint of it, much less order another one." This is certainly the case with salt in Gose. You need to have a subtle hand. You want people to notice its effect, but only enough to make the beer interesting. Salt's flavor contribution should accentuate other flavors and enhance mouthfeel, not create a salty brew.

When we first brewed our Gose at Anderson Valley Brewing we, the brewers, could not agree on how much salt we wanted to use. Some people (well, me) wanted less salt, some people wanted more, some people wanted it to taste like a salt lick. There were a lot of opinions and we could not reach a consensus. We agreed that we would let the people decide. So on a Friday afternoon, we set up a beer station in front of our tasting room and everyone that came in that day had to try four beers. Our base Gose with no salt added, a sample of the base Gose with 0.06 oz. (1.7 g) of salt per gallon, a sample with 0.12 oz. (3.4 g) per gallon, and a sample with (the seemingly unreasonable amount of) 0.24 oz. (6.8 g) per gallon. We had everyone rank the beers favorite to least favorite. We tallied the scores, plotted them on a graph and the perfect amount of salt was determined. And the proper amount of salt, per our less then highly scientific method, was determined to be right in the middle of our graph: 0.12 oz. (3.4 g) per gallon of finished beer (0.888 g/L or 888 ppm). This is a bit above average. For some historical perspective, we know that most Gose beers from the very early twentieth century had between 130 and 260 ppm of salt. The 888 ppm we settled on would be about 346 ppm of sodium and 542 ppm chloride, both above the recommended range for normal beers. Levels over 500 ppm chloride may effect fermentation with some yeast strains (Palmer and Kaminski 2013). The potential of negative effects on fermentation is one of many good reasons to add salt after fermentation is complete.

When deciding on how much salt you want to use, it is important to remember the goal: it's added to marry a subtle salinity with the clean and sharp tartness of the lactic acid and the mild undertone of the coriander. You want a mineral salinity to bring out the fullness of the wheat and pique the interest of the drinker. The salinity should be a nuance, not a distraction.

Figure 3.9. Anderson Valley Brewing uses this much salt in a pint of Gose.

Adding the Salt

Once you have decided what kind and how much, then you need to get it into your beer. You will need to get the salt into solution and homogenized throughout the solution. Like most solids, salt will not want to dissolve into a cold liquid. For that reason, it's easiest to add it to the kettle, but there may be some drawbacks to this. First, salt is not good for stainless steel, especially at warmer temperatures (for more detail on this, see the "Sanitation" section in chapter 4). Second, if you add the salt in the kettle, the higher salinity may cause fermentation problems with some yeast strains. So, if you are concerned with either of these potential problems, then the best time to add the salt is after fermentation is completed, but before you chill the beer.

We have found that the easiest way to add our salt is to first premix the salt in a small vessel. Once the salt is completely dissolved, we inject the salty solution into the fermentor through the bottom. We then gently blow some carbon dioxide through the bottom of the fermentation tank and the rising gas mixes the solution into the beer. Doing it at this phase of the brewing process has the added advantage of having a lot of dormant yeast still in solution, so any oxygen we inadvertently add with the salt is absorbed by the yeast. Another option would be to premix the salt and then dose the salt solution inline during the transfer to the secondary or conditioning tank. Do not add solid, crystallized salt to carbonated beer—it can cause a dramatic release of carbon dioxide that may be dangerous, or at the very least messy.

For a discussion on salt's potential effects on your brewing equipment, please see the "Equipment" sidebar in chapter 4 under the section on sanitation.

SOURING AGENTS

> *It [Gose] differs from other beers by its larger content of lactic acids. The*
> *method how this lactic acid is brought in the Gose, or how it develops in*
> *it is known as Einschlag, which is a well kept secret of Gose brewers until*
> *this very day.*
>
> —Otto Kröber, *Die Geschichte der Gose und die Chronik der Gosenschänke Leipzig*
> *Eutritzsch* (Translated by Adept Content Solutions)

Bacterial Souring Agents

Gose-style beers need to be sour. If you make a Gose and it is not sour, then you really have not made a Gose. It might be a very interesting wheat beer, but it is not a Gose. Lactic acid is one of the defining flavor characters of the Gose style. True, there has been some discussion about the original Gose beers not being sour beers, but realistically, more than 500 years ago, any but the youngest of beers was at least slightly sour and a piquant sourness is what Gose is known for. When it comes to making your Gose sour there are several choices open to the brewer.

Traditionally it was done with bacteria during or after the yeast fermentation. Today we have more options. All of the methods except the traditional method have the advantage of being safer from a cross-contamination standpoint, as the bacteria are never in the fermentation area of the brewery.

DEFINING 'TRADITIONAL' SOURING TECHNIQUES

When you are writing about a beer style like Gose that is approximately 1,000 years old, it is hard to define what traditional means with this style. Should that definition be what was done 1,000 years ago, or merely 300 years ago?

The most traditional and common method of souring is to use the lactic acid-producing bacteria *Lactobacillus*. Although *Pediococcus*[19] also produces lactic acid, it is a less desirable bacterium for the job as it also produces diacetyl—sometimes prodigious amounts of diacetyl—and can also produce ropiness. Diacetyl and ropiness are not part of Gose's flavor profile. Usually when *Pediococcus* is used as a souring bacteria, *Brettanomyces*[20] is

---

[19]   *Pediococcus* is a coccus-shaped bacteria that are often found in pairs or tetrads. *Pediococcus* is a Gram-positive, non-motile, homofermentative, facultative anaerobe that occurs in the wild on many types of plant material. It is a lactic acid-producing bacteria that can grow in low pH and some strains are hop tolerant.

[20]   *Brettanomyces* is sometimes referred to by the genus name of *Dekkera* or just Brett. It is a yeast, not a bacteria, that occurs in the wild. *Brettanomyces* produces significant flavor and aroma compounds and because of that it is often considered a spoilage agent in "clean" beers and wines.

also used in what is known as a mixed fermentation. This is because *Brettanomyces* will metabolize and reduce the diacetyl produced by *Pediococcus*. In addition to breaking down diacetyl, the *Brettanomyces* will also produce some distinctive aromas of its own. These aromas are often described as barnyard, horse blanket, and funky. They are aromas that we associate with some lambics and some American sours beers. Other aromas may be described as fruity pineapple, peach, or apricot. Unfortunately, these former flavors and aromas produced by *Brettanomyces* also do not really belong in a Gose. So this pretty much rules out the use of *Pediococcus* as a souring agent for Gose-style beer. Thus, we are left with *Lactobacillus* as the most appropriate souring agent.

Lactic Acid Bacteria

The term lactic acid bacteria (LAB) is conventionally applied to genera of the order Lactobacillales, which includes, notably, *Lactobacillus, Pediococcus, Lactococcus, Leuconostoc,* and several other lesser-known varieties. *Lactobacillus* is the most widely used and is the most well-known of the LAB.

Lactobacillus is best known for use in cheese making and souring milk to make yogurt. In fact, some brewers use a yogurt pitch to get their *Lactobacillus* for souring their beer (more on that in "Souring the Beer" in chapter 4). *Lactobacillus* is a straight or curved rod-shaped bacteria, occurring singly or in chains, and sometimes in filaments. *Lactobacillus* is a non-spore forming, Gram-positive,[21] catalase negative, anaerobic-to-facultative anaerobe bacteria that converts sugar to lactic acid. *Lactobacillus* is usually non-motile. Facultative anaerobe means that it does not require oxygen, but it can function in the presence of oxygen; it can also function just fine if oxygen is absent. Most species are homofermentative (producing only lactic acid from sugar), but some species are heterofermentative (producing lactic acid and other by-products from sugar). Heterofermentative varieties can produce other metabolites, including ethanol, acetic acid, and carbon dioxide, although lactic acid still makes up the majority (over 50 percent) of the by-products created. In some species of *Lactobacillus*, the level of acetic acid created will be above the taste threshold, and so will be noticeable in the finished beer; but, the production of lactic acid in these strains is approximately ten times higher than that of acetic acid, so lactic acid will still be the dominate acid flavor. In some species of *Lactobacillus*, small amounts of other acids may be formed, including formic, propionic, valerianic, and butyric acid (Boone and Castenholz 2001). *Lactobacillus* have complex nutritional requirements, meaning that they require an environment that includes sugars, amino acids, vitamins, purines, and pyrimidines.

---

[21] Gram-positive means no outer membrane.

Lactobacillus can be found throughout nature on fruits, plant material and grain husks, and in the mouths, digestive tracts, and on the skin of humans and animals. The genus *Lactobacillus* contains around 180 known species.[22] Most species of *Lactobacillus* are not hop tolerant. *Lactobacillus* is commonly used in the production of many foods including yogurt, cheese, cocoa, fermented vegetables like pickles, sauerkraut, and kimchi, sourdough bread, some aged meats, some sour beers, and some wines. Medically speaking, *Lactobacillus* is considered a friendly bacteria and is beneficial to human digestion, so it should not pose any problems for consumers. Although considered friendly to humans and some food processes, it can also be a food "spoiler" and a nuisance under other conditions, like when you are trying to make beer that is NOT sour.

It was not until the early part of the twentieth century that the concept and production of single-strain starter cultures of *Lactobacillus* to use in food came about. These starters were mostly used in dairy products. By mid-century the idea of using pure-strain starters was making its way into the preserved meat industry.

When it comes time to select the species of *Lactobacillus* that you would like to use in your beer, there are many choices, as noted, around 180. The main selection criteria should be flavor. Other considerations are speed of production, hop tolerance, temperature range, and whether they produce by-products that may affect other bacteria or your yeast's metabolism.

Flavor Contributions

There are some general flavor and aroma notes that can be discussed. Heterofermentative species of *Lactobacillus* generally produce four main metabolites: lactic acid, ethanol, carbon dioxide, and acetic acid. The amount of each metabolite is strain and environment dependent. *Lactobacillus* fermentations are often said to have a slightly musty aroma, and sometimes aromas that are referred to as dough-like or reminiscent of sourdough bread. A subject that is often discussed among brewers of sour beer is the quality of the sourness. Words like bright, sharp, or clean are often used as positive descriptors. Dull, musty, and earthy are negative descriptors that are sometimes used.

Both hetero- and homofermentative stains will produce a variety of secondary metabolite by-products that can have effects on both flavors

---

[22] Wikipedia, *s.v. "Lactobacillus,"* last modified May 17, 2018, 10:58, https://en.wikipedia.org/wiki/Lactobacillus.

and aromas. Some of the more common secondary metabolites can be diacetyl, acetaldehyde, ethyl acetate, or fusel alcohols. These may be expressed in flavors or aromas noted as buttery, green apple, fruity, or solvent, respectively. Other metabolites found in even smaller quantities that may be produced include norfuraneol (caramel flavors and aromas), ethyl 2-methylbutanoate (citrus), and 2-phenylethanol (rose). Aging can have a big impact on the aromas and flavors produced during fermentation. This impact is typically influenced by temperature, oxygen exposure, and the other by-products produced during fermentation.

Keep in mind that all of these flavors and aromas are on the lighter side, and they can easily be overpowered by stronger notes contributed by fruits, spices, yeast, and even some strong malt flavors. An exception to the above rule may be *L. plantarum* from Swanson's Probiotic Pills. It has been reported that this strain of *L. plantarum* (and possibly other strains of *L. plantarum*) can make some pretty funky flavors in the presence of oxygen.

TABLE 3.3 LACTIC ACID BACTERIA DEFINED BY FERMENTATION TYPE

Obligatory Homofermentative	Obligatory Heterofermentative	Facultatively Heterofermentative
Lactobacillus acidophilus	L. brevis	L. bavaricus
L. delbruekii	L. buchneri	L. casei
L. helveticas	L. cellobiosus	L. coryniformis
L. lactis	L. confusus	L. curvatus
L. leichmannii	L. coprophilus	L. plantarum
L. rhamnosus	L. fermentatum	L. sakei
L. salivarius	L. fermentum	L. paracasei
Pediococcus acidilactici	L. pontis	
P. damnosus	L. reuteri	
P. pentocacus	L. sanfranciscensis	
Streptococcus bovis		
S.thermophilus		

TABLE 3.4 LACTIC ACID BACTERIA STRAINS AND THEIR ACID AND ETHANOL CONTRIBUTIONS

Species	Lactic acid, g/L	Acetic acid, g/L	Ethanol, g/L
L. sanfranciscensis	2.88–3.79	0.27–0.35	1.45–1.78
L. brevis	2.12–3.56	0.17–0.27	0.73–1.39
L. fructivorans	1.12–1.79	0.13–0.20	0.33–0.46
L. fermentum	2.93–3.44	0.21–0.25	1.02–1.95
L. cellobiosus	2.81–3.27	0.15–0.35	1.19–1.95
L. plantarum	4.58–5.14	Trace	0
L. farciminis	3.58–4.27	Trace	0
L. alimentarius	3.48–3.95	0	0
L. acidophilus	3.11–4.19	0	0
L. delbrueckii	4.24–4.98	0	0
S. cerevisiae	0	0	8.88–9.41

Summary of end products for a simple fermentation of a minimal media of various *Lactobacillus (L.)* species compared to *Saccharomyces (S.) cerevisiae.*

Hop Tolerance

Hop components are known to have antimicrobial properties against gram-positive bacteria. Hops contain multiple compounds that act to stop bacteria from reproducing. The alpha acids are the best known and understood, but beta acids and a number of polyphenols and even some of the aromatic oils have been found to have some bacteria-inhibiting effects. In aged hops the alpha acids are almost completely absent, but other compounds, especially beta acids, are still present and that is why aged hops still retain their antimicrobial effects. It appears that all these hop compounds inhibit bacterial growth in the same way.

Hop tolerance is both species and strain dependent, but hop tolerance can be an inducible trait in many *Lactobacillus* species. That means that a hop intolerant strain can become more tolerant if it is repeatedly cultured with successively increasing levels of hop components. Conversely, a hop tolerant strain can become hop intolerant after several generations in a hop-free media. In general, the higher the level of hop components, the slower the pH of the beer will drop due to bacterial action.

Figure 3.10. Hexa-Iso Foam Test. This series of photos shows the foam quality of two *Lactobacillus*-soured beers, one with Hexa-Iso hop product added to the beer (left), the other with nothing added (right). Photo courtesy of Kristen England (used with permission).

Foam Degradation

There are some species or strains of *Lactobacillus* that will create all of the amino acids they require for normal growth; these are known as prototrophic strains. Other species or strains can only produce some of the amino acids they require for normal growth; these bacteria must obtain the other required amino acids from within their environment and are known as auxotrophic. It would be impossible to list them, as they change over time.

Auxotrophic *Lactobacillus* break down proteins in their environment in order to create the amino acids that they cannot make. Importantly, this includes foam-positive proteins in beer. This proteolysis (the breaking down of various proteins into polypeptides) and the subsequent peptidolysis (the breaking down of polypeptides into peptides and then amino acids) is enzyme dependent. This proteolytic activity has been observed in both homofermentative and heterofermentative species, and even different strains of the same species may have differing levels of this proteolytic capability.[23]

Some species of *Lactobacillus* have shown that this proteolytic activity decreases as the pH drops near or below 4.5. In brewhouse-soured worts, one might reduce the wort pH to a level of 5.0 or below with an acid addition or by using acidulated malts prior to pitching their *Lactobacillus*. This could help to retain some of the proteins necessary for foam formation. Another possible solution might be to sideline some of your wort and hold it separate (and unsoured) during the stage of bacterial fermentation. Then as you start to boil the soured wort, add the unsoured wort to your kettle. By boiling it, you have killed all the *Lactobacillus* bacteria and the sidelined, unsoured wort would retain the proteins helpful to foam formation. Be mindful that by adding in some unsoured wort you will also raise the pH of the whole wort being boiled. You will have needed to previously factor this

---

[23] Milk the Funk Wiki, *s.v.* "Lactobacillus," last modified May 26, 2018, 17:35, http://www.milkthefunk .com/wiki/Lactobacillus#Foam_Degradation

in and let your soured wort attain a low enough pH so that the pH of your final beer is where you want it to be.

Additionally, one can use ingredients that will increase head retention. Ingredients such as malted wheat, oats, Carafoam®, and hexa-iso-hop extracts have been successfully used to help increase head retention in *Lactobacillus*-soured beers (fig. 3.10).

Haze

There are some forms of LAB that can aggregate to form haze, and some non-aggregating bacteria are light enough to remain in suspension and cause clarity issues. Some other strains can have the opposite effect by producing the enzyme tannase. Tannase can break down certain haze-forming tannins, and thus could play a positive role in beer clarity. Some sources have claimed that of the 47 strains of LAB that they studied, *L. plantarum* produced the highest amount of the enzyme tannase (Matsuda et al. 2018).

Attributes of Common Lactic Acid Bacteria Strains of *Lactobacillus*

L. brevis. Heterofermentative: creates CO_2, ethanol, lactic acid, and can produce acetic acid. Some variants can be hop tolerant, making it a potential beer spoiler. Optimum temperature is 95–105°F (35–40°C). Typically produces more lactic acid than *L. delbrueckii.*
Lactic acid: 2.12–3.56 g/L
Acetic acid: 0.17–0.27 g/L
Ethanol: 0.73–1.39 g/L

L. delbrueckii. (Also known as *L. bulgaricus,* which is an L. delbrueckii subspecies.) Used in yogurt production, optimum temperature 83–90°F (28–32°C). Prefers lactose over sucrose or maltose. Produces a moderate amount of lactic acid. Clean, lactic sourness. Known for heat tolerance. May produce trace amounts of diacetyl. *L. delbrueckii* subspecies *lactis* can consume trehalose. Trehalose is an off-flavor released when *Saccharomyces* cells autolyze, thus, this subspecies could be used advantageously in longer (or barrel) aged sour beers.
Lactic acid: 4.24–4.98 g/L
Acetic acid: 0
Ethanol: 0

L. acidophilus. Homofermentative, microaerophilic, optimum growth temperature around 99°F (37°C). Used in soured dairy products like yogurt. Known to inhibit other organisms.
Lactic acid: 3.11–4.19 g/L
Acetic acid: 0
Ethanol: 0

L. plantarum. Aerotolerant, optimum temperature 83–90°F (28–32°C), but will grow at lower temperatures of about 60°F (16°C); will also grown at higher temperatures, but has some difficulty performing above 115°F (45°C). Can ferment a variety of sugars, can produce other by-products (CO_2, alcohol, acetic acid). Does not like hops. Commonly used in food production, notably cheddar cheese. Very high tolerance to low pH (~3.0)
Lactic acid: 4.58–5.14 g/L
Acetic acid: trace
Ethanol: 0

L. sanfranciscensis. Important in sourdough production.
Lactic acid: 2.88–3.79 g/L
Acetic acid: 0.27–0.35 g/L
Ethanol: 1.45–1.78 g/L

L. buchneri. Heterofermentative, may produce acetic acid.

L. casei. Has a wide pH and temperature range. Used in yogurt and cheese production. Ferments lactose, maltose, and mannitol.

Pediococcus. Homofermentative cocci that form tetrads. Used in sauerkraut and pickle production.

4

BREWHOUSE OPERATIONS

The precise method of brewing Gose was of great secrecy in the eighteenth and nineteenth centuries. The beer's popularity (and the premium price that it commanded) made it an attractive proposition for any brewery. Naturally, those already in the business of making it weren't too keen on their rivals getting in on the act. The tricky part was getting the addition of lactic acid bacteria right. Sometimes during the boil, the precise moment was of great importance, a powder was added to the wort (according to a source of 1872).

—As reported by Ron Pattinson, "Leipzig Pub Guide: Leipziger Gose," European Beer Guide (website).

A thousand years ago, when the first Gose-style beers were first being brewed, the world was a very different place in many ways. Brewers were often also maltsters, and sometimes even farmers. Milling the malt would probably have taken place at a community mill shared with the local baker; lucky brewers may have had their own mill driven by a donkey walking endlessly in circles.

MILLING

Today, almost all brewers get their grain already malted, some get it pre-milled, and some even use malt extract. For most brewers, all that is required of their malt is that it is properly cracked and captured in a grist case. To do this there are many good mill options, from benchtop homebrew mills, to the Roskamp two-row mill, to the Kunzel six-roll for the larger breweries. The key difference between Gose-style beers and other beers is that you are milling approximately 50 percent wheat and 50 percent barley. The kernel size of these two grains may be different enough that the roller gap of the mill will need to be adjusted. The other main difference between the two grains is that wheat is a huskless grain and can be more finely milled.

However you mill your grain, the goal is to crack open the kernel and expose the inner starch. Most of the malt husks should be relatively intact, split into halves or quarters, and not pulverized. The chalky inner starch should be exposed and broken. In a proper grind from a two- or even four-roll mill, you can expect to see a few uncracked kernels, but not many; aim for less than one percent.

Figure 4.1. Properly milled barley malt. Note that there are not very many whole grain kernels and the majority of the husks are broken open, but not pulverized.

Too coarse of a grind will lead to insufficient amino acids and low sugar yields in your wort. Too fine of a grind will lead to more phenols and husky flavors (at least for the barley portion of the grist) and longer lauter times.

If you have the ability to steam condition your malt, or if you are able to wet mill, both these hydrating processes will help to keep the starch-encapsulating layers of the wheat and the husks of the barley malt more intact. This in turn will help to keep the mash bed looser during lautering and make for an easier runoff to the kettle.

Detour 1: Sour Mashing

It is at this point that that we hit our first fork in the road. What method of souring are you planning to use? Will it be a sour mash, a kettle sour, or will you sour post-brewhouse operations? If you chose number one, come back to this section after you have read the first section on "Souring the Beer" (which starts on page 118). If you have chosen either of the latter two options, please continue reading.

MASH-IN

Mashing in a Gose needs to be done with care. Although this is a relatively low-gravity beer, it is at least 40 percent wheat and can be as much as 60 percent wheat, or even 100 percent if you are making an all-wheat Gose from the Middle Ages. This is pertinent, because the viscosity of the wort created from wheat malt is higher than that from barley malt, and because wheat is a naked grain and has no husk to help build a filter bed in the lauter tun. With a grist bill that is 40 percent wheat malt or greater, you will have 40 percent less husk material to aid runoff. Because of the lack of husks, a Gose or other wheat beer mash will not form the same kind of constructed mash bed that a 100 percent barley malt mash will. This, coupled with the higher protein content of wheat, can make for a very dense, sticky mash and you can expect to have some lautering difficulties. To alleviate some of these issues, a brewer may choose to conduct a protein rest around 122°F (50°C). This rest will allow for some for the high molecular weight proteins to be broken down and thus decrease wort viscosity. This can easily be done using a step-infusion mash regime. Brewers who are planning on using more than 50 percent wheat malt in their grain bill, especially when used in conjunction with under-modified malts, may opt to use a non-traditional decoction mash regime. Decoction mashing is usually accomplished by doughing-in at around 122°F (50°C) for a protein rest, waiting for 20–30 minutes, then removing one third of the mash, sending it to another vessel, and bringing it to a boil. The boiled portion is then returned to the main mash and blended to attain a temperature of 148–156°F (64.5–69°C). This process will give you maximum protein degradation, and will break down starch as well. Decoction mashing is complicated, time consuming, difficult, and involves a lot of mixing that can cause further problems with lautering. You will have to decide if your brewing equipment is suited to the task, and if the benefits of the extra steps are justifiable. If not done properly, decoction mashing can lead to a scorched mash, darker beer color, denatured enzymes, and husky or burnt flavors.

Another option for reducing lautering difficulties is to use rice hulls (or spelt hulls) in your mash. Rice hulls are flavorless and will not impact the color of your beer. They will help you establish a suitable mash bed matrix that will allow for acceptable wort flow, runoff times, and mash tun efficiencies. I suggest using between 0.2 and 1 oz. (6–28 g) of hull material per pound of malt in the mash, depending on your grain bill and lauter system. Mix the rice hulls in with the rest of your grain so that they are evenly dispersed throughout the mash. For those brewers in Europe who have a hard time finding rice hulls, spelt hulls are more accessible and work well too. It is suggested that you soak the spelt hulls for 4–12 hours before using them.

In my opinion, it is better to use 50 percent or less wheat malt in your grain bill with highly modified barley malt, employ a single temperature mash, and throw in some rice hulls. With today's well-modified malts, using a complex mash regime is avoidable and probably unnecessary. All that is required for a Gose mash is an infusion rest at 148–152°F (64.5–66.7°C)

Keep in mind that the ABV on these beers is between 3 and 5.5 percent. Original gravities should be low as well—between 8 and 13°P (1.032–1.052). This equates to about 1.5–2.2 lb. per gallon (~0.18–0.26 kg/L) of wort post boil, depending on your desired gravity and equipment capabilities. Finishing gravities in a Gose should be low at 1.5–3°P (1.006–1.012). A saccharification rest at 148–152°F (64.5–66.7°C) is recommended to achieve this.

When doughing-in, or mixing your grain with hot liquor, the key word is gentle. Do not over stir your mash, as excessive mixing will beat out the entrained air attached to your grain particles. This air helps buoy up your mash bed, and that will be a good thing during lautering. If you remove the air by overmixing, it will lead to a compacted mash bed, and too long (and in some cases very long) lautering times.

It's important to remember throughout the process to measure the pH in your brewhouse. A proper pH is especially important in the mash tun. Alpha- and beta-amylase enzymes work best under specific pH ranges. If your pH is too high or too low, your enzyme activity will be hampered or even possibly eliminated.

Optimum hot liquor water pH: 6.7–7.6
Optimum mash pH (unsoured):   5.1–5.6 (should not go below 4.8)

Water and mineral additions are covered in the "Water" section in chapter 3.
Before proceeding with recirculation, an iodine test should be done to confirm full starch conversion has taken place.

VORLAUF

Vorlauf (recirculation) should be done gently and with care so as to avoid a stuck mash. It is important to recirculate long enough to establish a good filter bed, but not so long as to compact the mash bed too much. Start off slowly, and gradually increase the recirculation rate until the wort is flowing at about your desired runoff speed. Continue recirculating until the wort is running relatively clear and free of most medium-sized grain particles. If the filter bed is not well established and the wort is not properly clarified before running to the kettle, small particles of grain and starch will be washed over to the kettle where boiling can cause haze and harsh, astringent flavors in the final beer.

PARTI-GYLE BREWING

In the Middle Ages, brewers did not sparge the grains. Instead, they used the parti-gyle system whereby they mashed the same grains several times. Below is a description from a newspaper article in 1869.

> *Every time the beer was finished cooking, the pan was filled with water and put onto the spent grain and mashed again. In this fashion, the following qualities where produced:*
> *1. Werth [wort]* (Bestekrug) *2. Werth 3. Werth 4. Werth* (Hüppig). *To the* Hüppig, *some malt or colour malt was added.*
>
> —From "Lokales aus der Provinz und aus den Nachbarstaaten: Goslarsche Gose," *Goslarsche Zeitung*, February 17, 1882, quoted by Benedikt Rausch [nacron, pseud.], "Gosslarsche Gose," *Wilder Wald* (blog), February 15, 2017, http://wilder-wald.com/2017/02/15/gosslarsche-gose/.

LAUTERING AND SPARGING

Lautering should also be done with care. Even with the addition of rice hulls, lautering too fast can set the mash bed and lead to a long and difficult runoff. After you are satisfied with the clarity of your wort during recirculation, start lautering to the kettle at the same flow rate. When the first kernels of grain are exposed on top of the mash bed, start your sparge. The sparge water temperature should be 166–170°F (74.5–76.5°C). Do not exceed 170°F (76.5°C) or you will begin to leach tannins and husky flavors. Temperatures above 170°F (76.5°C) will also begin to wash unconverted starch over into the kettle. Keep one to two inches (2.5–5 cm) of sparge water above the grain bed. As your sparge continues and the sugars are rinsed from the grain, you can slowly increase the runoff speed. Lauter times should be around 60–90 minutes and lautering pH should be kept between 5.2 and 5.6 for an unsoured mash.

The lower starting gravity of Gose-style beers means there is not a lot of malt in your lauter tun compared to what you might be used to. You will have to be careful not to oversparge. I recommend stopping runoff when the wort runnings get to 2°P. Collecting wort after the gravity has dropped below 2°P (1.008 SG) will lead to harsh tannins, polyphenols, and husky flavors in the beer.

Detour 2: Kettle Souring
This option will be discussed in the "Souring the Beer" section below. If you plan on souring your beer in the kettle, please rejoin the rest of us after reading that section.

Figure 4.2. A selection of kettle-soured beers including Berliner *weisse* and *Gose*. Photo courtesy of Phil Cassella, Craft Beer Cellar.

THE BOIL
We boil the wort for several reasons: to sanitize it, to halt enzymatic activity, to extract hop bitterness and make it water soluble, to coagulate and precipitate proteins, and to volatilize and drive off unwanted compounds such as dimethyl sulfide (DMS). Boiling will concentrate wort flavors as water evaporates, reduce wort volume, and especially with direct-fired kettles, can caramelize sugars and add to color formation. Some white beers, Gose among them, were often not boiled for very long; some sources say as little as 10 minutes. Other later sources maintain Gose-style beers were boiled for two hours.[1] How long

---

[1] Jürgen Reuß, "Die Goslarer Gose," Bier aus eigener Küche (website), September 28, 2004, http://www.bierauseigenerkueche.de/Goslarer%20Gose.html

you decide to boil will depend on what you want the boil to achieve. If you are planning on an extended boil time, you should not boil the hops for more than 60 minutes, as this can extract unwanted compounds that will negatively affect the flavor of the finished beer. Boil times of two hours or greater can actually cause some of the proteins coagulated in the first 90 minutes of the boil to disassociate, causing problems downstream.

A short boil will not thoroughly precipitate your proteins, or provide sufficient hop utilization, and may leave you with some unwanted sulfur compounds. But if you want to recreate the white Gose-style beers from the Middle Ages, a short boil may be part of your process. And because hop bitterness extraction and haze formation are of less concern with Gose than with some other beer styles, you may elect to shorten the boil time some. For brewing twenty-first century Gose-style beer, I would recommend boiling the wort as you would with your other beers. A 90-minute boil is standard for most beers, with hops added for the last 60 minutes. Wheat beers have more protein and less hops (which assist with protein coagulation), so if you are looking for a clearer Gose, you may want to consider a boil time of at least 90 minutes. Additionally, the vigor of the boil can affect all of the aforementioned activities, but especially the coagulation of proteins; the more vigorous the boil, the better the protein coagulation. With normal brewing equipment, anything less than a 45-minute boil negatively affects protein coagulation and hot break formation. Some advanced brewing systems claim the ability to accomplish both in about that time; but with more traditional kettles, a lengthier boil is recommended. Irish moss or Whirlfloc™ can and should be used if you are hoping to remove some additional proteins. But again, if you don't coagulate proteins in an adequate boil (i.e., 45–90 minutes) then clarifying agents are less effective.

Shortening the boil time somewhat from 90 minutes may be a consideration for brewers with direct-fired kettles who want to keep color formation to a minimum. For brewers using malt extract, boil times can be shortened to as little as 30 minutes without worrying about the above issues.

Kettle Hops

Hops are usually added at three stages in the brewhouse: boiling hops for bittering; flavor hops during the last 2–30 minutes; and aroma hops after the boil, while the wort is still hot. Since Gose beers are not hop forward, brewers may elect to eliminate one, two, or even all three of these additions, although I would advise the use of enough bittering hops to adequately balance malt sweetness. The decision to eliminate a hop addition will be based on the other spices you use in the beer and/or the qualities you wish to get from the hops.

Bittering hops should be boiled for a minimum of 30 and a maximum of 60 minutes. As noted previously, boiling hops for more than 60 minutes can extract harsh and unpleasant flavors (Cantwell and Allen 1998).

Optimal wort pH range post boil, unsoured: 5.0–5.4

Optimal wort pH range post boil, soured: 3.4–4.0

The choice of a finishing hop is more subjective. Try to find aromas that are pleasing to you and that blend well with any spices that you have chosen. Hop growers and merchants will tell you that the best way to determine a hop variety's aroma contribution is to take a hop cone or pellet and rub it vigorously between your palms, then cup your hands and smell. This method works well for both finishing hops added to the hot side and dry hops added post-fermentation, though use of the latter is not typical in traditional Gose-style beer.

If you have not already soured your beer in the mash or the kettle and you are planning on souring post-brewhouse, it is important to know that most strains of *Lactobacillus* are not very hop tolerant. You should know how hop tolerant your *Lactobacillus* strain is, and adjust the hop additions accordingly so as not to inhibit *Lactobacillus* growth later in the fermentor.

WHIRLPOOL AND HEAT EXCHANGE

After the boil is complete, it is important to remove the trub or hot break from your wort prior to pitching yeast. Allowing the trub to be transferred over to your fermentor can negatively impact the flavor of both wort and beer, as well as yeast vitality. Transferring too much hot break to the fermentor may also increase the production of fusel alcohols. Centrifuging your wort is an easy and effective way to remove the hot break and can be done in most kettles (except those with an internal calandria) or in a separate whirlpool vessel. In smaller brewing systems (300 gal. [9.7 bbl., or 11.4 hL] or less) getting an acceptable rotation can be achieved manually with a paddle. In larger systems you will need to use a pump, which draws wort off from the center of the vessel and pumps it back in tangentially to the side wall. This spinning of the wort will cause the heavier particulates and coagulated proteins to gather in a cone-shaped mass at the middle of the vessel's base. The optimal rate of wort rotation is 12 to 15 revolutions per minute. Once you have achieved that rate of spin, stop stirring or recirculating the wort. The wort should be allowed to stop spinning naturally (usually that takes about 20 minutes). The clear, hot wort is drawn off from the side and sent to the heat exchanger, leaving the solids behind in the middle of the vessel. Today some breweries elect to put the wort through a mechanical centrifuge separator. Mechanical centrifugation can be faster and more effective at removing trub solids than using a whirlpool.

After separating the clear wort from the solids, cooling of the wort should happen as quickly as possible. For modern Gose, that means a heat exchange to bring the wort from around 212°F (100°C) to fermentation temperature of 66–72°F (19–22°C), depending on the yeast choice and the desired flavor profile.

It is necessary to add oxygen to the wort right after cooling. Without adequate oxygenation, the yeast will not fully attenuate the beer. This oxygen can be added using sterile filtered air, or medical-grade or aviator-grade oxygen. The recommended amount of oxygen in cooled wort is 8–10 ppm. Air is about 21 percent oxygen, so if you use sterile air, the maximum amount of oxygen that you will be able to get into solution at fermentation temperature is about 8 ppm. If you use pure oxygen, you will be able to get slightly higher amounts dissolved into the wort, but you will never need more than about 10–12 ppm. Don't attempt to dissolve more than 12 ppm—it's just a waste of oxygen. Henry's law states that the solubility of a gas in a liquid is dependent on a constant temperature, the partial pressure of the gas over the liquid, the nature of the liquid, and the nature of the gas. The key parameters are temperature and pressure. At fermentation temperature, the liquid (wort) will only hold so much gas (oxygen); any extra gas will just bubble through the solution. Henry's law will again be useful when discussing carbonation of the beer.

This is also a good point to confirm the original gravity of your wort. Starting gravities should be 9–13°P (1.036–1.053).

If you are planning on using a coolship (*koelschip* in Flemish/Dutch, or *Kühlschiff* in German) and spontaneously fermenting or naturally innoculating your Gose, here is where you take your detour. Send your clear, hot wort into a shallow, open metal (usually copper) pan. The large surface area of the pan facilitates fairly rapid cooling and acceptable oxygen pickup. The wort will cool over the next several hours. The rate of cooling will depend on many variables, including ambient temperature, coolship size, the type and thickness of the metal used to construct it, and other variables of construction. Allow the wort to sit undisturbed in the coolship for two to seven days, or until you see signs of fermentation. Once actively fermenting, you can transfer the beer into another vessel.[2] Alternatively, in colder months, one can allow the beer to sit in the coolship for 12 to 24 hours and then transfer the beer into foeders or barrels, which can then be moved to a warmer location and allowed to ferment.

---

[2]   http://www.milkthefunk.com/wiki/Coolship and http://www.milkthefunk.com/wiki/Spontaneous_Fermentation#Cooling

THEN

(Gose) differs from other beers by its larger content of lactic acids. The method of how this lactic acid is brought into the Gose, or how it develops in it, is known as Einschlag, which is a well kept secret to Gose brewers until this very day.

—Otto Kröber, *Die Geschichte der Gose und die Chronik der Gosenschänke Leipzig-Eutritzsch.* (Translated by Adept Content Solutions.)

NOW

What I like about brewers is that your colleagues tell you a lot," he says humbly. "That's how I was able to learn a lot. Winegrowers or distillers don't do that, they keep everything a secret.

—Matthias Richter, brewmaster at Gosebrauerei Bayerischer Bahnhof as quoted on the Bayerischen Bahnhof website "The Master Brewer". http://www.gose.de/popup/the-master-brewer/. (Circa 2015).

SOURING THE BEER

There are many methods for souring beer, some of them easier and more effective than others. Originally, Gose was a spontaneously fermented beer, as were most beers 600 or more years ago. A description in 1740 stated, "*Die Gose stellt sich selber ohne Zutuung Hefe oder Ges,*" or, "Gose ferments itself without the addition of yeast."[3] And this reference was a relatively recent one in the 5,000-year history of brewing. That Gose was originally a spontaneously fermented beer makes sense, since Gose is an ancient beverage originally brewed prior to a complete understanding of yeast's part in fermentation. And although at some point in the late early Middle Ages brewers understood that "yeast," the sludge at the bottom of the fermentation vessel, was necessary for the next batch of beer, it was not until 1680 that Van Leeuwenhoek first observed yeast under a microscope. Van Leeuwenhoek incorrectly attributed yeast to being part of the cereals used to brew beer (Nanninga 2010). It was not until the French chemist Louis Pasteur's work of 1857 that the true nature of yeast and its part in fermentation was understood. In fact, it was Pasteur who also did the groundbreaking work on lactic acid production. He demonstrated that when different microorganisms contaminate wine lactic acid is produced, thus making the wine sour (Ligon 2002). He wrote in 1857, "I intend to establish that, just as there is an alcoholic ferment, the yeast

---

3   Wikipedia contributors. "Gose" *Wikipedia, The Free Encyclopedia.* https://en.wikipedia.org/w/index.php?title=Gose&oldid=845794675. (accessed June 15, 2018).

of beer, which is found everywhere that sugar is decomposed into alcohol and carbonic acid, so also there is a particular ferment, a lactic yeast [bacteria] always present when sugar becomes lactic acid" (quoted in Manchester 2007). Yes, we brewers have a great many things to thank Louis Pasteur for.

We know that by 1910 Gose-style beers were being soured in the brewhouse as described briefly by Max Delbrück in his *Illustriertes Brauerei Lexikon* of that same year. Since the majority of brewers today are using some variation of brewhouse souring to produce their Gose, we will focus on those options and only later will we discuss souring through spontaneous souring and fermentation or mixed fermentations.

Souring Mash

This process is used traditionally in German breweries that want to reduce their mash pH but also want to adhere to the tenets of the *Reinheitsgebot*. The mash is allowed to rest 100–120°F (38–49°C) until the pH drops to the desired level, which traditionally would be 5.2–5.5, but for our purposes is as low as 3.5 pH. There are several problems associated with this method of souring for anything more than just a minor mash pH adjustment. After you have soured the mash to your desired pH, you need to be able to heat it fairly quickly to get up to the proper saccharification temperature of 148–155°F (64–68°C), either in the mash tun or kettle. Moving your mash around can be difficult if you do not have the proper equipment to do so. Done improperly, it can lead to a stuck mash or excessive lautering times. Another problem with this method of souring is that there are many types of bacteria on the grain that will also be active at that temperature. Of the many, a notable one is *Enterobacter*. When exposed to oxygen, *Enterobacter* can cause some fairly unpleasant aromas such as butyric acid. They are aerobes, and thus their effects can be reduced by attempting to exclude oxygen from the mash tun by "blanketing" the top of the mash with an inert gas, such as carbon dioxide, nitrogen, or argon. But it is not possible to exclude all the oxygen, as there is a lot of air entrained in the mash mixture itself. This oxygen clings to the grain particles and in a normal mash is beneficial, in that it helps buoy up or "float" the mash bed. If you excessively mix your mash, it is possible to reduce the air that is clinging to the grain particles and thus reduce oxygen in the mash. But the downside to overmixing is, as we have discussed, that you are then left with a much denser mash bed that is much more difficult to lauter.

Fortunately, *Enterobacter* do not like to function at a pH below 4.5, so another way to exclude their unpleasant aromas from the beer is to lower the mash pH as rapidly as possible. Some brewers will add some acidulated malt to the mash to expedite acidification. The lower pH will minimize *Enterobacter's* impact. A brewer could also acidify the mash pH with an acid addition to the mash itself, or to the mash-in liquor. But one has to be careful, because a mash pH below 5.2 creates problems of its own, for example, denaturing mash enzymes, which can result in an incomplete saccharification of starch later in the mashing process.

Another option is to mash in at saccharification temperatures of 148–155°F (64–68°C), rest 30–90 minutes, then cool the mash down to 100–120°F (38–49°C), for an acid rest. The problem here is, how do you cool down the mash? What about the inevitable mixing of the mash as you cool it down—is it excessive? You could add cold water, but this can thin the mash too much. Using a heat exchanger can be problematic as well, as most heat exchangers are not designed for semi-solid material like mash. And I would never run unboiled, bacteria-laden wort through my main heat exchange—that would be asking for a systemic infection later on. The answer would be to have a separate heat exchanger not used for post-boil wort. And again you would have issues of excessive mixing.

So what's a brewer to do? Not to worry, there are other, more practical ways to acidify in the brewhouse.

Kettle Souring

Kettle souring is done, as you might guess, in the brew kettle. There are several methods we will discuss a little bit later, but they all begin with the same mashing procedure as one would use with a regular beer. Once the wort is separated from the grain, it is cooled to the proper temperature, and run into the kettle. There, the brewer pitches a source of *Lactobacillus* into the wort, which is held at a temperature 100–120°F (38–49°C). The brewer allows the *Lactobacillus* to do its work until the pH drops to the desired level. At that point the wort can be boiled like a normal brew. The bacteria are killed by the heat of the boil, and the wort can be transferred for fermentation—with proper care there should be little worry of contaminating other beers.

Figure 4.4. Mango-Spruce Gose collaboration beer. Label courtesy of Freigeist Bierkultur.

The advantages of kettle souring, as opposed to post-kettle souring, are several. First, since the soured wort gets boiled before being transferred to fermentation, no live *Lactobacillus* is sent into the cellar. Second, it enables you to fix the level of acidity desired with a good degree of accuracy. Third, you can add a little more hop bitterness to your beer, because the usually hop-intolerant *Lactobacillus* has already done the souring prior to your hop additions. It is important to remember that as little as 5 IBUs can retard *Lactobacillus* growth, and that Gose beers are not supposed to be too hoppy.

Variations on the kettle souring methods are the source of the *Lactobacillus* and how you process the wort in the brewhouse. I will outline these various methods and talk about some specific breweries and how they go about souring their wort in the brewhouse. Some are more complicated than others, but each has points of interest, and pros and cons.

SAUERGUT

Sauergut is a traditional German method of producing soured wort without using acidulated malt that remains within the *Reinheitsgebot*. Some brewers believe this method enhances malt character in the beer, but it is more commonly used for making sour starters than for kettle souring. It uses *Lactobacillus* that naturally occurs on the outside of malt to sour wort that can be added to a brew later. The lactic acid bacteria strain found on malt is hop-sensitive, thermophilic, homofermentative, and is capable of fermenting maltose and some dextrins. To produce Sauergut, make a low-oxygen wort of about 12°P (1.048) and transfer it into an oxygen-purged container—you can purge it with carbon dioxide, nitrogen, or argon. It is imperative that you exclude oxygen from this process.

Bring the wort to a temperature of 115–120°F (46–49°C). Place unmilled pale or Pilsner malt into the container at a ratio of approximately 0.1–0.2 kg of malt per liter of wort. Hold for 72 hours at 115–120°F (46–49°C). Using sanitary methods, strain the liquid from the grain and avoid adding any oxygen. This will be your stock acid solution of Sauergut. It should be at a pH of about 3.3 to 3.6. Its volume can be increased using the same method as above, but substituting the stock solution for the un-milled malt. For best results, use a ratio of Sauergut solution to fresh, unsoured wort of approximately 1 to 5. Continuous, gentle agitation will increase productivity. The bacteria multiply best at a lactic acid concentration of less than 0.5 percent, and will stop producing lactic acid once the solution reaches an acid content of about two percent (Kunze 2004). It should be noted that this process can be used to make brewhouse-soured wort for Gose production, or for addition to other beers for pH adjustment. It has been shown that biological pH adjustment of this kind carries with it a great many benefits to beer flavor, stability, and processing (*Technology of Brewing and Malting*, 2004, Wolfgang Kunze).

Also see: "A Sauergut Reactor," *Low Oxygen Brewing* (blog), October 28, 2016, http://www.lowoxygenbrewing.com/ingredients/a-sauergut-reactor/.

The Clean and Careful Method

There are quite a few breweries that use this method to produce some very good beers. Mash your grains in using your usual temperature and process. After your normal mash rest period, lauter and sparge to the kettle just like you would with a non-sour beer. Once the wort is in the kettle, you have two options. One is to bring the temperature up to 160–180°F (71–82°C) to pasteurize the wort. Be sure to keep recirculating so as to be sure it is thoroughly homogenized. Your other option is to bring the wort to a boil for 5 to 10 minutes to pasteurize it. This pasteurization step does add a bit of time to the process, but brewers do it for two reasons. First is to assure that all the "bad" bacteria that was on the grain has been killed off. The second is that heating, especially boiling, helps drive out some of the oxygen in the wort. After you heat the wort, let it rest for a few minutes. This assures pasteurization and allows you some time to get everything else set up. This pasteurizing of the wort is why I call this the "clean and careful method"—you start off with sanitary wort. This method produces a cleaner flavor profile. If you decide to forego this step, you may get a little bit more funk in your final beer, but it might not be the funk you want.

At this point you will have to lower the temperature to one that is conducive to *Lactobacillus* growth. This is done by running the hot wort through a heat exchanger. You may choose to execute Option 1 here (see "Other Operational Options" sidebar). Monitor the temperature of the wort as it decreases. When the temperature reaches about 130°F (54°C), take a pH reading. You may want to exercise Option 2 (below) at this point. It is very important to remember to adjust your wort sample temperature before measuring its pH. As discussed earlier, pH drops as temperature rises, so a sample at 180°F (82°C) will read a lower pH (higher acidity) than the same sample at 120°F (49°C). The wort will be at the proper temperature in the kettle usually between 100°F and 120°F (38–49°C), but consult with your *Lactobacillus* supplier, as it varies depending on strain. You have reached the optimal temperature for *Lactobacillus* growth.

OTHER OPERATIONAL OPTIONS

Option 1: Some brewers like to hook up a carbon dioxide line to a carbonation stone. This stone is put in line as the wort returns to the kettle during its cooling recirculation.

The reasons for doing this are twofold. First, it achieves a more uniform temperature in the kettle during the chilling process, as the carbon dioxide helps to mix the wort. Second, the gas also helps to remove any residual oxygen from the kettle and, as carbon dioxide is heavier than air, stays in the vessel and forms a blanket over the top of the wort; this helps to suppress aerobic bacteria activity during the souring process.

Option 2: Check the pH and, if it is above 5.1, adjust it to 4.5–5.0 with lactic acid concentrate. This will help to suppress some of the less pleasant tasting and smelling bacteria, such as *Enterobacter.* Recirculate well when adding lactic acid to completely homogenize the acid throughout the wort. You don't want pockets of very low or high pH.

Option 3: For those concerned about foam stability in the final beer, check the pH and, if it is above 4.9, adjust to 4.5–4.8 with lactic acid. This will help to suppress some of the less pleasant tasting and smelling bacteria as mentioned above. It will also help promote foam stability in the final beer. Again, the adding of lactic acid requires good recirculation to completely homogenize the acid in the wort.

Option 4: Near the end of wort cooling, when your wort is around 125°F (52°C), take a carbon dioxide line and gently flow in carbon dioxide to blanket the top of the wort in the kettle. The carbon dioxide line can also be hooked up to the clean-in-place (CIP) valve to allow carbon dioxide to trickle in from the top of the kettle. Remember to close the kettle door and the stack vent (if you have one). Also it is VERY important to not seal off the vessel entirely—never cool wort, or any liquid, in a sealed tank. Always make sure your vessel is properly vented to avoid collapsing it by drawing a vacuum. Vacuum-collapsing a tank is surprisingly easy to do.

Now that you have made it to this point, you have some other options. These are the different ways to start souring the wort.

Method 1: Sour with uncrushed grain (pale or Pilsner malt is best) so as not to add color or flavor to the wort. Most brewers use 0.5–2 lb. (225–910 g) of grain per barrel (1.17 hL) of beer. Put the malt in a mesh bag or purpose-built stainless steel screen basket. Lower it into the wort and allow the grain to steep. Take periodic pH readings until you reach your desired pH (usually 3.2–3.6). This method usually takes 35–55 hours to sour. For faster souring times, one would need to use substantially more grain, probably at a rate of 5–10 lb. per barrel (2.27–4.54 kg/1.17 hL). See "Sauergut" sidebar for more details.

Method 2: Sour with plain, live-culture yogurt, containing *L. acidophilus* and possibly other *Lactobacillus* strains. A surprising number of brewers use yogurt to sour their wort. It certainly gets the job done and I have tasted many great beers soured with yogurt. But, I have two concerns with this method. The first regards the bacteria used in making yogurt. When souring milk to produce yogurt, dairies often uses different strains of other bacteria and with strains of *Lactobacillus* to do their work. For example, many yogurts include the bacteria *Streptococcus thermophiles* along with *L. bulgaricus* (Hui 2004). Some dairies

THE MAKING OF
≡FRUITLANDS≡
AT MODERN TIMES BREWERY

ADD **FOUR DIFFERENT** LACTOBACILLUS SPECIES

WEEE!

BREW KETTLE

INCUBATE FOR
48 HOURS AT 100°F

BLEND WITH MICHIGAN MONTMORENCY
CHERRIES

BOIL & ADD SALT

DRINK FRESH!

FERMENTER

Figure 4.5. Modern Times flowchart. The pH will rise during lautering if your water is above the mash pH of 5.5 (by Palmer and Kaminski 2013). Image courtesy of Modern Times Beer.

use other strains of *Lactobacillus*. Dairies may change the strains of bacteria they use without notice. There is also some use of genetically modified (GMO) strains of bacteria in yogurt production. I like to know what strains I am adding to my wort and have more control over that choice. Different strains of bacteria will behave differently and that in turn will produce different flavors. These variations may be minor, but they may not be. I am also not sure I want *Streptococcus thermophiles* in my beer at all. The other concern is the lactose that I would be adding to my beer. To get a good pitching rate for a rapid souring, one has to pitch a lot of yogurt and this may lead to flavor issues. Also, your beer is no longer lactose free (if one worries about such things). But again, maybe these worries are really non-issues—the proof is in the pudding (or beer)—but they are worth considering.

SOME BREWERIES HAVE SUCCESS WITH YOGURT

While some people may not be comfortable using yogurt cultures, Phil Markowski at Two Roads Brewing Company has used yogurt cultures to sour some of their pilot-scale brews that are made for their tasting room. Markowski states that they have found this method to be surprisingly reliable, convenient, and certainly less expensive than purchasing pure lactic bacteria cultures. He feels that the lactic character is generally very clean and sometimes possesses a "pleasant funk" that adds a note of complexity. A super clean lactic fermentation, as of the type produced by a single LAB strain, such as *L. delbrueckii* or *L. brevis,* can sometimes come across as too "one note." Markowski was wary about adding milk protein solids to wort and subsequently boiling that wort, but he says they have never noted any off-flavors or deleterious effects on head formation that they would attribute to using yogurt as a source of souring bacteria.

Important: Please note that the addition of yogurt in the brewing of beer is not listed on the Tax and Trade Bureau (TTB) list of, "Exempt Ingredients and Processes Determined to be Traditional Under TTB Ruling 2015–1," and as such would require formula submission and approval by TTB prior to use in the brewing process. Consider that yogurt/dairy products/lactose are allergens to many; accordingly, a brewer should consider adding an allergen warning to the beer label. Current regulations under the Federal Alcohol Administration Act do not require the disclosure of major food allergens on alcohol beverage labels. Major food allergens used in the production of a malt beverage product may, on a voluntary basis, be declared on any label affixed to the container. However, if any one major food allergen is voluntarily declared, all major food allergens used in production of the malt beverage product, including major food allergens used as fining or processing agents, must be declared, except when covered by a petition for exemption approved by the appropriate TTB officer.

Method 3: Sour with live probiotics. There are live, non-dairy probiotics available that contain *L. plantarum* and other strains. Some brewers use these to add lactic acid bacteria (LAB) to their wort for souring. Advantages to using them are that they are easily available, pharmaceutical grade, and do not have other matter as a media, as does yogurt.

Method 4: Pure-strain LAB pitch. For this option you have choices too. There are five or six main strains of *Lactobacillus* to choose from: *L. brevis, L. delbrueckii, L. acidophilus, L. plantarum, L. bulgaricus,* and *L. casei.* These pure culture strains should be available from your local yeast supplier. Your choice of *Lactobacillus* strain will depend on what you want from the strain. Actually, there are over a 150 strains of LAB to choose from, depending on how far down that rabbit hole you want to go, and the variety of LAB you pitch can have some pretty interesting effects on the beer you brew. For more on *Lactobacillus*, see the "Bacterial Souring Agents" section in chapter 3.

Pitching rates for all these methods can vary greatly. We have found that for a fast pH drop (6–8 hours) you will need to achieve a pitching rate of approximately

Figure 4.6. Salt of the Earth Gose beer brewed with coriander and truffle salt by The Bruery in Placentia, Orange County, California.

1×10^8 cells per mL (100,000,000 cells/mL) of lactic bacteria. A pitching rate of about 1×10^6 cells/mL takes about 18–22 hours. Brewers pitching less bacteria than stated above will experience longer times to achieve the desired pH. Once the pH drops below about 4.5, it is safe from contamination by harmful bacteria or molds. Wort left to sour for more than 48 hours can be risky. If the pH is still above 4.5 after 48 hours, I would recommend dumping the wort and starting over again.

For all the above methods you will need to take pH readings to confirm that your bacteria are working, and be sure to take more frequent pH readings as you approach your desired level of acidity so that you do not over-sour your beer.

Anderson Valley Brewing Company Method

At Anderson Valley Brewing Company (AVBC) we have developed what I think is the simplest way to achieve a good and consistent souring of the wort. It produces a clean, sharp, well-defined sourness in a short period of time. The AVBC method differs in a several ways from the Clean and Careful Method.

We mash the grains as per a normal brew. After a 60-minute rest, we recirculate the wort until it clears—this usually takes about 20 to 30 minutes. We then proceed with runoff into the kettle, leaving the spent grain behind. We believe getting the wort off the grain is important, as the grain contains a lot of bacteria: the *Lactobacillus* that we want, as well as some other bacteria that can produce those unpleasant flavors and aromas. As the kettle fills, we introduce an inert gas, usually argon,[4] into the kettle. This helps exclude oxygen from the top layer of the wort. We do this by putting a 3/8th-inch hose (~1 cm) through the kettle door and flowing argon in at a

---

[4] When using any gas in an attempt to exclude oxygen from an environment, it is imperative that you do not subject yourself or others to that environment. Argon and carbon dioxide will all displace oxygen and in doing so can cause asphyxiation. So when using these gases to evacuate oxygen from the kettle, it should be done in an area that is adequately ventilated with outside air.

rate of about 1–2 psi (6.9–13.8 kPa). When runoff is nearing completion, we take a temperature reading. It is usually about 145°F (63°C). We then make a temperature adjustment by adding chilled house water to bring the wort down to a temperature of about 120°F (49°C).

It should be noted here that we have made a high-gravity brew, which allows us to easily cool the kettle wort with chilled water. At this point, with the wort at optimum temperature for *Lactobacillus* growth, we pitch a substantial amount of bacteria. This pitch has previously been grown up from a lab sample acquired from our friendly yeast and bacteria supplier, White Labs. Our propagated LAB pitch is about 2 bbl. (2.35 hL) of bacteria at 1×10^8 cells/mL. This two-barrel pitch is for about 115 bbl. (135 hL) of hot, unboiled wort—somewhat less than two percent of the total. The 115 bbl. of hot wort ends up being about 100 bbl. (117 hL) of cooled wort for the fermentor after the boil, accounting for approximately 11 percent boil evaporation and four percent shrinkage from cooling.

We continue the argon "sparge" for the duration of the souring process. We monitor the pH drop over the next 6 to 12 hours, six hours being very fast for us, and 12 hours being on the long side.

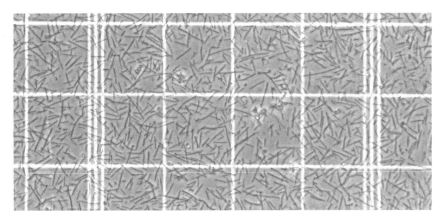

Figure 4.7. A *Lactobacillus* propagation on a hemocytometer under the microscope. As you can see from the photo, it can be very difficult to count bacteria at the proper pitching rate. Photo by Federico Guazzone.

If we are producing a double batch of approximately 200 bbl. (235 hL), when the pH reaches around 3.9 we know that the growth phase of the *Lactobacillus* is nearly finished. We then pull off 15 bbl. (17.6 hL) from kettle #1 and transfer it to kettle #2, which has been waiting with about 85 bbl. (100 hL) of fresh, unsoured Gose wort at 122°F (50°C). The amount of bacteria is somewhat lower in the 15-bbl. pitch than it was in the 2-bbl. pitch, hence the larger amount. We continue to monitor kettle #1 until it reaches a pH of 3.4.

Once the pH reaches 3.4, we bring the wort to a boil and proceed as with any other beer. We continue to monitor kettle #2 until it too reaches 3.4, or sometimes a bit lower depending on the pH of the first batch, and then we proceed to boil.

When the wort has boiled for 60 minutes, it is completely sterilized and we can proceed to the whirlpool. Once the whirlpool is full and spinning at 12 rpm or faster, we allow the wort rotation to come to a stop. This usually takes about 20 minutes. When the whirlpool is finished, we then proceed to cool the wort to 68°F (20°C).

We ferment the beer with our house yeast, which is an English ale variety. Our house yeast has no problem fermenting at that pH. Some yeast strains will not do as well with a pH that low. Be mindful of the yeast you use to brew your Gose, and be sure it can tolerate the acidity of Gose wort and still produce good flavors.

The main advantages of the AVBC method is that it is easy, produces good acidity, is relatively fast, gets the wort off of the grain to contain undesirable bacteria, and has a low risk of infecting our other beers.

The main disadvantage of the ABVC method is that once our yeast has finished fermenting a Gose, it

Figure 4.8. The Kimmie, the Yink, and the Holy Gose Ale by Anderson Valley Brewing Company in California.

cannot be repitched in any other house beers. Our house yeast produces nice flavors at pH levels as low as 3.1, but yeast harvested and repitched from our Gose never makes acceptable tasting beer again. The house yeast from a Gose ferment is essentially burned-out by the low pH. In the beginning, this was not a problem for us, but as we produce more and more Gose-style beers it has become an issue we have had to address. We now have to propagate more yeast than we used to. Another less worrisome issue is that we spend a fair amount of time and effort propping up *Lactobacillus* bacteria so that we can have a large, healthy pitch. I have been told by some brewers that the yeast they use to brew their Gose-style beers can be repitched without any difficulties. I would assume that the question of whether or not a yeast is affected by the low pH of a Gose is strain-specific, and also related to how low of a pH wort it had to ferment.

Alternative Method

Some brewers do a normal mash and runoff to the kettle, cool the wort through a heat exchanger or by adding cold water until it reaches 122°F (50°C) and then just let the wort rest without further assistance. They figure that there is enough souring bacteria on the grain that has carried over to the wort, which is true to some degree. But the amount of *Lactobacillus* bacteria coming over in the wort from your mash is not really sufficient for rapid souring—and I recommend a fairly rapid souring. Souring by this slower method can take up to two or even three days to sour to an appropriate pH of 3.6 or lower. For most breweries, three days is too long a time to wait to sour a beer, and this long period of time can also allow other bacteria that were on the grain to produce off-flavors. But brewers who use this method say they do not want to add yogurt or pitch extraneous bacteria culture. They want just what's on the grain.

High-Acidity Brewing

This method requires a separate area for making a high-acidity brew of *Lactobacillus*-soured wort. The high-acidity wort is then injected into a regular, unsoured brew in the kettle. Then the whole kettle is boiled to sterilize the wort so that the soured wort addition doesn't further acidify the rest of the batch. The brewer relies on getting the initial sour wort to an extremely high level of acidity, then blending at a set ratio of 25 percent soured wort to 75 percent sweet, unsoured wort to hit the target final acidity in the fermentor. Souring bacteria for the high-acidity wort can come from any of the sources mentioned above, although a straight pitch of *Lactobacillus*, especially strains with a high acidity tolerance, would work best. This method is very similar to the method Sierra Nevada uses to make their award-winning Otra Vez Gose.

Figure 4.9. Otra Vez, a Gose-style ale brewed with cactus and grapefruit by Sierra Nevada Brewing Co., Chico, California.

Conclusions to Using Bacteria as a Souring Agent

After much research, discussion with many brewers, reading many articles, and tasting many brewhouse-soured beers, I think that the biggest issue of using bacteria as a souring agent is the potential for off-flavors and aromas produced by aerobic bacteria. These flavors and aromas result from the development of isovaleric acid (dirty gym socks), butyric acid (vomit), and in some cases an excess of acetic acid (vinegar). These flavors and aromas are not produced by *Lactobacillus*, even in the presence of oxygen. The best options for avoiding these undesirable flavors are to keep non-lactic acid bacteria from metabolizing sugars by: 1) excluding oxygen; 2) dropping the pH below 5.0 as fast as possible;[5] and 3) pitching a sufficient amount of *Lactobacillus*. It is also critical to get the wort off the grain as soon as possible, because the grain has a lot of those other bacteria on it, and, as we've discussed, a normal grain bed holds in little pockets of air, and oxygen in that air allows undesirable bacteria to do their thing.

MAKING A LACTOBACILLUS *STARTER*

Each strain of *Lactobacillus* may require different conditions for optimal growth. This is a general guide to making a happy and healthy starter. Counting *Lactobacillus* under the microscope can be problematic due to the small size of the cells and how crowded it gets when you are near the proper pitching rate (fig. 4.7). So for bacteria, starter volumes can be used when talking about pitching rate. A pitching rate of 0.75 to 1 liter of starter culture per 20 liters of wort is a good rule of thumb (approximately 1–1.5 gal. of starter per barrel of wort).

Grow your starter in a wort-based media. Starters should be approximately 10°P (1.040 SG) and made up of 90 percent malt and 10 percent apple juice, with an addition of 10 g/L of calcium carbonate ($CaCO_3$) and approximately 2 g/L of yeast nutrient. Calcium carbonate has maximum buffering capacity at about pH 4.6, which, as it turns out, is ideal for the growth of *Lactobacillus*; and $CaCO_3$ precipitates out well. The math on building your starter works out to about 100 g of dried malt extract to 900 mL of water plus 100 mL of apple juice, plus the $CaCO_3$ and nutrients. Large, happy, healthy starters will lower the pH of the wort rapidly, and one of the really important reasons to drop the pH to below 5.0 as fast as possible is that it will help prevent off-flavor development by bacteria that thrive in conditions above pH 5.

---

[5]   Most of the unwanted bacteria will not, or in some cases cannot, carry out life functions (and produce unwanted metabolites) at a pH lower than five.

Procedure

Boil the malt extract in the water to sterilize it. Remove it from the heat source add the yeast nutrient and calcium carbonate; stir. Then add the pasteurized apple juice (do not boil the apple juice). Staying as sanitary as possible and excluding oxygen where possible,[6] cool the starter to the temperature best suited to the *Lactobacillus* strain you are using (see chapter 3 for specific tolerances of recommended strains of *Lactobacillus)*. Then pitch your bacteria culture. Incubate for 3–6 days. One indication of a slowing of growth is that the liquid will start to clear, starting from the top. After growth has slowed, decant all of the liquid starter into the main wort to be soured, leaving the calcium carbonate sediment behind. The calcium carbonate will precipitate out within a few hours of being added to the starter, which is ideal because you don't really want to transfer that calcium carbonate over to your main brew due to its continued buffering effects. You want to see a bacteria cell density of approximately 1×10^8 per mL or higher. The maximum cell density achievable by most *Lactobacillus* strains will be in the range of 1×10^8 to 9×10^8 cells/mL, depending on the nutrients available to them.[7] The amount the pH drops will depend upon the *Lactobacillus* strain.

Storage

It is recommended that both liquid and dry *Lactobacillus* cultures be stored at 35–45°F (1.7–7.2°C). Liquid cultures should be stored for less than two months. Cultures stored at room temperature will have their viability deteriorate significantly faster. Always consider making a starter if cultures are not fresh, or older than 30 days.

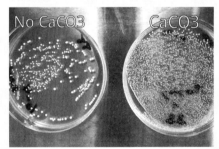

Figure 4.10.
Lactobacillus starters showing both growth with and without calcium carbonate ($CaCO_3$).

---

[6] You want to exclude oxygen here in the case of contamination from other unwanted bacteria. Oxygen doesn't significantly affect most species of *Lactobacillus*. Most varieties will grow and produce lactic acid regardless of the presence or lack of oxygen. They will not produce significant amounts of butyric or isovaleric acids in the presence of oxygen either, although some species may produce small amounts of acetic acid in aerobic conditions.

[7] L.C. Peyer et al., "Growth Study, Metabolite Development, and Organoleptic Profile of a Malt-Based Substrate Fermented by Lactic Acid Bacteria," *J. Am. Soc. Brew. Chem.* 73, no.4 (2015): 303, http://dx.doi.org/10.1094/ASBCJ-2015-0811-01.

Some Non-Bacterial Souring Options

For brewers who do not want, for whatever reason, to go through the process of a bacterial fermentation, there are other options.

Lactic Acid Addition

One can simply add lactic acid to the wort or beer. The advantage of this method of souring is that it is simple. It can even be done post-fermentation, thus leaving your yeast happy and healthy, and there is no danger of infecting any of your other beers with that pesky *Lactobacillus*. Unfortunately, there can be several problems associated with this method of souring your beer. The flavor is not the same as a bacterial fermentation; many people, myself included, assert that sour beers made this way are less complex. They do not have the depth of flavor that I hope to taste in a Gose. Also, concentrated lactic acid can be very syrupy and it can be very hard to mix into wort or beer, especially in cold, finished beer. For that reason, I recommend that you avoid mixing lactic acid concentrate into cold beer. Finally, it is not considered a very artisanal method of souring, and, in my experience, consumers frown on these sorts of additions to their craft beers. So this method may leave you with a bit of a marketing hot potato.

Acidulated Malts

Acidulated malts can be added to the grain bill to bring the pH down. The advantage to this souring method is that it is very easy, and since no live bacteria are involved there is no greater risk of infecting other beers than you would have with a regular mash. The disadvantage to this method is that it does not bring the pH down as much as some brewers would like; that is, unless you use a prodigious amount of acidulated malt, and this has flavor impacts that most people would find undesirable. Finally, this type of acidifying in the brewhouse leaves the brewer with the potential pitfall of subjecting the house yeast to an acidified wort to ferment. To drop the pH of the mash from 5.2 to 4.2, add approximately 8–15 percent acidulated malt to your total grist bill.

A combination of two or more of the above methods can be used to create a process unique to a brewery and thus add an acidity level that fits the brewery and the beer. For example, one could use a small portion of acidulated malt, do a brief kettle souring, and then add a little bit of lactic acid in the fermented beer to touch up the acidity. In the end it is all about finding the method or methods that work best to create the beer a brewer wants to brew.

Lactobacillus and Mixed Fermentations

For the very brave brewers out there—or for those producing sour beers exclusively—there is the opportunity to sour your beer in a more traditional way. This would be what is called a mixed fermentation. Mixed fermentation can refer to multiple yeast strains or multiple bacteria strains, but typically it refers to a fermentation with brewer's yeast and bacteria together. There are several options for mixed fermentation. A brewer could start with souring their wort in the brewhouse and then transferring the live, actively souring wort to the cellar, allowing the bacteria to continue to work during the main fermentation with pitched yeast. Or you could make a non-sour wort and then allow for a mixed culture fermentation in the cellar, featuring both yeast and either LAB or other microorganisms. The latter would be the more traditional way, and closer to how a Gose might have been made during the Middle Ages.

If you have transferred brewhouse-soured beer over into your cellar, all you would need to do would be to cool the wort to fermentation temperature and pitch your desired yeast strain. If you choose the more challenging, traditional method of a completely mixed fermentation, you could pitch a known bacteria and a known pure-culture yeast strain into your cooled wort; this would help to ensure unwanted bacteria and avoid off-flavors. Or you could let the microorganisms fall where they may and have a completely spontaneous fermentation. In either of the latter cases, it is best to have an IBU level less than 10 and preferably less than 6.

Should you decide to try out one of these methods, you should certainly keep in mind that fermenting with and growing up bacteria in a "clean" beer brewery has some serious dangers. Isolation of the sour beer and rigorous sanitation procedures need to be followed throughout the whole process so as not to spread microorganisms and contaminate your clean beers and yeast strain.

Some Potential Effects of a Mixed Fermentation

The presence of lactic acid can be a yeast stressor, so much so that the presence of *Lactobacillus* can stall or slow some yeast fermentations. This is likely the result of a combination of low pH and the ability of lactic acid (both L-lactic acid and D-lactic acid) to change the way yeast ferments. In a normal fermentation, the yeast will ferment glucose first before any other sugars. In the presence of high levels of acid, usually below a pH of 4.0, yeast may consume multiple types of sugars regardless of whether glucose is present or not. The presence of high levels of lactic acid has been shown to be responsible for stuck wine fermentations as far back as Louis Pasteur's time. This effect, known as "terminal acid shock," can affect some species of *Saccharomyces cerevisiae* and *Brettanomyces bruxellensis*.[8]

This presents a challenge to brewers making brewhouse-soured beers, or if they are planning on bottle conditioning those sour beers. Although yeast after sour fermentation may be around 80 percent viable, the surviving cells are small and are not budding. This indicates that they are not healthy and have ceased growing and entered the dormant phase.

Another consideration when doing a mixed fermentation is that some yeast strains can have similar effects on LAB. A study done by Hübbe showed that when *L. brevis* and *L. parabrevis* were co-fermented with *Brettanomyces*, the cell count of *L. brevis* was reduced by about 50 percent compared to when it was grown by itself, and that the growth rate of *L. parabrevis* was reduced even further, to as low as 15–20 percent of normal (Hübbe 2016). When co-fermented with both *Brettanomyces* and *S. cerevisiae*, the *Lactobacillus* growth was further diminished to between 2 and 13 percent of normal cell growth without competition. This shows that when used in a mixed fermentation, one can expect the activity of some species of LAB to be affected negatively and dramatically, and that the ability of *Lactobacillus* to compete with *Brettanomyces* appears to be species dependent. Interestingly, *Brettanomyces* activity was not affected by the presence of *Lactobacillus*, as some *Saccharomyces* strains are, but *Brettanomyces* was affected by the presence of *S. cerevisiae* in a mixed fermentation in low oxygen or anaerobic conditions.

One option to consider when using mixed fermentation is extended aging time. During a mixed fermentation not all the microorganisms hit their stride at the same time. For the most part, each yeast or bacteria will have its turn making use of the available energy sources. This will be very different depending on what mix is in your culture, but suffice it to say that these fermentations can take significantly longer than "clean beer" or brewhouse-soured beer fermentations. Extended aging times can be as short as two months for a piquant *saison* or as long as two to three years for complex barrel-aged beers. One reason for this is that some microorganisms can create off-flavors, such as sulfur compounds, that may take weeks or even months to be metabolized by other organisms. During aging, regardless of the nature of the vessels the beer resides in, it should be kept below 80°F (26.5°C) and above 55°F (13°C). Several brewers believe that the sweet spot is about 65°F (18°C).

---

[8]   Milk the Funk Wiki, *s.v.* "Lactobacillus," last modified May 26, 2018, 17:35, http://www.milkthefunk.com/wiki/Lactobacillus.

It is safe to say mixed fermentations are more complicated than producing conventional "clean" beer or brewhouse-soured beers. If you are planning to go down the mixed fermentation path, I would suggest exploring the Milk the Funk Wiki[9] and reading *American Sour Beers* by Michael Tonsmeire.

> *The first anxiety-causing aspect of brewing your first sour beer is not time, variability, or even the risk of bad beer—it is the fear that the 'wild' microbes will ruin other batches of clean beer. This is a legitimate concern.*
>
> —Michael Tonsmeire, *American Sour Beers* (Boulder: Brewers Publications, 2014), 16

CLEANING AND SANITATION

If you are using bacteria to create sourness in your Gose, then you will need to take some extra sanitation precautions. Of course, you will need to take all the normal precautions you would with any other beer so as not to infect it with unwanted bacteria or wild yeast—that is just good brewing practice. But when using wort- and beer-souring bacteria, you need extra special precautions. If you make the decision to intentionally bring souring bacteria into your brewery, that decision should be accompanied by a solid understanding of what consequences could come from it. *Lactobacillus* and *Pediococcus* are usually the brewer's sworn enemies. They must be kept completely separate from the main part of your non-sour brewing operations and all your other non-sour beers.

It is important to understand and remember that bacteria and wild yeast are able to metabolize dextrins and other carbohydrates that normal brewer's yeast cannot, and that it takes far fewer bacteria or wild yeast to have an impact on your beer's flavor. Bacteria and some wild yeast are also smaller than normal yeast and are thus able to "hide" and remain lodged in soil or crevices in areas that some sanitizers might not be able to get to. For all these reasons, great care must be taken to eliminate these microorganisms from your equipment before introducing your wort to it if you hope to make acceptable beer repeatedly.

When comparing brewhouse souring with mixed or spontaneous fermentation, brewhouse souring is the safer option. Brewhouse souring keeps all the LAB on the hot side of your operation. If at all possible, your brewhouse operations should be kept physically separated from your cellar operations. This is good brewing practice for any brewery, because milling and mashing can give rise to a lot of malt dust in the air. Malt dust contains LAB that will sour your beer. I know that in some smaller breweries the separation of the brewhouse and the cellar operations is not

---

9   Milk the Funk Wiki, *s.v.* "Mixed Fermentation," last modified May 16, 2018, 16:31, http://www.milkthefunk.com/wiki/Mixed_Fermentation.

always possible. Those brewers should give serious consideration to partitioning the two operations. If you cannot, you will need to take extra steps to keep your non-sour beers safe from souring bacteria. Special care should be taken with any equipment that is used to propagate or transfer LAB. Be sure to permanently mark all the equipment that you use for sour beers. This will help ensure that you keep the equipment separate from your non-sour beers equipment. At Anderson Valley, we are fortunate that our brewhouse is in a separate building. Anything used in souring wort or beer remains outside of our cellar building and packaging hall. We use a whole separate set of hoses, pumps, clamps, gaskets and tanks for culturing and transferring our *Lactobacillus* and non-sterilized sour beers. This is especially important for soft goods like hoses and clamps. We never mix our sour-designated equipment with our clean beer equipment. The only piece of equipment that gets used for both sour and non-sour beers is the boiling kettle. Once the wort has been boiled for 60 minutes, we consider it clean and sanitary and only then can it pass over into the cellar. Some breweries even go so far as to have their brewers change boots and gloves between their sour and non-sour operations.

If you decide you would like to go the more traditional route of souring your Gose post-brewhouse, I would recommend that you take extraordinary care. I would recommend you not only separate sour equipment from non-sour, but that you pitch and ferment in a separate, designated sour building. Many breweries have taken this approach: Firestone Walker's sour and non-sour facilities have different zip codes; The Bruery's two breweries are now separated by several miles; Anderson Valley uses two different buildings separated by over an acre. Trying to run a clean beer and sour beer operation in the same building can only lead to trouble. There is ample evidence of this, but one of the best-documented recent cases is that of The Bruery. After their issues arose, The Bruery separated their sour from non-sour beer programs and this, along with vigilant quality assurance and quality control (QA/QC) measures, has resolved the issue. Their honest transparency about it is to be applauded, as are the great lengths to which they went to rectify the problems. You can read about it on The Bruery's website.[10]

Cleaning

You will need to thoroughly clean and sanitize your equipment before and after every brew. Remember that you cannot properly sanitize equipment that is not first properly cleaned. If the equipment is not clean, you are leaving a place for unwanted

---

[10] Cleaning the slate — beer issues from 2013," The Bruery (website), December 23, 2013, http://www.thebruery.com/cleaning-the-slate-beer-issues-from-2013/.

bacterial and wild yeast to hide and grow. If your equipment is not clean, the soil on it may neutralize the sanitizer you are using. Clean your equipment and then sanitize it. Equipment should be cleaned with an appropriate agent to remove organic soils (trisodium phosphate, sodium hydroxide, Bru-R-Ez, Five Star PBW™, or similar products). Equipment should also be periodically cleaned with an acid-based cleaner to help remove any beerstone buildup. This is especially true of equipment used for post-fermentation beer. Beerstone is not broken down by traditional alkaline cleaners—you need an acid-based cleaner. Always follow the manufacturer's instruction when using cleaners. Adding more chemicals to your cleaning solution does not clean better, and in some cases can clean worse. Always wear the appropriate personal protective equipment (PPE) including gloves, safety glasses, footwear, chemical-resistant aprons, and face shields. Some people think that my concerns about cleaning are excessive. Maybe they are. But unless you want to make random, unrepeatable beers (though they certainly can have their place) you need to start with a clean slate every time—even if you are spontaneously fermenting your beer. To get a clean slate, you need to properly clean and sanitize your equipment.

Sanitation

Heat

There are several ways to sanitize your equipment. The best sanitizer is heat, preferably steam. Bacteria are very small and can hide in tiny cracks, or crevices in your equipment, especially in cracked hoses and gaskets. Heat gets to places other sanitizers cannot, and can penetrate those tiny crevices, cracks or scratches that other types of sanitizer might not be able to. With adequate heat, almost all known life-forms can be eliminated. But heat is dangerous, and it is hard on all your equipment, especially soft goods like hoses, gaskets, and plastic. Even stainless steel suffers when it is repeatedly heated and cooled over time. Great care should be taken if using heat with any sort of pressure. Heat plus pressure can be explosive, and pressurized hot liquid can remove skin instantly. Most brewers who use heat keep the temperature below 185°F (85°C).

Acid

Other brewers prefer to use an acid-based sanitizer. These sanitizers are safer, but are not as effective as heat. There are many options for acid-based sanitizers. Discuss with your local suppliers what options are open to you and which are best for you. There are also acid-based sanitizers with added iodine that can be more effective than solely acid-based sanitizers, but they have two main drawbacks. First, they lose their efficacy fairly quickly (18–48 hours) once pre-pared, and second, they can taint beer and cause off flavors, even when used at the recommended concentration. I have found it useful to occasionally change up sanitizers, as wild yeast and bacteria can occasionally build up resistance over time to a specific sanitizer. For all your cleaners and sanitizers, always follow the manufacturer-recommended instructions and safety procedures.

EQUIPMENT

If you are using plastic equipment, I recommend you upgrade to stainless steel. Plastic scratches too easily and after time cannot be properly cleaned or sanitized. Stainless is harder to scratch,[11] has a smoother surface, and is resistant to most chemicals, with the exception of chlorine—never use chlorine on your stainless steel equipment, as chlorine can damage and pit it. Stainless is also fairly cheap now. Beware of imported stainless steel products. Not all stainless is created equal, and in some countries they have different requirements for different grades. If you are planning on buying equipment from outside the USA or Europe, I would consider the quality of the stainless suspect (although suspect does not necessarily mean bad). In any case, it is always a good idea to get a written confirmation of the type and source of the steel used to manufacture your equipment. Stainless 304 series (European 14301–14306) and 316 series (European 14401–14404) are the most commonly used, and they are both acceptable for brewing equipment manufacture. The 304 series is for normal conditions. An "L" designation stands for low carbon in both these series. Low carbon gives better corrosion resistance at the expense of strength. The 316 series is for more corrosive environments than the 304 and it is used for equipment that will be exposed to extreme heat. The main difference between these two types of stainless is the addition of the corrosion-resistant element molybdenum to the 316 series. Stainless steels outside these two series may not be suitable for food production. Ask your supplier.

For breweries producing a lot of Gose-style beers, the above may be of particular interest. Salt is known to be corrosive to metals. Even though 304 may be resistant to most corrosives and chemicals, prolonged exposure to salt can still damage 304 series stainless. This would make the 304 series less suitable for equipment with repeated or prolonged exposure to salt or salt water. The 316 series is much more resistant to salt exposure and as such would be a better choice for saltwater or other corrosive environments, although many sources say even 316 is not resistant enough to use in ocean saltwater and that 317 might be a better option.[12]

---

[11] Stainless steel can be scratched or damaged. It is important that all your brewing staff know which scouring pads, or "scrubbies," are safe to use on stainless. Only white scrubbies are soft enough to use and will not scratch stainless steel. Green scrubbies are a bit harder; they will scratch stainless, and so should never be used for cleaning interior stainless surfaces. Red scrubbies are meant to be abrasive and cause fairly deep scratches on stainless steel, which may result in rusting.

[12] "Guidelines for Alloy Selection for Waters and Waste Water Service," Nickel Institute (website), last accessed June 9, 2018, https://www.nickelinstitute.org/NickelUseInSociety/MaterialsSelectionAndUse/Water/AlloySelection.aspx.

Equipment Concerns When Brewing Gose

I am not an expert in either metallurgy or chemistry, but here is what I was able to glean from people who are experts. Higher chloride levels will corrode and/or pit both 304 and, to a lesser degree, 316 stainless steel. This pitting process can be exacerbated by lower pH and warmer temperatures. A pH of less than 4.5 (normal beer) would be considered low; a pH of 3.4 (not uncommon for a Gose) would be considered very low. Fermentation temperatures around 68°F (20°C) would be considered moderately high, and conditioning tank temperatures would be considered low. Average seawater has approximately 35 g/L salt (35,000 ppm). Most Gose-style beers have less than 3 g/L (3,000 ppm) but more than 0.75 g/L (750 ppm). The upper limit for 304 stainless is less than 300 ppm chloride. Salt is sodium chloride in a close to 2:3 ratio by mass, with chlorine having a slightly higher molecular weight. Given the low pH and the relatively high salt content of Gose-style beers, and depending on when the salt is added (warm or cold), I think it would reasonable for a brewer planning to brew a lot of Gose-style beers to spend the extra money to have the interior of their tanks and their process piping manufactured with 316L. This 316L would give the tanks better protection against relatively high chloride levels in a low-pH environment, and would result in a longer life for those tanks.[13] Another concern is kettle-soured beers where salt is added to the kettle. The higher temperatures of boiling would cause stainless to be even more susceptible to corrosion or pitting. High chloride levels (from salt), lower pH (soured wort), and higher temperatures could all combine to result in stress cracking in just a matter of years in a stainless steel kettle. Of even greater concern would be the damage that might be done to the heat exchanger, where the metal is particularly thin by design. Brewers should also be mindful that if you are running a lot of Gose through your bottle or can filler, over time these low pH, relatively high-salt beers may cause pitting in the small stainless parts of your filler. This pitting will in turn create nucleation sites that could cause carbon dioxide breakout and improper filling.

---

[13] The average life of a 316 stainless steel fermentor is about 30–50 years depending on the number of cycles it sees and the temperature and type of chemicals used in the hot CIP. The average life of a 304 stainless steel kettle is about 20–30 years depending on similar variables. These estimates are for equipment not making sour salty beers.

5

CELLAR OPERATIONS

The beautiful properties of Gose
Made it beloved in Leipzig,
When drank as clear and pure as gold
It tastes like mild wine, so know,
For old and young, and thin and thick
Gose always is pure happiness.

(Der Gose schöne Eigenschaften
Sie sehr beliebt in Leipzig machten,
Als trank so klar und rein wie Gold
Schmeckt sie wie milder Wein, so hold,
Für alt und jung, und Schank und dick
Ist Gose stets das reine Glück.)

—From a Leipzig postcard circa 1930, translation courtesy of Randy Mosher

YEAST PITCHING

Once the wort goes through the heat exchanger, it passes over to cellar operations. While the wort was boiling in the kettle, you or one of your fellow brewers should have been preparing a fermentor and the yeast or mixed culture for pitching or adding to the cooled wort.

Whether you plan on using a single yeast strain, multiple yeast strains, or a mixed culture with yeast and bacteria, you will need an ample amount of healthy and viable microbes to ferment the beer. Preferably this will be from a recent, successful fermentation or from a culture that has been adequately propagated to a sufficient quantity ahead of time. It has been my experience over the last 30 years of brewing that no matter what a yeast supplier may tell you is in the package, pouch, or vial, it is always best to get the culture started yourself and grow up an adequate amount of microbes to pitch to get the job done right.

The proper pitching rate of yeast, for any beer, is one million cells per degree Plato per milliliter. So, for a 12°P (1.048) beer you will need 12 million healthy, viable yeast cells per milliliter of beer throughout the entire volume of liquid. This number increases slightly as gravities ascend past 13°P (1.053). The importance of having enough healthy, viable yeast pitched into your wort cannot be overemphasized. It may be even more important with a brewhouse-soured beer, as some yeast strains will not perform as well in a solution that acidic.

If you do not have a method for determining cell counts, I highly recommend you purchase a microscope, a hemocytometer, and some methylene blue dye. All these can be found easily online for less than US$300 total. This equipment will allow you to see your yeast, count the number of cells in solution, and ascertain if they are healthy enough to carry out a proper fermentation. There are some fairly decent articles archived online that explain all the basics of cell counting and yeast management (Allen 1994a; 1994b).[1]

If you are doing a post-brewhouse souring and will be pitching yeast and bacteria together, you should have similar amounts of bacteria as you do yeast in your mixed culture. That is approximately one million cells per milliliter of wort. There is a more in-depth discussion of bacteria pitching rates in the sections "Bacterial Souring Agents" (chapter 3) and "Souring the Beer" (chapter 4).

At the time of pitching, the temperature of both the yeast culture and the wort to be inoculated is important. If the wort is too cool, the yeast may stall and not completely attenuate during fermentation. If the wort is too hot, the yeast may experience thermal shock or even be killed. It is best if there is less than 20°F (11°C) difference between the temperature of the yeast culture being pitched and the temperature of the wort it is inoculating. A good temperature

---

[1]   Fal Allen, "The Microbrewery Laboratory Manual – A Practical Guide to Laboratory Techniques and Quality Control Procedures for Small-Scale Brewers, Part 1: Yeast Management," *Brewing Techniques,* July/August 1994, reproduced online, https://www.morebeer.com/brewingtechniques/library /backissues/issue2.4/allen.html.

range for ale yeast is 66–76°F (19–24.5°C). Yeast also need oxygen to get their life cycle started off. It is very important that you get enough oxygen into the wort so that the yeast get a good start on fermentation. If you are using bottled oxygen, it should be medical grade or aviator grade. If you are using air it should be sterile filtered. You want to achieve an absorbed oxygen level of about 8–10 ppm and no greater than 20 ppm for a wort of Gose strength. It is possible to over-oxygenate with bottled oxygen, which is 4.75 times more soluble in wort than air, since air is only 21 percent oxygen; but it would be near impossible to over-aerate, as wort will not hold that much gas at ale fermentation temperatures (Okert 2006). For homebrewers, one of the best methods for dissolving the proper amount of oxygen into wort is to use an aquarium aerator pump with the air pushed through a sterile in-line filter and into a sanitized defusing stone submersed in the cooled wort. Do this for about two minutes in your five-gallon (19 L) batch. For professional brewers it is best to add air (or oxygen) inline on the way to the fermentor, post heat exchange. Optimally, this will give the wort a chance to absorb the gas on the way to the fermentor. What you do not want is to create too many bubbles in the fermentor, as the bubbles will agitate the wort as they rise to the surface, and in doing so drive off volatile aroma components. This is why homebrewers should only inject air for no longer than about 2 minutes.

If you are spontaneously fermenting your beer, as it has been suggested Gose-style beers were during the Middle Ages and possibly beyond, then you may dispense with the above information regarding oxygenation and pitching rates—it will not apply to you. You have thrown caution to the wind, and you are depending on the wind to supply you with what you need. Of course, you should be starting this spontaneous fermenting thing in a shallow, open vessel—a coolship or the equivalent—and then transferring it to a different vessel for fermentation. Some research indicates that many of the microbes participating in most professional spontaneous fermentations reside not on the wind, but in cracks and crevices of wooden structures in a coolship room. This research suggests that the best way to achieve a good, repeatable spontaneous fermentation is to spray down the walls, ceiling, and beams of the coolship room with a lambic beer of your choice.[2] A good temperature range for spontaneous fermentations is 66–78°F (19–26°C), depending on ambient temperature.

---

[2]   Personal communication with Roger Mussche.

FERMENTATION

Once you have gotten the cooled and oxygenated wort into the fermentor and pitched healthy, viable yeast, there will be a brief lag period while the yeast take up oxygen, minerals, and amino acids from the wort and get ready to do their work. This lag phase should not last more than about 12 hours and may be as short as one. If the lag phase exceeds 12 hours, rouse the yeast by adding more sterile air or oxygen to the bottom of the fermentor. Once the lag phase has ended and the yeast has taken up most of the oxygen, fermentation will enter the exponential growth phase. During this phase, the yeast consume sugar from the wort and begin to produce alcohol, carbon dioxide, flavor components, and more yeast. This portion of the fermentation is exothermic and the temperature will begin to rise quickly. The generation of heat during this phase of fermentation is of particular concern with larger tanks, as they hold their thermal mass better; insulated tanks, for the same reason; and on days when the ambient temperature is over 80°F (27°C). Once this phase of fermentation starts, the beer will need to be temperature controlled and kept at 66–76°F (19–24.5°C). If the fermentation temperature is allowed to free rise, it could reach as high as 95°F (35°C) or more depending on the batch size and ambient temperature. Almost any fermentation that rises over about 76°F (24.5°C) begins to produce large amounts of fusel alcohols and esters, which are often harsh and solvent-like. The esters can vary from ripe fruit to banana to a heavy dose of butterscotch or butter (diacetyl). If wort is pitched at too high of a temperature and then allowed to cool down, it may also produce excessive diacetyl, so much so that the yeast may not be able to reduce it all later in the process. Excessive fruitiness, strong esters, fusel alcohols, and diacetyl are all considered defects in a Gose.

Level of pH During Fermentation

As the fermentation progresses, the pH will drop rapidly as yeast take up amino acids and create acidic components. For beers soured in the brewhouse, this drop will not appear to be as dramatic because pH is already low. Another potential concern for brewhouse-soured beers is that lower pH levels (below 3.9) can favor diacetyl and sulfur production with some yeast strains. If your yeast produces excessive diacetyl, be sure to address that in the secondary fermentation phase.

End of Fermentation pH

Optimum beer pH (unsoured):	3.9–4.6
Optimum beer pH (soured):	3.2–3.8

Secondary Fermentation

Once active primary fermentation has finished, marked by the end of rapid carbon dioxide evolution, the yeast still needs time to complete its processes. The warm secondary fermentation period should last two to four days. The temperature may drop on its own during this phase, but the beer should not be cooled. This time will allow the yeast to completely attenuate the beer, and reduce diacetyl and some other negative flavor components. At the end of fermentation, finishing gravities should be 1.2–3°P (1.005–1.012 FG). Take pH readings during this warm aging period. If the pH begins to rise, cool the beer. This slight rise in pH is due to the yeast cells autolyzing and releasing their slightly alkaline cytoplasm into the beer. Too much autolysis can have a negative flavor impact.

Additions

Additions of fruits and spices to the cold side are covered in their respective sections in chapter 3.

Figure 5.1. Now that the beer is safely in the secondary tank, you deserve a beer. A Gose brewery worker enjoys the fruits of his labor. Photo courtesy of Shelton Brothers Inc.

AGING AND CONDITIONING

The amount and nature of the aging you give your Gose will depend on a great many things, but mostly upon what characters you want for your beer. As discussed in other parts of this book, Gose was often served fresh from the barrel, and there are even some who insist that Gose (at least in Goslar) was never sour due to its freshness and rapid consumption. But, unless you are trying to recreate those fresh-served Gose beers of yore, you will want to give your beer a little time to mature.

Carbonation

Carbon dioxide (CO_2) is what gives beer its sparkle. It is an important part in the overall taste profile of a Gose. It influences mouthfeel, body, and flavor perception. You want your Gose to have enough carbonation to make it lively and effervescent. Without the proper amount of carbonation, your Gose will be lifeless and dull. Most brewers carbonate their beer in the tanks prior to packaging; a few others bottle- or keg-condition. Either way, you will need to understand the relationship between liquid and gas. Gas (in our case CO_2) saturation in a liquid (beer) is related to pressure and temperature. Your beer will need to be cold in order to hold enough carbonation. The proper amount of carbonation for a Gose is about 2.5–3.0 volumes (5–6 g/L) CO_2. To determine the amount of carbonation in beer, you will need to know the temperature of the beer and the amount of pressure in the tank or keg holding it. Then sufficient time must pass for the gas to stabilize and be fully absorbed by the liquid. Figure 5.2 is a chart for CO_2 in volumes as a function of temperature and pressure.

Once your beer has the desired amount of carbonation, it may be packaged in kegs, bottles, or cans (discussed in chapter 6, Packaging and Service). Be aware that packaging can cause carbonation to rise or fall depending on your process. An increase can result from overpressurizing the package. To avoid a loss of carbonation, make sure that the beer is cold enough to hold CO_2, and that the package is purged and pressurized properly.

Gosestraße, or Gose Street, in the town of Goslar.

Sent in 1899, this postcard showcases Leipzig's Ohne Bedenken. The artist took care to illustrate both interior scenes and the popular beer garden.

Gose at one of the most famous sources today, the Ohne Bedenken in Leipzig. It will make you say "Goseanna!"

Traditional Gose bottle.
Photo courtesy Dirk Van Esbroeck under Creative Commons License.

FRONT:

Certificate:

I am on the present day, the 19th day of the fifth month, 1913, in the Gose pub at Eutritzsch, Leipzig, thinking of you with a good Gose, and I emptied 60 glasses to your well-being. I send you my best greetings and remain in your friendship.

Your father

Translation by Dave Carpenter.

BACK:

Leipzig – Eutritzsch
19th May 1913
Evening, 9:15 p.m.

Dear Mother,

You have hopefully arrived safely home and are perhaps still lying on the sofa; think of me as I have just one more sip, and now it is gone. I'm doing quite well. My pain has decreased somewhat, and tomorrow it will hopefully be even better. Many heartfelt greetings.

Translation by Dave Carpenter.

Early nineteenth century postcard proclaiming, "Greetings from Leipzig!" and showcasing an artist's rendition of a traditional Gose bottle, Gose beers, and a shot of caraway liqueur. Image courtesy of Randy Mosher.

Brauhaus Goslar is serving up tradition in the town where Gose was born.

Even Ohne Bedenken is pushing the boundaries of Gose by producing a *maibock* Gose and an *Edel* Gose. Photo courtesy of Edgar Schmidke.

Figure 5.2. CO_2 solubility in beer as a function of pressure and temperature. This chart is used to determine solubility of CO_2 in beer when using a manual CO_2 measuring device. Solubility is given in volumes. Pressure is in psi and temperature in degrees Fahrenheit. Used with permission.

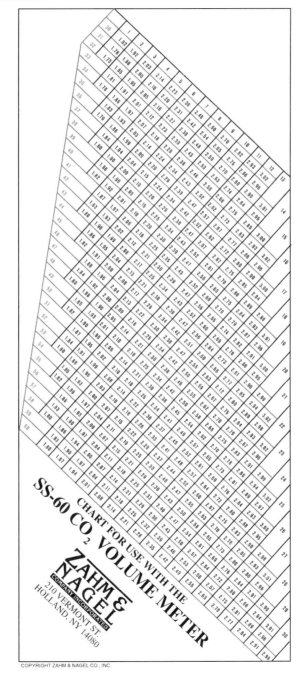

6

PACKAGING AND SERVICE

On the other hand, Gose should not mature too fast, otherwise something can happen that none of the tavern hosts is immune to: The sultriness before a summer storm can make a whole Gose supply turn into vinegar.

—Quoted by Axel Frey, Bernd Weinkauf, Dr. Hartmut Hennebach, *Gose Häppchen: 12 Kapitel Bier- und Kneipengeschichte.* (Translated by Adept Content Solutions)

Today, Gose can be packaged much like any other beer: in kegs, bottles, or cans. There is no need to worry about the acidity of the liquid affecting the crown of the bottle or the aluminum of the can, as Gose beers are less acidic than your average cola soft drink. There certainly are no longer the worries of packaging in traditional, slender-necked bottles and yeast plugs building up to contain the carbonation.

As any good brewer knows, oxygen is the enemy of any and all packaged beer. It will cause an unpleasant wet cardboard aroma and flavor. At Anderson Valley we do daily tasting of our beers and we incorporate aged beer (stored both warm and cold) into the tastings. We have found that Gose fares better during aging than all of our other non-sour beers. I do not know if it is the low hopping rate (highly hopped beers tend to pick up oxidized flavors faster), or if it is the lack of crystal malt (there is recent data supporting the anecdotal theory that crystal malt contributes to oxidation), or if it is the low pH; but, whatever the case, Gose tends to age better than IPA and other pale hoppy beers.

For those of you who are more traditional and would like to bottle condition your Gose, there are a few simple rules. For every gram of sugar fermented, 0.489 g of carbon dioxide will be created. So for a five-gallon batch of beer to go from 1 volume of CO_2 to around 2.75 volumes, you will need to add 5.1 oz. (145 g) priming sugar. Make sure that you have sufficient yeast in the beer, and that the beer is stored warm enough after priming, for the yeast to be able to re-ferment. Be sure not to over-prime your bottles—some yeast can actually build up enough pressure during fermentation to explode bottles.

Some brewers choose to use a different yeast for bottle conditioning than for the main fermentation. In contrast, others prefer to bottle condition without sugar and instead add actively fermenting beer. This method has the advantage of adding a known amount of healthy, active yeast to the beer along with the malt sugar from the wort. It can be a little tricky getting the fermenting beer at the right stage so that it contains the correct amount of both yeast and sugar, but the results are worth the trouble. The up side of bottle conditioning is that there is yeast left in the bottle, and this yeast will scavenge oxygen from the beer and keep it fresher longer. The down side is, that yeast can make the beer cloudy and a bit yeasty tasting when the beer is poured.

A HISTORICAL PERSPECTIVE ON GOSE PACKAGING

As Gose's popularity grew, brewers started exporting it to other towns and then on to other regions. The beer was transported by horse cart to the taverns where it would be served. This trip sometimes took four to six hours from the Döllnitz brewery just north of Leipzig, and longer for breweries farther afield. Typically, fully fermented beer was sent from the breweries, but in the mid-1800s the Döllnitz brewery started filling the barrels and then adding the yeast. They would then quickly load the barrels onto the horse carts and ship them off to taverns. This was best done in the cooler months. In warmer weather the trip had to be a fast one or the barrels would start fermenting. The occasional exploding barrel was not a rare occurrence in the hottest days of summer.

When a cartload arrived at the tavern, the barrels were put into the cellar, where temperatures were a more consistent 50–60°F (10°C–16°C), and the bunghole was opened up. This vented the pressure and allowed the yeast to rise up and out of the barrel. As the beer fermented in the barrels, much of the excess yeast was expelled. After the most active part of the fermentation slowed, and the yeast stopped foaming out of the barrels, the Gose was drained into a large tub. This tub served to help homogenize the barrels of Gose. From there, the beer was hand-filled into the characteristic longneck bottles. Gose was then matured in the bottle, which took from 6 to 18 days. During this time, yeast would come to the top of the bottles, push its way up the long neck, and form a seal there in the top of the bottle neck. This plug was impermeable enough to retain any carbon dioxide remaining in the beer. A small amount of yeast settled at the bottom of the bottle as well.

Some people have questioned whether a plug of top-fermenting yeast would have been strong enough to seal the bottle neck and hold in any real amount of carbonation. In the February 17th, 1882 edition of the *Goslarsche Zeitung*, the article titled "Lokales aus der Provinz und aus den Nachbarstaaten: Goslarsche Gose" found by Benedikt Rausch states, "There is no yeast pitched into the beer. Due to that fact, a thick layer of mold builds on top of it. The thicker this leather-like layer gets, the better the stability of the beer. The reason for that is that the mold layer blocks oxygen from getting into the beer. Only when the beer is given away is yeast pitched."[1] To me, this thick, leather-like layer sounds a lot like the symbiotic culture of bacteria and yeast (SCOBY) used to ferment kombucha. In experiments at home, I was able to grow up a fairly thick SCOBY layer in about three to four weeks for a high-alcohol Kombucha. This SCOBY was indeed leather-like, and it would certainly have been thick enough to exclude oxygen during aging and to plug the long neck of the traditional Gose bottle, and by doing so, retain some carbonation.

A normal pellicle would not be tough enough to plug the neck of a bottle. Possibly, if this pellicle were combined with some yeast, it might form a plug, but it seems unlikely to me that it would hold much carbonation. But, if Gose beers were in fact fermented by a SCOBY-like combination of bacteria and yeast, the resulting pellicle could certainly have formed a plug sufficient to hold carbonation. And if Gose beers of the day were fermented with a SCOBY-like group of microorganisms, it would have had a noticeable flavor impact on the final beer, almost certainly making it more acetic (Henneberg 1897, 223).

This would fit with some of the descriptions of more mature bottles of Gose being very sour, while other descriptions said that Gose beers (younger bottles that had not yet developed as much acetic acid) were not that sour at all. In my experiments with mixed-culture fermentations, *Lactobacillus* creates lactic acid fairly early on prior to *Acetobacter* creating acetic acid, which often happens two to four weeks after the main yeast fermentation is finished. This has been most notably true in mixed fermentations where there was a lot of good,

---

1   Quoted by Benedikt Rausch [nacron, pseud.], "Gosslarsche Gose," Wilder Wald (blog), February 15, 2017, http://wilder-wald.com/2017/02/15/gosslarsche-gose.

strong yeast present. As yeast creates carbon dioxide, it blankets the surface of the beer and excludes oxygen from it and *Acetobacter* requires oxygen to create acetic acid.

When it came time to serve the beer, the yeast plug would be quickly "swashed away," and the beer gently poured from the bottle. To achieve the best flavors, the bottled Gose is best kept at moderate temperatures around 60°F (15°C).

SCOBY

A symbiotic culture of bacteria and yeast (SCOBY) is usually associated with the drink kombucha, a fermented tea beverage. The SCOBY carries out a cross-feeding mixed fermentation where the anaerobic yeast fermentation produces ethanol, and the bacteria produce acetic acid through oxidizing ethanol (Villarreal-Soto et al. 2017). All this takes place simultaneously along an oxygen gradient created in part by the pellicle that is formed. This pellicle is a cellulose-based gelatinous biofilm that forms mostly at the air-liquid interface and it can be very sturdy.[2] The color and yeast populations in SCOBYs can vary greatly and may include *Brettanomyces bruxellensis*, *Candida stellata*, *Schizosaccharomyces pombe*, *Torulaspora delbrueckii*, *zygosaccharomyces bailii*, and other domesticated strains.[3] Bacteria strains can be just as numerous.

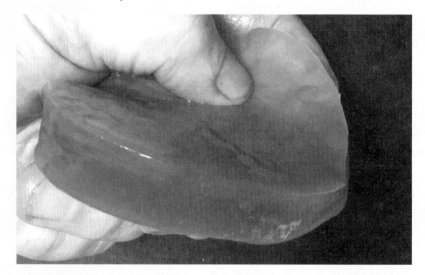

Figure 6.1. A thick, leather-like SCOBY grown by the author for kombucha. It was thick enough to have excluded oxygen and plugged the long neck of a traditional Gose bottle.

---

[2] Matthew Humbard, "Beer Microbiology – What is a pellicle?," A Ph.D in Beer (blog), January 30, 2015, https://phdinbeer.com/2015/01/30/beer-microbiology-what-is-a-pellicle/; Wikipedia, s.v. "Kombucha," last modified June 7, 2018, 02:39, https://en.wikipedia.org/wiki/Kombucha.

[3] "What is a Kombucha Scoby," Happy Kombucha (website), copyright 2018, https://happykombucha.co.uk/pages/what-is-a-kombucha-scoby.

The cellar temperature had a significant effect on the duration of the maturation process. The maturation would be much shorter at higher temperatures during the summer, and slower in the cool of winter. Once the Gose was bottled, it wouldn't have been kept any more than three weeks in the summer. It is said that in the heat of summer, Gose would be considered undrinkable after three weeks, suggesting that *Acetobacter* had done its work turning the lemony Gose into something akin to malt vinegar. For other seasons, Gose would have lasted four to five weeks in the bottle during spring or fall, and up to six weeks in the cold winter months. After those maturation periods, the Gose was said to be suitable only for real Gose lovers—those who really liked sour beers. It is written that caution had to be used to prevent the Gose from maturing too fast, otherwise "the sultriness before a summer storm" could make it turn to pure vinegar (i.e., be overly infected with *Acetobacter*). The spring and fall were the best times to mature the beer. For the tavern owner, the trick was to have the beer ready and serve it all at the right time. Some tavern owners went to the trouble of stocking several differing degrees of maturity, serving the fresher, less sour beers to those not accustomed to Gose, and saving the more mature sour bottles for Gose aficionados. So the final taste and sourness of Gose was as much a part of the tavern manager's guardianship of the beer as it was the brewer's art.

i Tagesverbrauch in der Gosen-Schänke.

Figure 6.2. Gose bottles are cleaned for reuse. Photo courtesy of Shelton Brothers Inc.

There were names for the stages of the maturation of bottled Gose. *Birnbruhe* (loosely translated as "hangover drink") was too early, and Gose drank at this yeasty stage was notorious for giving one fairly explosive gas and sometimes possibly more. *Limonade mit Geist* (lemonade with spirit) or *Mittelgose* (middle Gose) was the sweet spot, where the beer was tangy, tart, and effervescent—delicious to most people and akin to champagne. And the *Essig* (vinegar) was the stage where the Gose was old enough and had taken up enough air to start producing acetic acid. It was very much up to the tavern manager to properly maintain a stock of Gose with some bottles in each of these stages. The manager would then know what stage was best to serve to customers to give them the best Gose drinking experience. Some taverns (mostly in Halle, the town just north of Leipzig) added an extra step to the process: once the beer reached the *Birnbruhe* stage, they would transfer the beer to champagne bottles and then cork them. They were then called *Stöpselgose*, or corked Gose. This process helped exclude oxygen, thus diminishing the production of acetic acid, and resulted in more effervescence in the beer. This type of Gose was very highly praised for its closeness to French sparkling wine.

SERVICE

> In Gose service, "The yeast plug should be quickly swashed away right before serving the beer. While emptying the bottle, one should be careful to pour slowly; the cloudy sediment, originating from the fermentation process, has to remain in the bottle. Best taste is achieved at moderate temperatures around 15°C."
>
> —Otto Kröber, *Die Geschichte der Gose und die Chronik der Gosenschänke Leipzig-Eutritzsch.* (Translated by Adept Content Solutions.)

Through the Middle Ages, Gose was served from the cask or sometimes from earthenware jugs in which the beer remained softly carbonated (Frey et al. 1999). During this period, Gose was served in containers made from wood, horn, leather, metal, or ceramics. Although glass bottles had been around since at least 1,000 BC they were not in common use until the mid-1600s. This is mainly because the nature of glass at that time did not allow for bottle walls to be thick enough to hold much pressure (Brückmann and Kohl 1735). It was not until the invention of the coal-burning furnace in the seventeenth century that glass bottles with thick enough walls could be regularly produced.[4] The early accounts of bottle use are from that time. Writing in 1615, Gervaise Markham advises that when bottling their beer, house brewers "should put it into round bottles with narrow mouths, and then, stopping them close with corks, set them in a cold cellar up to the waist in sand, and be sure that the corks be fast tied with strong pack thread, for fear of rising out and taking vent, which is the utter spoil of the ale."[5]

By the time Gose became famous in Leipzig in the mid-eighteenth century, glass bottles were readily available and able to withstand pressures of three to four volumes of CO_2. Leipzig Gose was traditionally served from bottles in which it built up carbonation. It was drunk from a long, cylindrical glass resembling a large *Stange* used to serve Kölsch beer.

To properly serve a Gose, pour the beer slowly into a tall cylindrical glass or other similar aroma-promoting glass. Gose-style beers are often unfiltered, and thus may contain sediment in the bottom of the bottle or keg. For kegs, this can often be dealt with by letting the keg sit a few day before dispensing. Often sediment will fall out and the first very cloudy pint can be decanted off. If serving from the bottle, there may also be some accumulated sediment on the bottom. Some drinkers may prefer to swirl the sediment and add it to the beer. I would suggest against this practice, as Gose sediment is mostly dead yeast cells and precipitated proteinaceous matter. It can taste chalky and bitter, and tends to blur the other flavors of the beer rather than enhance them.

Figure 6.3. A Gose beer postcard from the early 1900s. Note the tall cylindrical glass and the long-necked bottles.

---

4   "A History of the Glass Wine Bottle," by Robyn, September 26, 2013, http://www.wallafaces.com/a-history-of-the-glass-wine-bottle/.

5   Quoted in Martyn Cornell, "A Short History of Bottled Beer," Zythophile (blog), January 15, 2010, http://zythophile.co.uk/2010/01/15/a-short-history-of-bottled-beer/.

PUB MIX-UPS

> *Gose, Like Berliner Weisse, the beer is available with Raspberry syrup or essence of woodruff or even fortified with sherry. I especially enjoyed it laced with the local version of the caraway liqueur,* Kümmel.
>
> —Michael Jackson, "Salty trail of Germany's link with wild beer"

In the past, Gose was often served with an addition of flavoring. Often this was caraway liqueur, or *Kümmel*. The Kümmel was served in small octagonal-shaped glasses that look like little folded umbrellas. Caraway liqueur was once one of the most popular drinks in Germany, leading to the phrase "Einen kümmeln gehn", meaning "to go out drinking caraway drinks," became a synonym for a pub visit in Leipzig.

> *Many recipes were invented to further improve and refine the taste of Gose. One of the most popular practices is to add caraway liqueur.….. Since caraway and Gose are blended together in the stomach anyway, one can also try this in the glass. This experiment was clearly a success. Caraway was served in small octagonal thick-walled glasses that looked just like folded umbrellas. If the customer wanted to have Gose laced with caraway, they had to order "Gose with an umbrella."*
>
> *One Gose Brother mentioned that you should order a "heavy cloudburst" if you preferred a stronger drink.*
>
> —Frey et al., *Gose Häppchen: 100 Jahre Gosenschenke Ohne Bedenken, Leipzig.* (Translated by Adept Content Solutions)

> *"Even though it was quite desirable that the youth would be aware of this patriotic drink very early on, its taste and effects were kept away from infants."*
>
> —ibid.

Gose was considered a good "marital beer," or *Ehestandsbier,* meaning that it was a beer that mixed well with other beverages. For

Figure 6.4. Advertisement for the Gosenshänke. Note the octagonal Kümmel glass at the lower right side.

example, a cocktail known as *Frauenfreundliche*, or "friendly to women," was invented specifically for the ladies. It was a Gose laced with a little cherry liqueur or cherry fruit syrup. If the cherry liqueur was replaced with one made from blackcurrants, the Gose drink was known as *schwarze Johanna*, or "black Johanna," or it was sometimes called the "wicked black soul." So the modern day impulse to mix fruits and flavors into Gose is one that has had a long tradition, and even today in Germany one can find both Gose-style beers fruited at the brewery and straight Gose blended at the point of service in the pubs.

> *Like Berliner Weisse, Gose is not only drunk straight, but also mixed with various kinds of fruit syrups, etc. [In December of 2005] The Ohne Bedenken offers Gose with mashed banana, strawberry juice, sweet white wine, and so on. I didn't try any of those alternatives, but Frederic Andres did, and thought highly of the banana alternative.*
>
> —Lars Marius Garshol , *Larsblog*

> *The Gose is an interesting style of beer more in the different ways in which it is consumed. Most locals to the Saxony state will drink a Gose from a bar or restaurant split with fruit-infused syrups and brandy. Splitting the sour puckering Gose with a sweeter syrup or brandy helps balance out the drinking experience for the consumer.*
>
> —Schuyler Ward, "Gasthaus & Gosebrauerei Bayerischer Bahnhof – Leipzig Germany"

FOOD PAIRING

Goses are acidic beers no doubt, but usually no more acidic than white wines. A white wine's pH is usually in the area of 3.0–3.4. Red wines are somewhat higher, at 3.3–3.7. So, generally speaking, Gose pairs well with many of the foods that go with white wine. They are a great complement to seafood, cheeses, and green salads. Gose's bright acidity allows it to counter or cut through oily or heavy flavors like salmon, salted mackerel, or a strong cheese such as *buratta*. Its salinity brings out the richness in both the beer flavors and the food you pair it with. On the seafood front, one of my favorite pairings is Gose with mussels. If you like, you can even steam your mussels in the Gose, much like the Belgians steam their mussels in *gueuze*. I also enjoy Gose pairings with mahi-mahi in butter with garlic, spicy ceviche, oysters on the half shell, or oysters lightly barbequed with garlic butter—all good choices.

Figure 6.5. Brewer carrying Gose bottles. Photo courtesy of Shelton Brothers Inc.

Other good matches are fried petrale sole, shrimp, crab, or lobster (in my book pretty much everything goes well with lobster). Gose is also big enough in flavor to stand up to spices. Try a Gose with Thai papaya salad or a spicy noodle dish. You can also match Gose's coriander with Indian curries.

Of course, the fruited Goses will pair well with things that echo or hookup with the fruits in them, for example, an orange sauce over fish paired with an orange Gose. And I know it may seem like sacrilege, but you have to go with what tastes good—fruited Gose beers can also be used as mixers in beer cocktails. Substitute Gose for champagne in a mimosa (would that be a gomosa or a migose?), or substitute ginger Gose for ginger ale in a slightly sour Moscow mule. Gose really is a marital beer.

7

GOSE RECIPES

SeaQuench Sour (For 5 US gallons [19 L])

Sam Calagione, Dogfish Head Craft Brewery, Delaware, USA

Original gravity: 1.044 (11°P)
Final gravity: 1.012 (3.1°P)
Bitterness: 10 IBU
Alcohol: 4.9% by volume
Apparent attenuation: 72%

MALTS
4.15 lb. (1.89 kg) Pilsner malt
3.7 lb. (1.68 kg) white wheat malt
0.96 lb. (0.44 kg) acidulated malt

HOPS
0.5 oz. (14 g) Cascade, 5% AA @ 60 min.
*Lactic acid to adjust pH as necessary to get down to pH 4.5 at end of boil

YEAST
Ale

ADDITIONAL ITEMS
0.26 oz. (7 g) crushed/smashed black limes @ 10 min.
0.54 oz. (15 g) sea salt @ 10 min.
0.48 oz. (13 g) crushed/smashed black limes @ flameout
2.6 oz. (73 g) coconut, in primary, warm addition
1 lime, zest+juice, in primary, warm addition
8.6 oz. (241 g) coconut, in secondary, cold addition

SOURING AGENT
Lactobacillus plantarum in the form of 1-2 GoodBelly StraightShots® per 5
gallons (19 L)

BREWING NOTES
Mash Target mash temp: 154°F (68°C)
Boil 60 minutes
Knockout @120°F (49°C) into purged fermentor, no aeration. Pitch
   Lactobacillus.
After the pH reaches 3.5 or lower (16–20 hours), aerate the wort by recirculating
   the wort in the fermentor and injecting oxygen inline. During that process,
   pitch ale yeast and ferment until you hit final gravity (usually 3–5 days).
Add first coconut and the lime zest and juice while the fermentor is still at
   room temperature. After 2–3 days, crash to 33°F (0.5°C) and rack into a
   secondary tank that has another dose of coconut waiting for the beer. After
   3 days of soaking with coconut, the beer is ready to serve.

"Strong English" Gose (all-grain) (For 5 US gallons [19 L])

Gordon Strong, BJCP Director, USA

Original gravity: 1.042 (10.5°P)
Final gravity: 1.008 (2.1°P)
Bitterness: 9 IBU
Alcohol: 4.5% by volume
Apparent attenuation: 80%

MALTS
5.0 lb. (2.3 kg) German wheat malt
3.5 lb. (1.6 kg) Belgian Pilsner malt

HOPS
0.7 oz. (20 g) Czech Saaz, 3% AA first wort hop

WATER
Reverse osmosis (RO) water
0.25 tsp. 10% phosphoric acid per 5 gallons (19 L) or until pH 5.5 at room
    temperature
1 tsp. (5 g) calcium chloride ($CaCl_2$) to the mash

YEAST
Wyeast 1007 (German Ale) or White Labs WLP029 (German Ale/Kölsch) yeast*
*Two days before brew day, make a 1 qt. (1 L) yeast starter with the German
ale strain, aerating the wort thoroughly (preferably with oxygen) before
pitching the yeast.

ADDITIONAL ITEMS
0.26 oz. (7.5 g) coriander seed, freshly ground @ 0 min.
0.35 oz. (10 g) kosher salt @ 0 min.

SOURING AGENT
19 capsules Swanson's Probiotic *Lactobacillus plantarum* Inner Bowel Support
    (10B cells/capsule)

BREWING NOTES
Mash Target mash temp: 149°F (65°C)
Boil 10 min.
On brew day, mash the malts at 149°F (65°C) in 13 qts. (12 L) of water, and
    hold this temperature for 60 minutes. Raise the temperature by infusion or
    direct heating to 168°F (76°C) to mash out. Recirculate for 20 min. Sparge
    with 168°F (76°C) water until 6.5 gallons (25 L) of wort is collected.

Raise the wort to a boil and hold for 10 minutes. Do not add the hops at this time. After the boil, chill to 95°F (35°C). Add the powder from 19 capsules of Swanson's Probiotic *L. plantarum* Inner Bowel Support (10B cells/capsule). Do not pitch the German ale yeast at this time. Purge the kettle with CO_2 and cover. Hold for 12 to 24 hours at 95°F (35°C), or until pH drops to 3.4. Add the hops, bring the wort to a boil, and boil for 90 minutes. Turn off the heat, then add the coriander in a mesh bag and the salt. Steep for 5 minutes then remove the bag. Chill to 64°F (18°C), pitch the yeast starter, and ferment until complete. Rack the beer. Prime and bottle condition, or keg and force carbonate to 3 volumes CO_2. Use 1 cup (132 g) corn sugar if priming.

Haarlemmermeer "K"ose *(For 5 US gallons [19 L])*

Kristian England PhD, BJCP Education Liaison and Bent Brewstillery, Minnesota, USA

Original gravity: 1.042 (10.5° P)
Final gravity: 1.008 (2.1° P)
Bitterness: 9 IBU
Color: 2 SRM
Alcohol: 4.5% by volume
Titratable acidity: 8–9 mg/L

MALTS
3.21 lb. (1.46 kg) Canadian Superior Oat malt (NOT flaked oats)
2.81 lb. (1.28 kg) Rahr Old World Pilsner malt
2.0 lb. (0.9 kg) Rahr red wheat malt

HOPS
1 oz. (28 g) Czech Saaz, 3% AA First wort hopping (FWH)

ADDITIONAL ITEMS
0.32 oz. (9 g) coriander seed, freshly ground @ 0 min.
0.35 oz. (10 g) kosher salt @ 0 min.

YEAST

0.28 oz. (8 g) Fermentis K-97 yeast, NOT rehydrated, sprinkled on top. DO NOT OVER PITCH. Any neutral strain will do fine.

SOURING AGENT

House lacto blend (or your favorite method)

RECIPE NOTES

A little twist on your Leipzig-style Gose. Grist is for a Dutch Kuyt beer (40% oat malt, 35% Pilsner, 25% wheat) but plays really nicely in a Gose. Don't be afraid of the loads of oats—as long as you use oat malt, and not flaked/rolled/naked oats you'll be fine. This is a basic Gose recipe but below you'll find some neat twists and variations.

BREWING NOTES

Mash Target mash temp: 153°F (67°C)

Boil 75 min.

Dough in to reach 153°F (67°C) at 1.3 qt/lb. Rest 5–10 min. Vorlauf 5–10 min. Iodine test for conversion. No mash out. Collect 6 gal (23 L) in the kettle sparging at 166°F (74°C). Boil until it breaks (10–12 min). Chill to 110°F (43°C) and run wort back into kettle injecting CO_2 through oxygenation stone. Pitch adequate souring bugs. Terminal pH 3.2–3.4 in 12–18 hours. Raise and boil for 75 min. Add salt and spice at flameout. Whirlpool 10 min, let stand 10 min. Chill to 62°F (17°C) and pitch yeast. Package at 2.7–3 volumes CO_2. Titratable acidity should be around 8–9 mg/L (0.8–0.9%).

VARIATIONS

Greyhound: 3 ruby red grapefruits, zest (0 min), juice into primary. Double salt but add after primary. May not want to let the wort get too sour, as the grapefruit brings loads of acid to the party.

Brohx Gose: Swap yeast for Fermentis BE-256 (0.17oz., or 5 g). At bottling, add *Brettanomyces bruxellensis* at 1 million cells/mL. Condition 3 weeks.

Genever (1.055 OG, 6% ABV):—Increase grist proportionally to reach new gravity. 2–3 oz. (56–84 g) crushed Juniper added in mash. 5″–10″ (13–26 cm) Black Swan toasted white oak in primary, remove on racking. A shot of genever (Dutch gin) in the finished pint does nice things.

Triple X FunkDown (1.060 OG, 6.5% ABV):—No boil. Sparge directly into vessel and add salt and let spices steep for 10 min then pull them. Chill to 110°F (43°C) and proceed with your spontaneous ferment or chuck in a bunch of mixed culture. (Check out *American Sour Beers* by Michael Tonsemeire for more information on spontaneous fermentations.)

T.N.D.M.M. (Topknot Neckbeard Dutchbag Mosaic Moutere) (1.084 OG, 10% ABV): Fire up the 'fixie' and throw all common sense out the window. Double all grist, kettle hops, and yeast. Add: 1.77 oz. (50 g) Mosaic cryo pellets in whirlpool; 3.5 oz. (100 g) Mosaic cryo pellets in primary, at half gravity; 1.77 oz. (50 g) Mosaic cryo pellets in secondary; and 7.75 oz. (220 g) Moutere pellets in secondary (+3 days).

Yuja Gose (For 5 US gallons [19 L])

Ryan Blocker, Galmegi Brewing Co., South Korea

Original gravity: 1.043 (10.5°P)
Final gravity: 1.008 (2.1°P)
Bitterness: low
Alcohol: 4.6% by volume
Apparent attenuation: 81%

MALTS
3.8 lb. (1.72 kg) wheat malt
4.66 lb. (2.12 kg) base malt

HOPS
0.17 oz. (4.75 g) Nugget, 13.0% AA @ 5 min.

YEAST
House ale yeast (a neutral ale yeast is an appropriate substitute)

ADDITIONAL ITEMS
0.17 oz. (4.75 g) coriander, freshly ground
0.27 oz. (7.6 g) roasted sea salt
3.5 oz. (104 mL) yuja fruit (called yuzu in Japanese)

SOURING AGENT

10 capsules Swanson's Probiotic *Lactobacillus plantarum* Inner Bowel Support (10B cells/capsule)

BREWING NOTES

Mash Target mash temp: 153°F (67°C)

Boil 60 min.

Mash as normal and runoff to the kettle. Boil wort for 10 minutes to sanitize and drive off any oxygen. During this boil, pre-sour the wort to 4.5 pH with a lactic acid addition. Blanket kettle headspace with CO_2 then chill wort to 113°F (45°C) and pitch *L. plantarum*. The kettle is allowed to free-fall in temperature overnight to about 40°C (104°F). Target wort pH of 3.4 in about 18–24 hours, then boil and proceed as normal. (See "Souring the Beer" in chapter 4 for more information on *Lactobacillus* rates.) Steep salt, hops, and coriander for 5 min. (whirlpool). Cool to 70°F (21°C) and ferment as normal with your house yeast culture. Beer is infused with yuja (the Korean name for yuzu, a type a citrus fruit) after fermentation, but before chilling.

Rueben's Gose (For 5 US gallons [19 L])

Adam Robbings, Reuben's Brews, Washington, USA

Original gravity: 1.042 (10.5°P)
Final gravity: 1.010 (2.6°P)
Bitterness: 6 IBU
Alcohol: 4.2% by volume
Apparent attenuation: 76%

MALTS

54% Pilsner
44% white wheat
2% rice hulls

HOPS

0.3 oz. (8 g) Mt. Hood, 5% AA @ 60 min.
Sea salt and Indian coriander in last 2 minutes of the boil

YEAST
Wyeast 1056 American Ale yeast.

SOURING AGENT
Lactobacillus

BREWING NOTES
Mash Target mash temp: 152°F (67°C)
Boil 10 min.
Mash, lauter, and sparge like a normal beer. Adjust mash pH to 5.3 with lactic acid.
Bring wort to 180°F (82°C) for 10 minutes to pasteurize.
Crash cool the wort to 110°F (43°C), adjust pH to 4.5 with lactic acid.
Purge the kettle with CO_2. Continuously blanket the wort during souring.
Inoculate with *Lactobacillus* taken from a prior batch.
When the wort hits pH 3.5 then harvest *Lactobacillus* for your next batch.
> Turn the burner on and start the rest of the process just as if it's a normal beer post lauter. (See "Souring the Beer" in chapter 4 for more information on *Lactobacillus* fermentations.)

Tiny Bubbles (For 5 US gallons [19 L])

Eric Rose, Hollister Brewing Company, California, USA

Original gravity: 1.044 (11°P)
Final gravity: 1.010 (2.6°P)
Bitterness: 3 IBU
Alcohol: 4.5% by volume
Apparent attenuation: 77%

MALTS
2.27 lb. (1.03 kg) Pilsner
4.6 lb. (2.09 kg) white wheat malt
0.79 lb. (0.36 kg) Munich malt
0.83 lb. (0.38 kg) acidulated malt
0.25 lb. (114 g) rice hulls

HOPS
5.16 oz. (144 g) Saaz, in the mash

YEAST
Bavarian *hefeweizen* yeast

ADDITIONAL ITEMS
0.21 oz. (5.9 g) sea salt, last 5 min. of the boil
1.0 oz. (28 g) Indian coriander, last 5 min. of the boil

SOURING AGENT
Lactobacillus delbrueckii

BREWING NOTES
Mash Target mash temp: 149–150°F (65°C)
Boil 45 min.
Brewhouse operation as normal beer and as per above.
At the end of whirlpool, cool the wort to 95° F (35°C). Exclude oxygen. Send
    the wort to the fermentor. Pitch *L. delbrueckii*.
Check pH every 12 hours.
Allow the wort to sour to desired taste (I am guessing from experience that
    this will be around pH 3.3–3.5 and would be reached in about 2–4 days).
Cool fermentation to 78°F (25.5°C) and pitch Bavarian hefeweizen yeast.
Maintain 78°F (25.5°C) for approximately 8 days. At the end of fermentation
    cool to 33°F (0.5°C).

Guimas Gose (For 5 US gallons [19 L])

Lucas Hendricks, The Cebruery, Philippines

Original gravity: 1.033 (8.3°P)
Final gravity: 1.010 (2.6°P)
Bitterness: 8 IBU
Color: 4.5 SRM
Alcohol: 4.2% by volume
Apparent attenuation: 69%

MALTS
3.0 lb. (1.37 kg) Pilsner malt
3.0 lb. (1.37 kg) white wheat malt
6.7 oz. (190 g) caramel aromatic malt

HOPS
0.15 oz. (4 g) Topaz, 14% AA @ 60 min.

YEAST
German Kölsch ale yeast

ADDITIONAL ITEMS
0.84 oz. (23.8 g) sea salt, in boil
0.84 oz. (23.8 g) coriander, in boil
26 oz. (0.75 L) mango puree, in secondary

SOURING AGENT
Lactobacillus and other microbes from Pilsner malt

BREWING NOTES
Mash Target mash temp: 142–150°F (61–65°C)
Boil 10 min.
Post sparging, let the wort naturally cool from mash-out temps down to 110°F
(43°C)(this usually takes about 18 hours) keeping a blanket CO_2 on the
wort. During this time acidify the wort using food-grade lactic acid from
~5.2 pH down to about ~4.6 pH. Inoculate with Pilsner malt and some
active sour wort from the last batch. (You can also explore other souring
techniques in chapter 4). Rest for 24–48 hours, checking pH every 12 hours.
Boil for 10 minutes with your bittering hop, and add equal parts local sea
salt and coriander. Pitch ale yeast. Ferment for 15 days, then do a secondary
fermentation on mango puree, (usually about 4% by volume) for 5 days.
This increases the gravity slightly, which ferments out nearly completely.
Then we add sodium citrate and benzoates to stabilize.

Bullpen Hijinks Sunflower Seed Gose (For 5 US gallons [19 L])

Will Meyers (with Alex Corona and Kevin Dwyer), Cambridge Brewing Co., Massachusetts, USA

Original gravity: 1.040 (10°P)
Final gravity: 1.008 (2.1°P)
Bitterness: 12 IBU
Alcohol: 4.2% by volume
Apparent attenuation: 79%

MALTS
5 lb. (2.27 kg) wheat malt
3 lb. (1.36 kg) 2-row pale malt
0.25 lb. (114 g) melanoidin malt
0.15 lb. (68 g) acidulated malt
2 lb. (0.91 kg) malted sunflower seeds, cracked
 OR
2 lb. (0.91 kg) roasted unsalted sunflower seeds, cracked

HOPS
0.75 oz. (21 g) Hallertauer, 4% AA @ 60 min.

YEAST
London ale or California ale yeast

ADDITIONAL ITEMS
0.50 oz. (14 g) ground coriander @ 5 min.
0.63 oz. (18 g) sea salt @ 5 min.

SOURING AGENT
Lactobacillus from "live active culture" yogurt or pure *Lactobacillus* cultures
 from your local yeast supplier. See the "Souring the Beer" section in
 chapter 4 for more information.

BREWING NOTES

Mash Target mash temp: 148–149°F (65°C) for 60 min.

Boil 90 min.

The beer Bullpen Hijinks is brewed in the Leipzig Gose style with a twist. The remainders from sunflower oil production were malted by Andrea Christian of Valley Malt in Hadley, Massachusetts to create a unique ingredient.

Purge brew kettle with CO_2 at very low pressure to remove oxygen. Mash as normal. Sparge mash to collect a full kettle volume. Minimize splashing and agitation. Maintain a very low flow of CO_2 over surface of wort. Boil wort for 5 minutes to sterilize. Then cool wort in kettle to 110°F (43°C); measure your starting wort pH. Draw off some warm wort and fully mix in 4–6 oz. (114–170 g) of fresh "live active culture" yogurt.* Then gently pitch in to the kettle. Periodically over the next 24–36 hours, gently mix to keep lactic cultures in suspension. Monitor wort pH and temperature every 4–6 hours. When wort pH is at your desired level of acidity (around 3.4–3.8), bring the kettle to a boil. Boil hops for 60 minutes. Add coriander and sea salt in the last five minutes of the boil. Cool wort as normal and pitch London ale or California ale yeast.

* Alternately you can use pure *Lactobacillus* cultures from your local yeast supplier.

Geisterzug Gose (For 5 US gallons [19 L])

Sebastian Sauer, Bierkompass, Freigeist Bierkultur, Germany

Original gravity: 1.046 (11.6°P)
Final gravity: 1.008 (2.1°P)
Bitterness: 10 IBU
Alcohol: 5.1% by volume
Apparent attenuation: 82%

MALTS
4.65 lb. (2.11 kg) pale wheat malt
3.66 lb. (1.66 kg) Pilsner malt
0.42 lb. (190 g) pale malt

HOPS
0.4 oz. (11 g) Spalter Select, 6% AA @ 60 min.

YEAST
Ale, top-fermenting house yeast
Lactobacillus for kettle souring

ADDITIONAL ITEMS
5.5 oz. (157 g) coriander @ whirlpool
2.2 oz. (63 g) spruce tips @ whirlpool
2.2 oz. (63 g) salt @ whirlpool

SOURING AGENT
House *Lactobacillus* culture or pure *Lactobacillus* cultures from your local
yeast supplier

RECIPE NOTES
Geisterzug Gose is Freigeist Bierkultur's classic, historically inspired Gose. This
is a two step-infusion and kettle-soured Gose. Because there are historical
references to Gose containing spruce when brewing a Gose, we used spruce
twigs in the whirlpool in this beer. Freigeist Bierkultur's own top-fermenting
house yeast is used for sour beers like Berliner weisse and Gose. The main
fermentation temperature is 71°F (22°C) and the beer gets cooled down for
secondary fermentation.

BREWING NOTES
Mash 143.5°F (62°C) and hold it for 30 minutes at that temperature. Then
raise the temperature to 161.5°F (72°C) for another 30 minute rest. Mash
out at 172.5°F (78°C).

Boil 60 min.

Mash in with 143.5°F (62°C) and hold it for 30 minutes at that temperature.
Then raise the temperature to 161.5°F (72°C) for another 30 minute
rest. Mash out with 172.5°F (78°C) water. Then runoff to the kettle.
Once the kettle begins to fill, cool the wort and drop the temperature to
116.5°F (47°C). Add the house *Lactobacillus* culture or your favorite pure
Lactobacillus culture from your local yeast supplier for kettle souring.
When the wort gets to a pH of 3.2, bring the kettle to a boil.

Gose Long *(For 5 US gallons [19 L])*

Jennifer Talley, Auburn Ale House, California USA

Original gravity: 1.040 (10°P)
Final gravity: 1.002 (0.5°P)
Bitterness: 4–7 IBU
Alcohol: 4.9% by volume
Apparent attenuation: 95%

MALTS
3.96 lb. (1.8 kg) Pilsner malt
3.17 lb. (1.44 kg) malted wheat
0.95 lb. (0.43 kg) unmalted wheat

HOPS
0.33 oz. (9 g) Hallertau Mittelfrüh, 4% AA @ 60 min.

YEAST
Brettanomyces bruxellensis and low-attenuating saison yeast (Wyeast 3724
   Belgian Saison)

ADDITIONAL ITEMS
0.74 oz. (21 g) sea salt @ 5 min.
1.47 oz. (42 g) Indian coriander, freshly ground @ 2 min.

SOURING AGENT
Lactobacillus delbrueckii

BREWING NOTES
Mash 149–150°F (65–66°C)
Boil 60 min.

Fermentation Temp: *Lactobacillus* is grown in light-colored, unhopped wort of 7–10°P (1.028–1.040) strength one week prior to Gose brew day. On day of brew, pitch *Lactobacillus* into fermentor and knockout Gose brew at 95°F (35°C). No oxygen added at this point. After 3–4 days of fermentation, reduce temperature to 75–76°F (24°C) and pitch both *Brettanomyces* and low-attenuating saison yeast. The saison yeast will take off initially and then peter out; then the *Brettanomyces* will go the long haul and finish the beer. The total time of production should be about 1 month.

Finishing/Maturation/Carbonation

Once 0.5°P is achieved, drop temperature to 33°F (0.5°C) and cold condition 1 week. Transfer to serving vessel with no fining agents or filtration. Carbonate to 2.75 volumes CO_2 and serve.

Gosaic (100% Mosaic Dry-hopped Gose) *(For 5 US gallons [19 L])*

Alex Tweet, Fieldwork Brewing Company, California, USA

Original gravity: 1.041 (10.3°P)
Final gravity: 1.008 (2°P)
Bitterness: 11 IBU
Alcohol: 4.3% by volume
Apparent attenuation: 80%

MALTS

4.6 lb. (2.09 kg) Pilsner malt
3.17 lb. (1.39 kg) malted wheat
0.43 lb. (200 g) acidulated malt, moistened

HOPS

1.28 oz. (37 g) Mosaic hops @ whirlpool
5.12 oz. (146 g) Mosaic hops @ dry hop

YEAST

Wyeast 3711 French Saison and California Ale yeast blend.

ADDITIONAL ITEMS

0.20 oz. (5.9 g) gypsum @ mash

0.16 oz. (4.6 g) French grey sea salt @ post boil

1.5 tsp (6.6 g) yeast nutrient @ post boil

SOURING AGENT

Lactobacillus plantarum, *Lactobacillus brevis*, and *Lactobacillus delbrueckii*,
plus 5.6 oz. (160 g) Pilsner malt.

BREWING NOTES

Mash 148°F (64°C)

Boil 45 min.

To sour the beer, fill the kettle and boil the wort for 15 minutes. Then drop
the wort temperature down to 100°F (38°C) while running CO_2 through a
venturi injector to deoxygenate the wort. Flush the headspace of the kettle
with CO_2. When the wort is down to temp, pitch a blend of *Lactobacillus
plantarum*, *Lactobacillus brevis,* and *Lactobacillus delbrueckii*, and hang a
bag of Pilsner malt in wort. Let it sit over the weekend or until until pH
reaches 3.6. At pH 3.6, boil for 45 minutes with no bittering hops. Add
French grey sea salt and yeast nutrient (use triple the normal amount of
yeast nutrient to increase nitrogen content for the *Lactobacillus*) and add
Mosaic in the whirlpool. Ferment with ale yeast blend at 66°F (19°C).
After terminal gravity, dry hop with Mosaic. Five days later, cold crash
and carbonate the beer.

Keypunch Gose (For 5 US gallons [19 L])

Bret Kollmann Baker, Urban Artifact Brewing, Ohio, USA

Original gravity: 1.037 (9.25°P)

Final gravity: 1.004 (1°P)

Bitterness: 11 IBU

Alcohol: 4.3% by volume

Apparent attenuation: 89%

MALTS
2.87 lb. (1.30 kg) pale ale malt
2.80 lb. (1.27 kg) red wheat malt
1.69 lb. (0.77 kg) light Munich malt

HOPS
0.613 g of CO_2 hop extract

YEAST
Omega Yeast OYL-044 Kolsch II

ADDITIONAL ITEMS
0.11 oz. (3 g) fresh coriander @ flameout
0.77 oz. (22 g) sea salt @ flameout
1.69 lb. (0.77 kg) fresh key lime puree added to the fermentor on day three of
    fermentation

SOURING AGENT
Lactobacillus OYL-605

BREWING NOTES
Mash 148°F (64°C)
Boil 60 min.
Go through a pre-boil acidification with a house culture of *Lactobacillus* in a
    dedicated souring vessel. Mash and lauter like any normal beer, runoff to
    the boil kettle, and pasteurize the wort at 180°F (82°C). From there, run
    it into an acidification tank and chill to between 70–74°F (21–23°C) and
    pitch a pure culture of *Lactobacillus*. We have found that by keeping the
    temperature cooler we get a much cleaner sour flavor and character. The
    souring process takes about 1–2 days to reach target acidity.

(Frehmten) Bestekrug Gose (For 5 US gallons [19 L])

Benedikt Rausch, Frankfurt, Germany (http://wilder-wald.com)

Original gravity: 1.060 (14.7°P)
Final gravity: 1.014 (3.6°P)
Bitterness: 20 IBU
Alcohol: 6% by volume
Apparent attenuation: 76%

MALTS
11.9 lb. (5.4 kg) floor-malted wheat malt (Weyermann)
1.0 lb. (0.45 kg) rice hulls

HOPS
1.2 oz. (34 g) Hallertau, 4% AA @ 120 min.

YEAST
Yeast choice is a tricky one since originally they would let it ferment without adding any yeast, only relying on the dormant yeast of the wooden fermentor and the cellar. Since those yeast would survive in wood, an approximation would be to use kveik. Pitch something like Sigmund's Voss Kveik (Yeast Bay) when cooled to 35°C. The alternative route would be to spontaneously ferment over and over in a wooden vessel and let a culture develop. Another way would be to use an open fermentor and do a wild fermentation for 24–48 hours, then transfer to a carboy or barrel. Let it ferment out for 2–3 weeks.

WATER
Suggested water profile from RO water (all in ppm): calcium 20, magnesium 6, sodium 28, sulfate 22, chloride 45, bicarbonate 60.

SOURING AGENT
None

BEER NOTES

This is a recipe that attempts to recreate an early Golsarian Gose that was
made without the use of the kettle souring technique. Souring would
have been done by yeast and or bacteria after the wort was cooled. This
would be called *Bestekrug* (best jug) and would represent the best quality
Gose that was served in Goslar in the late Middle Ages. If you want to
make something special you can alter it using tinctures of wormwood
and cinnamon (see amounts below)—this is called a *Frehmtenbestekrug*.
Wormwood and cinnamon aromas go very well together, especially in
combination with the older spruce twigs. Be cautious with wormwood,
it is really potent. I recommend 5 mL (1 tsp) of wormwood tincture for
5 gallons. You can be heavier handed with cinnamon and use between
30–50 mL (1–1.7 fl. oz.) tincture. Usually this beer would be served
directly from the cask, like real ale. But some sources state that stone
bottles were filled and given a second fermentation.

BREWING NOTES

Mash 149°F (65°C)

Boil 120 min.

After boiling, run through a filter stuffed with spruce twigs. Use younger
twigs for a more citrus character and older for a more resinous aroma.

Gruit Gose (For 5 US gallons [19 L])

Tim Bray and Jeff Neumeier, Foggy Coast Brewers, California, USA

Original gravity: 1.033 (8.3°P)
Final gravity: 1.005 (1.3°P)
Bitterness: very low to none
Alcohol: 3.7% by volume
Apparent attenuation: 85%

MALTS

3.27 lb. (1.48 kg) Pilsner malt
3.27 lb. (1.48 kg) white wheat malt

HOPS
None.

ADDITIONAL ITEMS
0.63 oz. (18 g) coriander
0.32 oz. (9 g) sea salt

GRUIT
1.54 oz. (44 g) dried dandelion root
0.77 oz. (22 g) fresh or dried yarrow flowers
0.39 oz. (11 g) dried mugwort
0.35 oz. (10 g) dried chamomile flowers (optional)

SOURING AGENT
Lactobacillus plantarum (Make starter 24 hours before brewing.)

YEAST
White Labs WLP644 *Sacchromyces* "Brux" Trois

BEER NOTES
This recipe is for a light, dry base beer with restrained tartness and light
    salinity, providing the background for a little earthiness from the dan-
    delion root, an herbal tea quality from the mugwort, and a bright floral
    character from the coriander and yarrow. The quantities in this recipe
    will leave noticeable but restrained herbal character that enhances the
    Gose character.

BREWING NOTES
Mash Mash temp 148°F (64°C)
Boil 1 min.
Mash at 145–150°F (63–65°C) for one hour; mash out, vorlauf, runoff wort
    as usual. Add salt, bring to boil, turn off heat and chill to 120°F (49°C).
    Add active *Lactobacillus* culture; blanket the wort with CO_2. Cover kettle
    to exclude air, and insulate it to keep warm for 24 to 36 hours or until pH
    drops below 3.7 (ideally 3.5). On the second day make a tisane* with the
    herbs. Add the tisane to the wort, heat to 180°F (82°C), then chill and
    transfer to the fermentor. Aerate/oxygenate and pitch yeast. Ferment at
    70–75°F (21–24°C) for 5 to 7 days or until finished. Chill, transfer to keg

and carbonate to 3 volumes. (If bottling, transfer to secondary container and mix in 150 g (5 oz.) corn sugar, bottle and condition at room temperature for 14 days, then chill.)

*The best way to control herbal additions is to make a tisane. Add dandelion root to 1 L of water, bring to boil and simmer 5 minutes. Add remaining herbs, turn off heat and steep 5 minutes, then strain and add to kettle at flameout. Be careful not to boil the herbs, except the dandelion root, to prevent bittering.

Moroccan Preserved Lemon Gose (For 5 US gallons [19 L])

Jim Crooks, Barrelworks/Firestone Walker Brewing Company, California, USA
Base beer: Bretta Weisse

Original gravity: 1.042 (10.5°P)
Final gravity: 1.012 (2.5°P)
Bitterness: 8 IBU
Alcohol: 4.6% by volume
Apparent attenuation: 71%

MALTS
2.63 lb. (1.19 kg) Pilsner malt
2.63 lb. (1.19 kg) white wheat
1.20 lb. (0.54 kg) acidulated malt
1.0 lb. (0.45 kg) torrified wheat
0.62 lb. (290 g) Carapils® malt
0.38 lb. (170 g) Munich malt

HOPS
0.33 oz. (9 g) Mt. Hood, 5.5% AA @ 60min

YEAST
Mixed culture of *Brettanomyces bruxellensis* var. Drei and *Lactobacillus delbrueckii*. Pitch rate @ 0.7 million cells/mL/Plato. 2nd round *Brettanomyces lambicus* at 13 fl. oz. (384 mL).
(13 fl. oz. is 2% by total beer volume)

SOURING AGENT

Lactobacillus delbrueckii found through Brewing Science Inst. Used in
primary fermentation. Pitch rate @ 0.7 million cells/mL/Plato.

BEER NOTES

This beer takes some planning. It is a beer in three parts; first preserving the
lemons (this takes 3 months), then brewing the base Bretta Weisse beer,
and finally adding the preserved lemons to the beer. Preserved lemons are
also available commercially and purchasing them will save you a step.

ADDITIONAL ITEMS

0.3 lb./gal. (35 g/L) freshly harvested Meyer lemons
10% (by weight) coarse kosher salt
1 food-grade bucket with lid, ceramic fermentation crock, or Ball® mason jar
3 fresh Meyer lemons for zest
To make the preserved lemons, you will need 0.3 lb./gal. (35 g/L) freshly
harvested Meyer lemons and 10% by weight coarse kosher salt. Roll lemons
under palm on work surface until they feel soft. This helps the lemon
express its juice. Keeping the stem side of the lemon intact, cross-cut the
lemon so that one side opens into quarters. Evenly coat the inner flesh of
the lemon with the coarse salt and place into the bucket. Repeat this until
all the salted lemons are packed tightly into the fermentation bucket.
If you are using a crock, place the ceramic weights onto top of the resting
lemons to keep them from floating in their own juices. If using a bucket,
using small ceramic plates as weights can achieve the same goal. Make
sure to vent lids using a fermentation lock or by cracking the lid to release
pressure. This is an active fermentation producing carbon dioxide.
After 3 months at a controlled temperature of 65–70°F (18–21°C), the lemons
will be ready to use for the secondary fermentation step. You can then
make the Bretta Weisse base beer.

BREWING NOTES

Mash Mash at 110°F (43°C) for 5 min., 121°F (49°C) for 10 min., 158°F
(70°C) for 60 minutes, 169°F (76°C) drop to lauter
Lauter 4 deep cuts are made during the runoff to promote turbidity.
Boil 65 min. No kettle finings.
Kettle pH 4.84
Whirlpool pH 4.75

Yeast pitching temp 65°F (18°C). Allow beer to free rise to 75°F (24°C). Fermentation active for 8 days. After primary fermentation, beer pH should be 3.5.

To a clean and purged fermentation vessel, add 0.3 lb./gal. preserved lemons, actively purging the vessel with carbon dioxide during the transfer. Add Bretta Weisse. Add *Brettanomyces lambicus* at 2% by total beer volume. Zest the entirety of 3 fresh Meyer lemons. Put zest into a food grade mesh bag and tie off, or weigh down bag in secondary fermentor. Allow secondary fermentation to mature for a minimum of 2 months at 65°F (18°C).

Heretic & Fuller's Collaboration Blackberry Gose (For 5 US gallons [19 L])

Jamil Zainasheff, Heretic Brewing, California, USA

Original gravity: 1.042 (10.5°P)
Final gravity: 1.010 (2.5°P)
Bitterness: 5 IBU
Alcohol: 4.6% by volume
Apparent attenuation: 76%

MALTS
5 lb. (2.27 kg) wheat malt
3.33 lb. (1.51 kg) Fullers pale ale malt

HOPS
0.35 oz. (10 g) Saaz, 3.5% AA @ 60 min.

YEAST
Fuller's ale yeast (White Labs WLP002 or Wyeast 1968)

ADDITIONAL ITEMS
0.83 lb. (0.39 kg) oat hulls (in mash)
0.07 oz. (2 g) salt
0.11 oz. (3.0 g) coriander, with very lemony character

SOURING AGENT
Lactobacillus plantarum

BREWING NOTES
Mash 152°F (67°C)
Boil 60 min.
Boil runoff for 15 minutes, chill down to 99°F (37°C), and pitch 1 L
  Lactobacillus plantarum culture grown up from probiotic capsules. Hold
  for 24 hours or sour until you reach a pH of 3.3.
Cool to 70°F (21°C) and pitch Fullers ale yeast. Ferment at 70°F (21°C). Add
  blackberry syrup to taste post-fermentation.

Yuzu Isuzu (For 5 US gallons [19 L])

Ron Jefferies, Jolly Pumpkin Brewing, Michigan, USA

Original gravity: 1.045 (11.2°P)
Final gravity: 1.006 (1.5°P)
Bitterness: 11 IBU
Alcohol: 5% by volume

MALTS
5.78 lb. (2.62 kg) Pilsner malt
3.9 lb. (1.36 kg) raw wheat
0.5 lb. (227 g) flaked oats

HOPS
0.516 oz. (14.63 g) Willamette, 4% AA @ 60 min.
3.17 oz. (89.87 g) Strisselspalt, 4% AA @ 30 min.

ADDITIONAL ITEMS
0.33 oz. (9.4 g) yuzu zest (whirlpool)
0.06 oz. (1.7 g) pink Himalayan or red Hawaiian salt (whirlpool)
0.45 oz. (13 g) coriander, ground (whirlpool)

SOURING AGENT
The Jolly Pumpkin funk and other *Lactobacillus*

YEAST
Ale yeast; Safbrew T-58 as the packaging yeast

BREWING NOTES
Mash 147°F (64°C)
Boil 60 min.
Let the ferment free rise into the 77–78°F range (25°C). At the end of
fermentation, chill down to 55°F (13°C) for four days then move into a
foeder, where the JP funk and lacto take it from there. Age until it's ready
to package (depends on the foeder), then keg/bottle condition using T-58
as the packaging yeast.

Supermarket Gose (For 5 US gallons [19 L])

Phil Markowski, Two Roads Brewing Co., Connecticut, USA

Original gravity: 1.042 (10.5°P)
Final gravity: 1.008 (2.1°P)
Bitterness: 12 IBU
Alcohol: 4.4% by volume
Apparent attenuation: 85%

MALTS
4 lb. (1.82 kg) Pilsner malt
3.94 lb. (1.79 kg) raw wheat
0.44 lb. (200 g) acidulated malt
0.47 lb. (213 g) flaked rye
0.48 lb. (220 g) light dried malt extract

HOPS
0.75 oz. (21 g) Hallertauer Herzbrucker, 3.6% AA @ 60 min.

YEAST
0.45 oz. (12.9 g) Fleishmann's Bread Yeast (or Safale 05, or equivalent)

ADDITIONAL ITEMS
0.16 oz. (4.6 g) kosher salt

SOURING AGENT

3.87 oz. (114 mL) Fage Greek-style Plain Yogurt or equivalent

NOTES

Mash 149°F (65°C)

Boil 60 min.

This modern-style Gose sources some key ingredients from a typical super-market. The ending pH should be in the range of pH 3.40–3.45. Gravity at souring should be in the range of 1.036–1.038 (9–9.5°P) to facilitate rapid lactic fermentation using yogurt cultures. Extract will be boosted post-souring by using dried malt extract (DME).

Runoff and boil the unhopped extract for 10 minutes to sanitize the wort. Cool to 105°F (40.5°C) and transfer off of the hot break. Inoculate with yogurt. Maintain temperature to within ±5°F until pH hits 3.40–3.50 range, typically 24–48 hours. Bring wort to boil to denature lactic bac-teria. Add hops, kosher salt and DME, continue to boil for 45 minutes. Target OG in the range of 1.042–1.044 (10.5–11°P).

Cool to 70°F (21°C) and pitch a neutral yeast such as Fleishmann's Bread Yeast (or Safale 05, or equivalent). Ferment at 72–74°F (22–23°C) until fermentation is complete (5–7 days). Allow yeast to settle an additional 2–3 days then rack to secondary to separate from dregs.

Cool and carbonate beer per your usual method when beer settles but retains the desired slight haze.

The Traveling Plum—Li Hing Mui-inspired Gose (For 5 US gallons [19 L])

The Bruery and Bruery Terreux® Team, Bruery Terreux, California, USA

Original gravity: 1.060 (14.7°P)

Final gravity: 1.011 (2.8°P)

Bitterness: 5 IBU

Alcohol: 6.2% by volume

MALTS

5.38 lb. (2.44 kg) domestic 2-row of your choice

3.0 lb. (1.36 kg) Weyermann pale wheat malt

3.36 lb. (1.53 kg) Briess red wheat flakes

0.6 lb. (0.27 kg) Briess Carapils

HOPS

2.25 oz. (63.7 g) Czech Saaz, 3% AA @ 60 minutes

YEAST

White Labs WLP001 California ale yeast

ADDITIONAL ITEMS

0.26 oz. (7.4 g) salt @ whirlpool

1.61 oz. (46 g) dried plum (a.k.a. prune) juice concentrate @ whirlpool

0.11 oz. (3 g) Chinese five-spice powder @ whirlpool

rice hulls as needed (in mash)

lactic acid as needed to adjust whirlpool pH to 4.5 or less (to minimize
    Lactobacillus proteolytic activity, which helps with foam retention)

SOURING AGENT

Lactobacillus brevis and *L. plantarum*

BREWING NOTES

Mash 152°F (67°C)

Boil 60 min.

Knockout of kettle at 80°F (27°C) into a purged fermentor without aeration.
    Pitch *L. brevis* and *L.plantarum*. Once beer is at pH 3.6 or less, cool
    tank to 68°F (20°C), and aerate or oxygenate. Once at temperature,
    pitch WLP001 California ale yeast at 0.75 million cells/mL/°P. When
    fermentation is complete, crash cool* the tank to 32°F (0°C). Either force
    carbonate or bottle condition to 2.8 volumes of CO_2.

*Author's note: It is extremely important that when cooling any vessel it
    should either be open to the atmosphere or be under pressure with gas
    inflow, because as the liquid cools it will contract and even a very small
    amount of vacuum can collapse a tank.

Blood Orange Gose (For 5 US gallons [19 L])

Asbjorn Gerlach, Veza Sur Brewery, Florida, USA

Original gravity: 1.036 (9°P)
Final gravity: 1.016 (4.1°P)
Bitterness: 8 IBU
Alcohol: 3.6% by volume

MALTS
3.83 lb. (1.74 kg) 2-row malt
2.27 lb. (1.03 kg) Bohemian floor-malted wheat
0.83 lb. (0.38 kg) acidulated malt

HOPS
0.33 oz. (9 g) Mandarina Bavaria, 5.9% AA @ 60 min.

YEAST
White Labs WLP001 California Ale yeast

ADDITIONAL ITEMS
4.5 lb. (2.04 kg) Purfect Puree blood orange concentrate (in secondary)
0.21 lb. (95 g) rice hulls (in mash)
0.11 oz. (3 g) sea salt @ 0 min.
0.15 oz. (4.25 g) coriander seed, freshly ground @ 0 min.
0.06 oz. (1.7 g) sweet orange peel @ 0 min.
0.06 oz. (1.7 g) bitter orange peel @ 0 min.
0.05 oz. (1.5 g) Superfood® yeast nutrient @ 0 min.

SOURING AGENT
Active *Lactobacillus delbrueckii* culture

BREWING NOTES
Mash Single step infusion at 152°F (67°C)
Boil 10 min. without hops, then 50 minutes more with hops

Cool to 115°F (46°C) injecting with CO_2. Plug the vent stack to minimize contact with oxygen. When wort reaches 115°F (46°C), add about 2 qts. (2 L) of active *Lactobacillus delbrueckii* culture (cultivated from last batch in 9° P wort, pH 3.6). This drops the overall pH of wort to 4.2. Hold at 112°F (44°C) and let the wort sour until pH reaches 3.2–3.4. At a pitching rate of 8–10% volume of Lacto culture, this should take 24–36 hours. When target pH is achieved, boil for 60 min. Spices and salt added at the end of the boil

Ferment at 66°F (19°C). On second day of fermentation, add blood orange concentrate. A final gravity of 4.2°P (1.017) should be reached on day 5, at a pH of 3.4. When the beer reaches terminal gravity, fine it and crash cool the tank to 35°F (1.6°C). On day 7, transfer to the bright beer tank, and carbonate to 2.65 volumes CO_2 on day 12. Also works well to substitute the blood orange with pink guava puree.

Water Chopper Gose (For 5 US gallons [19 L])

7 Seas Brewing, Washington, USA

Original gravity: 1.042 (10.5°P)
Final gravity: 1.005 (1.25°P)
Bitterness: 7 IBU
Alcohol: 4.8% by volume

MALTS
2.92 lb. (1.33 kg) white wheat malt
2.5 lb. (1.14 kg) 2-row pale malt
2.5 lb. (1.14 kg) Pilsner malt
0.36 lb. (160 g) dextrose

HOPS
0.15 oz. (4 g) Magnum, 9% AA @ 45 min.
0.15 oz. (4 g) US-grown East Kent Golding, 5% AA @ 30 min.

YEAST
House ale yeast strain

SOURING AGENT
Lactobacillus culture

BREWING NOTES

Mash Single step infusion at 151–152°F (66–67°C).

Boil 60 min., with hop additions at 45 and 30 min.

After mash rest, vorlauf and sparge to collect wort. Boil vigorously for 20 minutes, then chill to 105°F (40.5°C). Pitch *Lactobacillus* at a rate of 1 qt. (1 L) per 5 gallons (~19L). Maintain CO_2 in tank headspace at 1–2 psi (6.9–13.8 kPa) for duration of souring process. After 48 hours, monitor pH until it hits 3.3–3.4. This generally requires 60–72 hours. Transfer the soured Gose wort back into the kettle and boil 60 minutes. Add hops at 45 and 30 min. At 15 minutes from the end, add locally sourced, San Juan Island coarse sea salt directly to the boil. Add freshly cracked coriander in the whirlpool

After a 30-minute whirlpool, cool the wort down to 65°F (18°C) and aerate. Pitch house ale strain and ferment. On day 14, transfer beer to a bright tank and make a small addition of Biocloud* to help preserve a slight degree of haze. Carbonate to 2.54–2.64 volumes CO_2.

*Biocloud is a yeast-derived cloud system, extracted from primary grown *Saccharomyces cerevisiae* cells. Biocloud is added post-filtration at between 40 and 100 g/hL to help preserve haze in beer.

Salvation Mountain Gose (For 5 US gallons [19 L])

Eagle Rock Brewery, California, USA

Original gravity: 1.041 (10.2°P)
Final gravity: 1.011 (2.8°P)
Bitterness: 6 IBU
Alcohol: 3.9% by volume
Overall attenuation: 73%

MALTS

5.32 lb. (2.42 kg) Weyermann Pilsner malt
1.81 lb. (0.83 kg) flaked rye
0.63 lb. (0.29 kg) Weyermann acidulated malt
0.61 lb. (0.28 kg) flaked oats

HOPS
0.75 oz. (21 g) Citra, 14% AA @ flameout

YEAST
Wyeast 1272 American Ale II

ADDITIONAL ITEMS
13.3 oz. (0.38 kg) peeled/pureed prickly pear fruit @ 10 min.
0.83 oz. (24 g) sea salt @ 10 min.
Lactic acid to adjust pH as necessary to get down to a pre-boil boil pH of 4.8

SOURING AGENT
Lactobacillus from probiotic yogurt

BREWING NOTES
Mash 147°F (64°C)
Boil Two boils: #1 for 20 min., #2 for 45 min.
Boil #1—Kettle Additions
Bring wort to boil for 20 minutes to sterilize. Recirculate wort through heat exchanger back into the kettle and cool to 110°F (43°C) while injecting CO_2 inline. Blanket wort with CO_2 and then pitch 2.5 oz. (72 mL) of probiotic yogurt and cap the kettle. Insulate the kettle to maintain temperature.
Boil #2—Kettle Additions
After the pH reaches 3.6, which typically takes at least 20 hours, bring the wort back to a boil for 45 minutes to kill off the yogurt culture. Knockout @ 68°F (20°C), pitch yeast and treat like a regular clean ale fermentation (Wyeast 1272 American Ale II @ 0.75 million cells/mL/°P). Final gravity should be reached in 4–5 days and pH should be approximately 3.4. On day 4 of primary fermentation, add 6.7 oz. (195 mL) of aseptic pink guava puree directly to the fermentor.
Begin cooling the beer to 34°F (1°C) on day 7 or 8. Transfer to bright tank after 5 days of conditioning, carbonate and enjoy!

The Kimmie Gose (For 5 US gallons [19 L])

Anderson Valley Brew Crew, Anderson Valley Brewing Company, California, USA

Original gravity: 1.040 (10°P)
Final gravity: 1.007 (1.8°P)
Bitterness: 8 IBU
Alcohol: 4.1% by volume
Apparent attenuation: 73%

MALTS
5.15 lb. (2.34 kg) pale barley malt
2.77 lb. (1.26 kg) red wheat malt

HOPS
0.15 oz. (4 g) Nugget, 13.5% AA @ 60 min

YEAST
House ale yeast (English variety)

ADDITIONAL ITEMS
~2 oz. (57 g) rice hulls (in mash)
0.02 oz. (0.5 g) coriander, finely ground, end of the boil
0.62 oz. (17.6 g) sea salt (added) after fermentation

SOURING AGENT
Lactobacillus culture from White Labs

BREWING NOTES
Mash 152°F
Boil 60 min.
Mash in at 152°F (66.6°C), rest 60 minutes and proceed as normal. As the kettle fills, begin to introduce an inert gas (usually argon or nitrogen*) into the top of the kettle. Stop runoff at 1.008 (2°P). Once the wort is in the kettle, mix in cooled water to achieve a temperature of 118°F (48°C) and a gravity of about 1.034 (8.5°P). Pitch *Lactobacillus* culture at a rate of ~500 mL at 100 million cells per milliliter (or approx. 100 million total). Allow to sour to desired pH (3.2–3.4). Once the pH is reached, boil the wort for 60

minutes. Then proceed as normal to fermentation. Pitch English ale yeast at 68–70°F (20–21°C). At the end of fermentation add the fully hydrated salt solution at a rate of 0.124 oz. (17.6 g) per gallon.

Hard Case Gose (For 5 US gallons [19 L])

Fal Allen, NorCal Brewing Cooperative, California, CA

Original gravity: 1.042 (10°P)
Final gravity: 1.008 (2°P)
Bitterness: n/a
Alcohol: 4% by volume
Apparent attenuation: 70%

MALTS
4.5 lb. (2.04 kg) red wheat malt produced by air drying (see section on
    Luftmalz in chapter 3)
3.0 lb. (1.36 kg) pale barley malt
2.4 oz. (68 g) rice hulls

GRUIT
0.4 oz. (10 g) dried mugwort
0.7 oz. (20 g) dried sweetgale
0.4 oz. (10 g) dried dandelion root
0.4 oz. (10 g) fresh ginger root
0.4 oz. (10 g) dried juniper berries

YEAST
House ale yeast (English variety)

ADDITIONAL ITEMS
0.4 oz. (10 g) sea salt

SOURING AGENT
Mixed bacteria/wild yeast. You can culture the property around the brewery
    and propagate in advance of brewing or select a strain from your local
    yeast supplier.

BREWING NOTES

Mash 150°F (66°C)

Boil 20 min.

Mash in at 152°F (66.6°C), rest 60 minutes and lauter as normal. Boil for
15 minutes, turn off the heat and add spices and salt. Rest for 5 minutes
before whirlpooling. Cool the wort to 76°F (24.5°C) and send to the
fermentor. Add the mixed culture propagation. Allow to ferment and
sour to desired pH (3.2–3.4), usually about 7 to 10 days. Prime and bottle
condition for 3–10 weeks or keg and force carbonate to 2.8 volumes CO_2.

Deep End Gose (For 5 US gallons [19 L])

Mike Luparello, Homebrewer, California, USA

Original gravity: 1.048 (11.9°P)
Final gravity: 1.010 (2.6°P)
Bitterness: 2 IBU
Alcohol: 5% by volume

MALTS

5.34 lb. (2.44 kg) wheat malt
3.55 lb. (1.61 kg) Pilsner malt
0.25 lb. (114 g) melanoidin malt
0.49 lb. (220 g) flaked oats

HOPS

1.3 oz. (37 g) Crystal hops, in mash

ADDITIONAL ITEMS

0.42 oz. (12 g) sea salt, 5 min.
0.42 oz. (12 g) coriander 5 min.

SOURING AGENT

Lactobacillus delbrueckii

YEAST

Wyeast 1007 German ale yeast

BREWING NOTES

Mash Mash in at 131°F (55°C). Ramp to 162°F (72°C) over 90 min. Mash out at 168°F (76°C).

Boil 90 min.

Cool to 100°F (38°C) into CO_2 purged fermentor. Pitch *Lactobacillus* and let cool to ambient temperature over 6 days. Pitch ale yeast and hold for additional 7 days @ 70°F (21°C). Bottle condition with *Brettanomyces* at a cell count of about 0.3 million cell/mL, or about one White labs vial (35 mL) per five-gallon batch. The target carbonation is 4 volumes of CO_2.

Lemonaze Gose (For 5 US gallons [19 L])

Dick Cantwell, Magnolia Brewing Co., California, USA

Original gravity: 1.040 (10°P)
Final gravity: 1.012 (3.1°P)
Bitterness: 10 IBU
Color: 4 SRM
Alcohol: 5.3% by volume

MALTS
3.56 lb. (1.62 kg) Pilsner malt
3.56 lb. (1.62 kg) white wheat malt
0.79 lb. (0.36 kg) Munich malt

HOPS
2.0 oz. (5.7 g) Mandarina Bavaria, 3.5% AA @ boil
1 oz. (28.3 g) Mandarina Bavaria, 3.5% AA (dry hop, the day before terminal)
1.5 oz. (42.5 g) Mandarina Bavaria, 3.5% AA (dry hop, the day after terminal)

YEAST
Imperial Yeast A07 Flagship

ADDITIONAL ITEMS
1.19 oz. (34 g) sea salt at boil
17 oz. (500 mL) lemon juice at transfer
0.25 mL Super Lemon Haze cannabis terpene blend per 5 gallons at transfer

SOURING AGENT
Liquid collected from Sauergut, pitched in kettle once wort is cooled to 110°F (43°C) (see brewing notes below)

BREWING NOTES
Mash 152°F (67°C)
Boil 30 min.
Two days before sour brew, mash an amount of malt equivalent to 10–15% of total mash of crushed Pilsner malt in a thin mash at 105°–110°F (40.5–43°C); hold in closed container (such as a picnic cooler) for 2 days, and when ready to pitch to kettle (once wort has been cooled from pasteurization to 110°F/43°C) strain off liquid and discard grains (or you may use them in the mash for an additional tang).
On brew day, mash grains at 153°F (67°C) for 1 hour; runoff as normal and collect wort. Bring to pasteurization temperature of at least 165°F (74°C) and hold for 15 minutes; cool to 110°F (43°C). Return wort to clean kettle and pitch Sauergut liquid; cover wort with a blanket of CO_2 and cover/close kettle. Allow to sour 2–3 days, checking pH periodically. Bring to boil, and add boiling hops and salt; boil 30 min. Cool and pitch ale yeast; ferment normally. Dry hop once as terminal gravity nears, and once again the day after that; allow for a diacetyl rest and then chill. Transfer off yeast and add terpene blend and lemon juice. Force carbonate.

Otra Vez Prickly Pear and Grapefruit Gose *(For 5 US gallons [19 L])*

Ken Grossman, Sierra Nevada Brewing Co., California, USA

Original gravity: 1.042 (10.5°P)
Final gravity: 1.008 (1.8°P)
Bitterness: 5 IBU
Alcohol: 4.5% by volume

MALTS
4.6 lb. (2.09 kg) pale malt
3.9 lb. (1.77 kg) wheat malt

HOPS

1.44 oz. (40.8 g) Steiner experimental 04190 hops @ 60 minutes

1.12 oz. (31.75 g) Cascade @ end of boil

YEAST

SNBC ale fermented @ 70°F. (After fermentation this yeast is not harvested
for re-pitching.)

ADDITIONAL ITEMS

2.4 oz. (68 g) coriander @ 75 min

4.0 oz. (113.2 g) grapefruit peel @ 75 min

0.5 fl. oz. (15 mL) prickly pear concentrate @ 75 min

SOURING AGENT

Lactobacillus casei isolated from a mixed culture purchased from White Labs.
Add volume of sour wort targeting 0.5% titratable acidity.

BREWING NOTES

Mash Target mash temp: 150°F (66°C). Mash out at 168°F (76°C).

Boil 75 min.

Rather than doing a traditional kettle souring, we have a separate Lacto
fermentation cellar where we create a sour wort. The wort is cooled to and
incubated at 100°F (38°C), which we found to be the optimum incubation
temperature for our lactic species. We rely on titratable acidity as our
metric for sour wort, since the pH levels off at about 3.2 after a few days,
but the acidity continues to drop for about a week.

After the wort sours below 3.2 pH, we send it to our regular kettle where it is
sterilized upon addition to the now sour boiling wort we have made—this
way the soured wort doesn't acidify the main batch of wort any further.
We rely on getting our sour wort to an extremely high acidity. We then
blend it in at a set ratio of 25% sour to 75% not sour. That way we hit our
target final acidity in the fermentor.

BIBLIOGRAPHY

Albers, Ulrich. "Überlieferung des Domstifts," Stadtarchiv Goslar (2017), attributed in Daniel J. Leonard, "Gose and Gueuze: A Tale of Two Sours- Act 1," *Beer Syndicate,* September 19, 2014, https://www.beersyndicate.com/blog /gose-and-gueuze-a-tale-of-two-sours-act-1/.

Allen, Fal. 1994a. "The Microbrewery Laboratory Manual – A Practical Guide to Laboratory Techniques and Quality Control Procedures for Small-Scale Brewers, Part 1: Yeast Management." *Brewing Techniques* 2, no.4 (July/August). Republished online at https://www.morebeer.com/brewingtechniques/library /backissues/issue2.4/allen.html.

———. 1994b. "The Microbrewery Laboratory Manual - Part II: Bacteria Detection, Enumeration, and Identification." *Brewing Techniques* 2, no.5 (September/October). Republished online at https://www.morebeer.com /brewingtechniques/library/backissues/issue2.5/allen.html.

Allen, Fal, Dick Cantwell. 1998. *Barley Wine.* Boulder: Brewers Association.

Alworth, Jeff. 2015. *The Beer Bible.* New York: Workman Publishing Co.

Arnold, John P. 1911. *Origin and History of Beer and Brewing : From Prehistoric Times to the Beginning of Brewing Science and Technology; a Critical Essay.* Chicago: Alumni Association of the Wahl-Henius Institute of Fermentology.

Bennett, Judith M. 1996. *Ale, Beer, and Brewsters in England: Women's Work in a Changing World, 1300-1600.* Oxford: University Press.

Bibra, Sigmund von, ed. 1791. "Fortsetzung der Topographie der Kaiserlichen freyen Reichsstadt Goslar." *Journal von und für Deutschland.* Frankfurt am Main: Hermann. 8.Jg., 1.St. [vol. 8, no. 1]: 361–99.

Bickerdyke, John. 1889. *The Curiosities of Ale & Beer: An Entertaining History.* London: Swan Sonnenschein & Co.

Biendl, Martin, Bernhard Engelhard, Adrian Forster, Andreas Gahr, Anton Lutz, Willi Mitter, Roland Schmidt, and Christina Schonberger. 2014. *Hops: Their Cultivation, Composition, and Usage.* Nuremburg: Fachverlag Hans Carl.

Bitterman, Mark. 2010. *Salted: A Manifesto on the World's Most Essential Mineral, with Recipes.* New York: Random House.

Boone, David R., and Richard W. Castenholz, eds. 2001. *Bergey's Manual of Systematic Bacteriology.* Vol. 1, *The Archaea and the Deeply Branching and Phototrophic Bacteria.* 2nd ed. New York: Springer-Verlag.

Bradford, Thomas Lindsley. 1999. *The Life and Letters of Dr. Samuel Hahnemann.* New Delhi: Jain.

Briggs, D.E., J.S. Hough, R. Stevens, and T.W. Young. 1981. *Malt and Sweet Wort.* 2nd ed. Vol. 1 of *Malting and Brewing Science.* New York: Kluwer Academic/Plenum.

Brinkmann, Hans. 1925. *Das Brauwesen der Kaiserlich freie Reichsstadt Goslar.* Beiträge zur Geschichte der Stadt Goslar, H. 3 [Contributions to the History of the City of Goslar, issue 3]. Goslar: Geschichts- und Heimatschutzverein.

Brückmann, Franz Ernst, and J. D. Kohl. 1735. *Epistola itineraria XXXVIII. De cerevisia goslariensi ad virum nobilissimum doctissimum atque clarissimum dominum.* Wolffenbuttelae.

Buhner, Stephen Harrod. 1998. *Sacred and Herbal Healing Beers: the Secrets of Ancient Fermentation.* Boulder: Siris Books.

Burnsed, Justin. 2011. "Brew a Gose." *Brew Your Own.* May/June. http://byo.com/hops/item/2349-gose.

Collard, Sneed B. III, 1999. *1,000 Years Ago on Planet Earth.* Boston: Houghton Mifflin Harcourt.

Corran, H.S. 1975. *A History of Brewing.* Vermont: David & Charles.

Delbrück, Max. 1910. *Illustriertes Brauerei Lexikon.* Berlin: P. Parey.

Doebner, Richard. 1882. *Die Städteprivilegien Herzog Otto des Kindes und die ältesten Statuten der Stadt Hannover.* Hannover: Hahnsche Buchhandlung.

Dornbusch, Horst. 1997. *Prost! The Story of German Beer.* Boulder: Brewers Association.

Elvert, Christian d'. 1870. *Zur Cultur-Geschichte Mährens und Oest. Schlesiens.* 3. 3. Brünn: Nitsch.

F.A. Brockhaus GmbH. 2001. *Brockhaus - die Enzyklopädie : in vierundzwanzig Bänden.* Bd. 7. Leipzig: Brockhaus.

Fahy, Ann, and Jim Spencer. 1999. "Wort Production." *The Practical Brewer: A Manual for the Brewing Industry*, 3rd ed. Edited by John T. McCabe, 99–146. Wauwatosa: Master Brewers Association of the Americas.

Faulkner, Frank. 1888. *The Theory and Practice of Modern Brewing: A Re-written and Much Enlarged Edition of "The Art of Brewing"; with a Complete and Fully Illustrated Appendix, Specially Written for the Present Period.* London: F. W. Lyon.

Frey, Axel, Bernd Weinkauf, and Hartmut Hennebach. 1999. *Gose Häppchen: 12 Kapitel Bier- und Kneipengeschichte. 100 Jahre Gosenschenke >> Ohne Bedenken <<.* Translated by Adept Content Solutions. Self-published, Gosenschenke, Leipzig.

Grenell. 1907. *Die Fabrikation obergäriger Biere in Praxis u. Theorie.* Berlin: Alfred Schneider.

Goslar, City of. 2015. "Goslarer Straßennamenkatalog - Stadtteil Goslar" ["Goslar street name catalog - Goslar district"]. http://www.goslar.de /strassenverzeichnis/goslar.

H.S. Rich & Co. (1903) 1974. *One Hundred Years of Brewing.* Reprint, New York: Arno Press.

Hedenus, Gottlob. 1817. *Cato: Ein Buch für junge Oeconomen und Guthsbesitzer.* Dresden.

Heiss, Philip. 1870. *Die Bierbrauerei mit besonderer Berücksichtigung der Dickmaischbrauerei.* Augsburg: Lampart & Co.

Henneberg, W. 1897. *Beiträge zur Kenntnis der Essigbakterien. Zentralbl. Bakteriol. Parasitenkd. Infektionskrank. Hyg Abt. II.* 2:223-231

Hieronymus, Stan. 2010. *Brewing with Wheat.* Boulder: Brewers Publications.

———. 2012. *For the Love of Hops: The Practical Guide to Aroma, Bitterness and the Culture of Hops.* Boulder: Brewers Publications.

Hollhuber, Dietrich and Wolfgang Kaul. 1993. *Die Biere Deutschlands.* Nuremberg: Hans Carl Verlag.

Hornsey, S. Ian. 2003. *A History of Beer and Brewing.* Cambridge, UK: Royal Society of Chemistry.

Hübbe, Thomas. 2016. "Effect of mixed cultures on microbiological development in Berliner Weisse." Master's thesis, Technische Universität Berlin, 2016.

Hui, Y. Hui. 2004. *Handbook of Food and Beverage Fermentation Technology.* New York: Marcel Dekker.

Jackson, Michael. 1982. *The World Guide to Beer.* London: New Burlington Books.

———. 1993. *Michael Jackson's Beer Companion*. London: Duncan Baird Publishing.

———. 1996. "Salty Trail of Germany's Link with Wild Beer." *What's Brewing*, October 1, 1996.

Janssen, Johannes, and M.A. Mitchell. 1910. *History of the German People at the Close of the Middle Ages, Volume 15*. London: Kegan Paul, Trench, Trubner & Co. Ltd.

Keil, Ernst. 1872. *Die Gartenlaube: illustrirtes Familienblatt*. Berlin: Scherl.

Knudsen, Finn B. 1999. "Fermentation, Principles and Practices." *The Practical Brewer: A Manual for the Brewing Industry*. 3rd ed. Edited by John T. McCabe, 235–61. Wauwatosa: Master Brewers Association of the Americas.

Kröber, Otto. 1912. *Die Geschichte der Gose und die Chronik der Gosenschänke Leipzig-Eutritzsch*. Translated by Adept Content Solutions. Leipzig.

Kunze, Wolfgang. 2004. *Technology Brewing and Malting*. Translated by Sue Pratt. 3rd int. ed. Berlin: VLB.

Lawrence, Margaret. 1990. *The Encircling Hop: A History of Hops and Brewing*. Sittingbourne: SAWD Publications.

Lewis, Michael J. 1997. "Quality Control in the Brewery." *BrewPub Magazine*, June 1997.

Ligon, B. Lee. 2002. "Biography: Louis Pasteur: A controversial figure in a debate on scientific ethics". *Seminars in Pediatric Infectious Diseases* 13 no. 2: 134–41.

Mallett, John. 2014. *Malt: A Practical Guide from Field to Brewhouse*. Boulder: Brewers Publications.

Manchester, K.L. 2007. "Louis Pasteur, Fermentation, and a Rival." *South African Journal of Science* 103, no. 9–10 (September/October): 377–80.

Marius Garshol, Lars. n.d. *Larsblog.* Last accessed May 25, 2018. http://www.garshol.priv.no/blog/.

Markowski, Phil. 2004. *Farmhouse Ales: Culture and Craftsmanship in the Belgian Tradition.* Boulder: Brewers Publications.

Matsuda, Mari, Yayoi Hirose, Makoto Kanauchi, Sakiko Hatanaka & Akira Totsuka. 2018. "Purification and Characteristics of Tannase Produced by Lactic Acid Bacteria, Lactobacillus Plantarum H78." *Journal of the American Society of Brewing Chemists,* 74:4, 258-266, DOI: 10.1094/ASBCJ-2016-4298-01.

McGregor, Nancy, and Christopher McGregor. 2017. "So the Story Goes – The Story of Gose, Part I." Technical Feature. *Brauwelt International* (March 15): S.16.

McGregor, Nancy, and Christopher McGregor. "So the Story Goes – The Story of Gose, Part II." Technical Feature. *Brauwelt International* (April 26): S.110.

McGregor, Nancy, and Christopher McGregor. "So the Story Goes – The Story of Gose, Part III." Technical Feature. *Brauwelt International* (June 21): S.174.

McGregor, Nancy, and Christopher McGregor. "So the Story Goes – The Story of Gose, Part IV." Technical Feature. *Brauwelt International* (August 24): S.246.

McGregor, Nancy, and Christopher McGregor. "So the Story Goes – The Story of Gose, Part V." Technical Feature. Brauwelt International (October 5): S.246.

Milk the Funk Wiki. 2018. "Main Page." Last modified May 16, 2018. http://www.milkthefunk.com/wiki/Main_Page

Milk the Funk Wiki. 2017. "Brettanomyces," accessed April 17, 2018. www.milkthefunk.com/wiki/Brettanomyces.

Moseley, James. 2006. *The Mystery of Herbs and Spices: Intimate Biographies of the World's Most Notorious Ingredients.* Philadelphia: Xlibris.

Mosher, Randy. 1994. "Parti-Gyle Brewing." *Brewing Techniques,* vol. 2, no.2 (March/April). Republished online athttp://www.morebeer.com

/brewingtechniques/library/backissues/issue2.2/mosher.html

Mosher, Randy. 2009. *Tasting Beer: An Insider's Guide to the World's Greatest Drink.* North Adams, MA: Storey Publishing.

Nanninga, Nanne. 2010. "Did van Leeuwenhoek Observe Yeast Cells in 1680?" *Small Things Considered* (blog). American Society for Microbiology (April 8, 2010). http://schaechter.asmblog.org/schaechter/2010/04/did -van-leeuwenhoek-observe-yeast-cells-in-1680.html.

Nelson, Max. 2005. *The Barbarian Beverage.* New York: Routledge.

Noonan, Gregory J. 1986. *Brewing Lager Beers.* Boulder: Brewers Publications.

Okert, Karl. 2006. *Fermentation, Cellaring, and Packaging Operations:* Saint Paul: Minnesota Master Brewers Association of the Americas.

Oliver, Garrett. 2003. *The Brewmaster's Table.* New York: HarperCollins.

Ost, Hermann. 1890. *Lehrbuch der Technischen Chemie.* Berlin: Robert Oppenheim.

Palmer, John, and Colin Kaminski. 2013. *Water: A Comprehensive Guide for Brewers.* Boulder: Brewers Publications.

Patino, Hugo. 1999. "Overview of Cellar Operations." *The Practical Brewer: A Manual for the Brewing Industry.* 3rd ed. Edited by John T. McCabe, 299–325. Wauwatosa: Master Brewers Association of the Americas.

Pattinson, Ron. n.d. European Beer Guide (website). Last accessed May 25, 2018. https://www.europeanbeerguide.net/.

Pellettieri, Mary. 2015. *Quality Management: Essential Planning for Breweries.* Boulder: Brewers Publications.

Raines, Maribeth. 1993. "Methods of Sanitization and Sterilization." Brewing Techniques, vol. 1, no. 2 (July/August). Republished online at http://www .morebeer.com/brewingtechniques/library/backissues/issue1.2/raines.html.

Rausch, Benedikt. n.d. *Wilder Wald* (blog). Last accessed May 25, 2018. http://wilder-wald.com/.

Rehberger, Arthur J. and Gary E. Luther. 1999. "Wort Boiling." In *The Practical Brewer: A Manual for the Brewing Industry.* 3rd ed. Edited by John T. McCabe, 165–99. Wauwatosa: Master Brewers Association of the Americas.

Reuß, Jürgen. 2007. "Die Goslarer Gose." *Bier Aus Eigener Küche.* Published online at http://www.bierauseigenerkueche.de/Goslarer%20Gose.html. Accessed June 15, 2018.

Romberg, Johann Andreas. 1861. *Die Wissenschaften im neunzehnten Jahrhundert, ihr Standpunket und die Resultate ihrer Forschungen.* Sondershausen: Verlag von G. Neuse.

Rosengarten, Fredrich Jr. 1969. *The Book of Spices.* New York: Jove Publications.

Sanchez, Gil W. 1999. "Water." In *The Practical Brewer: A Manual For The Brewing Industry.* 3rd ed. Edited by John T. McCabe, 33–52. Wauwatosa: Master Brewers Association of the Americas.

Schehrer, Russell. 1993. "Beer Style Workshop: Fruit Beer." *The New Brewer* Volume 10, Number 5.

Schiereck, Dirk, Christof Sigel-Grüb, and Christian Voigt. 2006. *The German Brewing Industry.* St. Gallen: SMG Publishing; Sternenfels: Verlag Wissenchaft & Praxis.

Scot, Reginald. 1574. *A perfite platforme of a Hoppe garden, and necessarie instructions for the making and mayntenaunce thereof, etc.* B.L. Pp. 56. C. Denham: London.

Sifferlin, Alexandra. 2017. "Does Pink Himalayan Salt Have Any Health Benefits?" In *TIME Magazine.* June 28, 2017.

Sparrow, Jeff. 2005. *Wild Brews: Beer Beyond the Influence of Brewer's Yeast.* Boulder: Brewers Publications.

Steele, Mitch. 2012. *IPA: Brewing Techniques, Recipes and the Evolution of India Pale Ale.* Boulder: Brewers Publications.

Tonsmeire, Michael. 2014. *American Sour Beers: Innovative Techniques for Mixed Fermentations.* Boulder: Brewer's Publications.

Unger, Richard W. 2004. *Beer in the Middle Ages and the Renaissance.* Philadelphia: University of Pennsylvania Press.

Villarreal-Soto, Silvia Alejandra, Sandra Beaufort, Jalloul Bouajila, Jean-Pierre Souchard, and Patricia Taillandier. 2017. "Understanding Kombucha Tea Fermentation: A Review." Journal of Food Science 83, no. 3: 580–88. doi: 10.1111/1750-3841.14068

Wahl, Robert, and Max Henius. 1908. *American Handy Book of the Brewing, Malting and Auxiliary Trades.* 3rd ed. Chicago: Wahl-Henius Institute.

Ward, Schuyler. 2015. "Gasthaus & Gosebrauerei Bayerischer Bahnhof – Leipzig Germany." *International Drink Collaborative Network* (blog), May 18. https://idcollab.weebly.com/blog /gasthaus-gosebrauerei-bayerischer-bahnhof-leipzig-germany.

Warner, Eric. 1992. *German Wheat Beer.* Boulder: Brewers Publications.

Weicker, Theodore, ed. 1899. *Merk's Report: A Practical Journal of Pharmacy, Materia Medica, and Chemistry.* Volume VIII. New York: Merck & Co.

White, Chris, and Jamil Zainasheff. 2010. *Yeast: The Practical Guide to Beer Fermentation.* Boulder: Brewers Publications.

Zückert, Johann Friedrich. 1762. *Die Naturgeschichte und Bergwerksverfassung des Ober-Hartzes.* Berlin: Friedrich Nicolai.

INDEX

hemocytometers, 142

Hendricks, Lucas: recipe by, 169-70

Hennebach, Hartmut, 25, 26, 27, 55; beer landscape and, 30; quote of, 149

Henry's law, 117

herbs, 8, 47, 52, 81; gruit, 73, 82, 85-86

Heretic & Fuller's Collaboration Blackberry Gose, recipe for, 183-84

Hermann, Johann Gottlieb, 19

heterofermentative, 100, 101, 105, 106

hexa-iso foam test, **104**

hexa-iso hop extracts, 105

Hieronymous, Stan, 74, 88

Hoegaarden *witbier*, 67

Holy Roman Empire, 13, 82

"Home Brew U" conference, 29

homofermentative, 100, 101

homogenization, 122, 150

hond, xvi

Hooper, Andy, 30, 31

hop cones, 116

hop pellets, 116

hop tolerance, 101, 103

Hopfkrug, 9

hoppiness, 43, 73, 75, 149

hops, 6, 8, 48, 52, 63, 74-75, 84, 86, 103; adding, 9, 75; alpha acid, 76; aroma, 115; bittering, 115, 116; boiling, 115, 116; Cascade, 76; citrus, 76; finishing, 14; fruity, 76; Hallertauer Mittelfrüh, 76; Hersbrucker, 76; kettle, 115-16; Magnum, 76; Nelson Sauvin, xv; Perle, 76; Saphir, 76; spicy, 76; using, 75-76, 115

Horse Tongue, xv

Hübbe, Thomas, 134

Hüppig, 9, 49

hydrogen, 36, 38, 39

Illustriertes Brauerei Lexikon (Delbrück), 119

Ilsenburg monastery, 14

India Pale Ale (IPA), xiii, xv, 30, 75, 149

iodized salt, described, 93

Jackson, Michael, xiii, 29, 54, 55; on Gose, 25; quote of, 156

Jänichen, Tilo, 28

Jefferies, Ron: recipe by, 184-85

juniper, 82, 85

Juniper Gose, 82

Kaiserpfalz (Imperial Palace), 13, 28

Kala Namak/Bire Noon, described, 94-95

Keevan-Lynch, John, 71

Keitzinger, Udolf Audenar, 19

Keypunch Gose, recipe for, 176-77

Kimmie Gose, The: recipe for, 192-93

Kimmie, the Yink, and the Holy Gose, The: **128**

Kirchberg, 45

Knaust, Doctor., 74

Kohl, J. D., 79

Kölsch, 77, 155

Kombucha, 151, 152

kosher salt, 93

Kröber, Otto: on Einschlag, 103; Gose Tavern of, **18**; quote of, 5, 118, 154

Kümmel, 156